Called Up

Called Up

*Ballplayers Remember
Becoming Major Leaguers*

Zak Ford

McFarland & Company, Inc., Publishers
Jefferson, North Carolina

ISBN (print) 978-1-4766-9279-1
ISBN (ebook) 978-1-4766-5085-2

LIBRARY OF CONGRESS AND BRITISH LIBRARY
CATALOGUING DATA ARE AVAILABLE

Library of Congress Control Number 2023042933

© 2023 Zachariah Ford. All rights reserved

No part of this book may be reproduced or transmitted in any form or by any means, electronic or mechanical, including photocopying or recording, or by any information storage and retrieval system, without permission in writing from the publisher.

Front cover photograph by Vasyl Shulga (Shutterstock)

Printed in the United States of America

*McFarland & Company, Inc., Publishers
Box 611, Jefferson, North Carolina 28640
www.mcfarlandpub.com*

For my parents, Tom and Debbie Ford.
Thanks for taking me to Candlestick Park,
the home of my best childhood memories.

Table of Contents

Preface 1

Introduction 3

1. 1960s and 1970s 5

Sam McDowell (Indians)	5	John D'Acquisto (Giants)	22
Bill Denehy (Mets)	7	Jack Kucek (White Sox)	24
Bill Plummer (Cubs)	8	Jim Kern (Indians)	25
Gene Tenace (Athletics)	9	Nyls Nyman (White Sox)	27
Jerry Reuss (Cardinals)	11	Randy Lerch (Phillies)	28
Bobby Grich (Orioles)	14	Al Woods (Blue Jays)	31
Roe Skidmore (Cubs)	16	Randy McGilberry (Royals)	32
Kurt Bevacqua (Indians)	19	Dave Machemer (Angels)	34
Steve Luebber (Twins)	21		

2. 1980s 38

Vance Law (Pirates)	38	Ed Hearn (Mets)	53
Chris Bourjos (Giants)	41	Greg Mathews (Cardinals)	54
Atlee Hammaker (Royals)	42	Ed Vosberg (Padres)	56
Jose Alvarez (Braves)	43	Mike Campbell (Mariners)	58
Ron Kittle (White Sox)	48	Jeff Schaefer (White Sox)	60
Bip Roberts (Padres)	49	Greg Litton (Giants)	62
Bobby Witt (Rangers)	50	Pat Combs (Phillies)	65
Bob Tewksbury (Yankees)	51		

3. 1990s 68

Bill Sampen (Expos)	68	Jeff Frye (Rangers)	82
Kip Gross (Reds)	69	Bret Boone (Mariners)	84
Joe Grahe (Angels)	71	Mike Trombley (Twins)	86
John Briscoe (Athletics)	74	Matt Walbeck (Cubs)	87
Jeff Nelson (Mariners)	75	Dave McCarty (Twins)	89
Jeff Reboulet (Twins)	77	Tim Worrell (Padres)	89
Kurt Knudsen (Tigers)	78	Jerry Spradlin (Reds)	90
Eric Fox (Athletics)	80	Scott Sanders (Padres)	92

Steve Trachsel (Cubs)	94	Rick DeHart (Expos)	119
Ray Holbert (Padres)	96	Mike Misuraca (Brewers)	122
Andy Carter (Phillies)	97	Steve Woodard (Brewers)	124
Jeff Cirillo (Brewers)	99	Sean Lowe (Cardinals)	127
Mark Acre (Athletics)	100	Kevin Millar (Marlins)	128
Marty Cordova (Twins)	103	Geoff Jenkins (Brewers)	129
Gary Wilson (Pirates)	104	Bob Howry (White Sox)	131
Jim Mecir (Mariners)	105	Creighton Gubanich	
Shawn Estes (Giants)	106	(Red Sox)	133
Jason Kendall (Pirates)	110	Ray King (Cubs)	135
Jason Hardtke (Mets)	112	David Lee (Rockies)	137
Scott Spiezio (Athletics)	114	Juan Alvarez (Angels)	139
Josh Booty (Marlins)	116	Chad Hermansen (Pirates)	141
Micah Franklin (Cardinals)	118		

4. Since 2000   143

Tarrik Brock (Cubs)	143	Zach McClellan (Rockies)	181
Scott Forster (Expos)	146	Ryan Rowland-Smith	
Jose Ortiz (Athletics)	147	(Mariners)	184
Tom Wilson (Athletics)	149	Josh Newman (Rockies)	186
Nick Johnson (Yankees)	150	Steve Holm (Giants)	188
Cory Aldridge (Braves)	151	Jonathan Van Every	
Jalal Leach (Giants)	154	(Red Sox)	190
Andy Shibilo (Padres)	157	Tim Dillard (Brewers)	192
Jason Jimenez (Devil Rays)	158	Jared Wells (Padres)	196
Jim Rushford (Brewers)	160	Justin Thomas (Mariners)	197
Josh Stewart (White Sox)	163	Freddy Sandoval (Angels)	198
Lance Niekro (Giants)	165	Casper Wells (Tigers)	201
Vinnie Chulk (Blue Jays)	167	Mike Belfiore (Orioles)	203
Travis Hughes (Rangers)	169	A.J. Achter (Twins)	205
Kameron Loe (Rangers)	170	Chris Heston (Giants)	207
Adam Greenberg (Cubs)	171	Deck McGuire (Reds)	208
Jason Bergmann (Nationals)	176	Nick Kingham (Pirates)	210
Craig Hansen (Red Sox)	179	Patrick Wisdom (Cardinals)	213
James Loney (Dodgers)	181		

Index   217

Preface

This is a collection of first-person, human-interest stories. While the theme is baseball, and specifically major league call-ups and debuts, stories rarely provide extensive game details. Every effort has been made to ensure that the details included are accurate. However, capturing detailed timelines of call-ups and debut games was not my goal for this book. My goal was to capture what can't be obtained through reading a box score—the feelings and emotions of becoming a major league baseball player.

The first question I asked players was, "When did you first realize you had the talent to become a major league baseball player?" My goal with this question was not necessarily for players to provide an age or timeline, and the answers are rarely included within stories. I knew this question would spark early memories about dreams, hard work, determination, and those who supported them on their journeys. Often, a player's answer to this question included references that would return later when they spoke of their call-ups and debuts.

Players were interviewed between the fall of 2019 and fall of 2022. My inclusion criteria? The broadest: If a player had been called up and was willing to talk, he was a candidate for the book. (For my purposes, the phrase "call-up" encompasses not just the summons of minor leaguers to the majors during a season, but also a big league roster spot earned in spring training, so long as the player in question had not previously played above Triple-A.) Therefore, major league service time ranges from just two days to more than two decades. Debuts range from 1961 to 2018. By pure coincidence, some teams are represented more than others. While I considered various ways to present stories, I ultimately chose to provide them in debut order.

These first-person narratives have been edited only minimally from the interview transcripts. Text has been selected and rearranged, but these are the words of the players. Stories will read like spoken word, not written word—so the occasional infelicity or grammar slip has not been changed, so long as the meaning is clear. Some stories may fluctuate between past and present tense. Additionally, many stories include baseball terms that may require a basic understanding of the sport.

    I hope you feel the emotions of the players as you hear their stories.

Introduction

As a young boy, I did not see major league baseball players as human. I wasn't aware of the hard work and dedication required for them to reach that level of play. They were essentially godlike superheroes put on baseball fields to exhibit superhuman powers. Like a boy pretending to be Superman flying through Metropolis, I pretended to be Will Clark hitting home runs at Candlestick Park.

Despite struggling to hit .200 throughout my Little League years, I spent much of my childhood dreaming of the day I'd become a major league baseball player. In fact, even in my mid–40s, and nearly 30 years removed from playing in a baseball game, I still occasionally dream of taking the field at Candlestick, which was demolished in 2015.

I was fortunate to discover Lawrence Ritter's classic book, *The Glory of Their Times*, as a young baseball fan. While many of the players included in the masterpiece were born nearly a century before me, Ritter presented their first-person narratives in a way that provided unique connections to them as human beings. Since I first opened it, the book has been my favorite. It developed a preference for obtaining historical information through oral histories. While a good writer can paint a great picture through biographical text, there is no substitute for the first-person account. I have always found a first-person narrative far superior when capturing the emotions of a story.

My great-uncle, Larry Powell, pitched in 14 professional seasons between 1937 and 1954. In 1946, he made the Boston Red Sox out of spring training. After two weeks, he was released before getting into a game. The next day, he was signed by the Boston Braves. A week later, he was released once again without making an appearance. He never returned to the big leagues.

I was always curious about the emotions Larry felt over those few weeks in the big leagues. However, knowing the disappointment he felt from not entering a game, I never asked him. His experience in baseball purgatory is one of my inspirations for this book.

Whether a player spent two decades in the big leagues, or their story is more like Larry's, they all overcame great odds. Sure, natural ability is required. However, a player's journey to the major leagues is not possible without extreme dedication and perseverance. Along the way, mentors play a large role. The thought of giving up may occur. Circumstances must align. Both physical and mental strength are necessary to endure the emotional rollercoaster. For only the elite few, the journey culminates with putting on a big league uniform.

There are 109 stories in this book. While all stories are about achieving the goal of becoming a major league baseball player, they are all different, as they are human stories.

1

1960s and 1970s

The 1960s and 1970s were decades of expansion for major league baseball. The 1960s began with 16 teams. By the end of the 1970s, there were 26 franchises, including two in Canada. The two leagues split into Eastern and Western Divisions, and the League Championship Series was created.

Often because of major league expansion, successful minor league cities lost teams. Additionally, many minor leagues disbanded. This impacted the exposure of young players working their way to the majors.

The first amateur draft was held. Offensive numbers dipped, and in an effort to boost hitting, the American League introduced the designated hitter. Multi-purpose stadiums with artificial turf became commonplace. Labor relations evolved considerably, improving player conditions, and creating opportunities to explore free agency.

Changes in baseball during this timeframe undeniably impacted the journeys of the 17 players whose stories follow.

Sam McDowell (Indians)

Sam McDowell made his major league debut on September 15, 1961, with the Cleveland Indians. He played in 15 big league seasons. In 2006 he was inducted into the Indians Hall of Fame.

I pitched my first major league game when I was 18.

When we were talking to all the scouts, my dad had an agreement that wherever I decided to go, I'd start at the bottom in D-Ball and earn my way up to the big leagues. Cleveland agreed, but after my first year at D-Ball, they immediately jumped me up to Triple-A because D-Ball wasn't a challenge for me. So they sent me to Triple-A, and then to the big leagues.

Back then it was common knowledge that you'd spend five to seven years in the minor leagues for seasoning. I never got that chance. I came to the big leagues after a year and a half and was expected to do well. I didn't know what the hell I was doing.

I spent the whole 1961 season at Salt Lake City in Triple-A. I was the only pitcher on the team with a winning record.

We knew every year they'd call up some players at the end of their season to finish out at the major league level and to give them a little taste of what it's like to be in the major leagues. However, we knew we weren't gonna stick in the major leagues. The word came down that five or six of us from the Salt Lake City team were gonna go to the major leagues.

I was wanting to go, and not wanting to go. As a high school kid, I wasn't used to that long of a baseball season. When I was in high school, I played five sports. Each sport was a different season, and usually only ran about 30 to 40 days long. Now I'm pitching on a team for six-and-a-half months, plus spring training for two-and-a-half months. It was challenging for me. Honestly, in my heart, I didn't care whether I went or not. I would've preferred going back home to see my girlfriend.

The first time I was called up was not really that big a thrill for me.

Freddie Fitzsimmons, who was the manager at Salt Lake City, brought the six of us into his office and told us that the Indians were calling us up. He gave us the options of either flying or driving there. I had my car, a brand-new, four-seater T-Bird. Max Alvis, Jim Lawrence, and me decided we'd save money on the airline ticket and take the money instead. They drove with me all the way to Cleveland, and we went straight through. We never stopped. Everyone took turns sleeping when the other ones drove.

When I first got there, they didn't have a locker for me. In the old Cleveland Indians locker room, they didn't have enough lockers for the six additional players. Fortunately, when we were looking around for a place to put our stuff, Chuck Essegian, an outfielder, came over and told me I could share his locker. I thought that was very gracious of him, because back in those days, there was no real interaction between a minor leaguer and a major leaguer. You had to earn your way.

I didn't stay long. Two days later, I started a game against the Minnesota Twins. To be frank, all I was interested in was not being embarrassed. I knew I was in the major leagues with players that were a lot better than me. My focus was solely on not wanting to be embarrassed, and trying to do the best I could, with what little I knew. That was it.

In the seventh inning, I broke two ribs because it was a cold night and I tried to throw too hard. They took me out of the game and sent me to the hospital. They found out I had two broken ribs, so they decided to send me home. Because I wasn't gonna pitch anymore, my call-up lasted three days.

Being 18 years old, I was in a fog. I did not appreciate where I was or what was going on. To me, I was just having fun, the same as I did in high school. I really wasn't aware of my surroundings.

Bill Denehy (Mets)

Bill Denehy made his major league debut on April 16, 1967, with the New York Mets. He played in three big league seasons. Following his rookie season with the Mets, he was traded to Washington for the Senators' manager, Gil Hodges.

I got to spring training in 1967, and no one had told me anything about possibly making the team, what my chances were, or anything like that.

I went to the ballpark one day and it turned out that Jack Fisher, who was our starting pitcher, was out. His daughter had an accident at a swimming pool, and they had to rush her to the hospital. The Mets said, "Here's your break, kid. You're gonna pitch today." I pitched against Pete Rose and the Cincinnati Reds. I pitched three innings, allowed one hit, and struck out seven.

They gave me another start against the White Sox, and I pitched well against them. Then Tom Seaver and I split a game against the Kansas City A's. He gave up one run in five innings and I pitched four scoreless innings. After that, they told me I was gonna be one of the five starters to go north with the team.

I wasn't nervous all week long, even though I knew I was pitching that Sunday. In fact, that Saturday night, I slept as good as I ever did. My roommate was Jerry Koosman. He was sitting up in bed when I rolled over, and I said, "Jerry, what's going on?" He says, "Aren't you nervous?" I said, "About what?" He says, "You're pitching today! Your first big league start!" I said, "I hadn't thought about it."

Obviously, as I got closer and closer to the game, the nervousness came on.

Back then you didn't warm up out in the bullpen. They had special flat mounds right in front of the dugout with the home plate being back towards the back stop. I was warming up for a few minutes and finally the catcher who was warming me up, John Sullivan, started laughing. He pointed towards the ball and threw it back. I had been throwing for a few minutes with a ball that had a Band-Aid on it. I didn't even notice it. When I warmed up that day, I didn't feel I had my best fastball. Nonetheless, I went out there.

John Briggs was the first hitter I faced. I ended up striking him out. I ended up striking out eight batters in six and a third innings, but I lost the game. We lost, 2–0.

Dick Allen hit a slider off me in the old Connie Mack Stadium. They had double-deck stands that ran all the way from left to center, and then they had a wall that ran from dead center field all the way to the right field line. They had signs on top of the roof of the second deck. The sign that was closest to dead center field was a Coca-Cola sign. I had walked Dick Groat and then Allen hit a line drive rocket that hit that sign. If it didn't hit the sign, that ball would have landed in Delaware.

Bill Plummer (Cubs)

Bill Plummer made his major league debut on April 19, 1968, with the Chicago Cubs. He played in 10 big league seasons. Plummer was Johnny Bench's backup catcher during the Big Red Machine years.

I was with the St. Louis organization in 1967. I played for Modesto in the California League and had a good year. As a matter of fact, Sparky Anderson was the manager. That December, I was a Rule 5 pick by the Cubs.

I was young. I turned 21 at the end of spring training. The Cubs wanted to send me down and make a deal [a trade or a sale] with St. Louis [but couldn't] so the Cubs had to keep me up [on their roster] all year.

In spring training, it was surreal. I was catching behind Willie McCovey and Willie Mays. They were my idols. I grew up listening to them in the backyard. My dad listened to every game out on the patio. It was pretty amazing to be where you were, when two years ago you were listening to them on the radio.

Leo Durocher never said much to me. One of his coaches said, "You're going north with us, but there are no guarantees." Ironically, my debut was against the Cardinals in St. Louis. I came in against a left-hander named Hal Gilson. I was nervous and hoping for a better experience, but he struck me out. That happens. You try to put it behind you and move on. Unfortunately, I had to wait another month for another at-bat.

I only had one at-bat in April and another one in May. A lot of people ask, "Is it a misprint that you only had two at-bats in 1968?" I say, "No." I was kind of a phantom catcher that year. No one really knew me. It was frustrating. You're a young kid and you want to play. It was a long year for me.

I worked 53 years in baseball. I went in at 18 and out at 70. I don't think I realized how lucky I was until later to have a full year in the big leagues. It was a great experience. I played with some great players and Hall of Famers. I look back at it and realize I was real fortunate at that age, 21.

Gene Tenace (Athletics)

Gene Tenace made his major league debut on May 29, 1969, with the Oakland Athletics. He played in 15 big league seasons. Tenace was the 1972 World Series MVP.

From '65 to '67, I was a utility guy. I wasn't goin' anywhere. In '67, I told the organization they had to make a decision with me, or I was just going to hang them up, go back home, and try to get a job or some kind of education. I couldn't kick around the minor leagues as a utility guy.

In '67, I'd get opportunities to play when a guy would get hurt. I'd swing the bat well, but they didn't have a position for me. In those days, the positions were pretty much locked up in the big leagues.

They finally approached me and said they wanted to convert me into a catcher because they didn't have any catching in the system. I'm going, "Oh my God, it's gonna take me forever to learn this." I said I'd give it a shot and go to instructional league. The next season, in '68, I started playin' every day. I had a good year offensively and defensively in the Carolina League.

In '69 I went to major league camp, and they sent me to Double-A in Birmingham, Alabama. I was having a great first six weeks. I think I was hitting like .370 with 10 home runs and 35 RBIs for the first six weeks.

We were in Montgomery, Alabama. After a game, a couple buddies and I went out. We were out after curfew and were coming back down the street. I looked down at the hotel, and the manager was standing out there in the front. I go, "Oh God, we're dead. We're gonna get nailed here." The guys said, "Well, what are we gonna do?" I said, "He knows we're out after curfew 'cause we're not in our rooms. We might as well just bite the bullet, take the consequences, and deal with it."

The three of us walked down to him, and he was very upset. He told the other two guys to get to their room and he'd deal with them later. Then he told me, "You get up to my room." I'm going, "Oh, God almighty." I get to his room, and he says, "I'll fix you a drink." I said, "Well, I don't drink hard liquor. I drink beer." He said, "Pour yourself a scotch. I've got to make a phone call." I said, "Okay." I figured if the manager says to pour yourself a scotch, you pour yourself a scotch even if you don't drink scotch.

I pour myself a little bit in a glass and he's on the phone. I couldn't tell who he was talking to. It was like 1:30 in the morning. He's saying,

"Yes, no, yes, yes." I'm thinking, "What's going on here?" Then I hear him say, "Yeah, he's here. I've got him." I thought, "Uh-oh. That doesn't sound good."

He gets off the phone and says to me, "Drink that stinkin' scotch. You're gonna need that scotch." I said, "What are you talkin' about?" He says, "In about 30 minutes, you're heading back to Birmingham, and then you're gonna catch a flight to Oakland. You're catching Catfish Hunter Thursday." I said, "Skip, I've only caught one year and six weeks. I don't think I'm ready for the big leagues yet defensively." He said, "You're ready. You're leaving."

The pitcher that had thrown that night had a car waiting. He was loaded up and ready. I packed my bags, got my equipment from the ballpark, and he drove me to Birmingham. I had called my wife from the hotel, told her I was coming in, and she should start getting my clothes ready because there wasn't much time before she'd have to run me to the airport.

I was in spring training with the guys for the last two years, so I knew everybody there and they knew me. They congratulated me for getting called up and accepted me with no problems.

I had only been catching for a year and six weeks. I hadn't really learned to call a ballgame yet as far as all the technical things that are involved. I go into the pitchers and catchers meeting prior to the game and say to Catfish, "Well, how do you want to pitch this guy?" He says, "Well, that's up to you." He goes, "You put the sign down and that's what I throw. I throw a fastball, slider, and changeup." I said, "Okay, that sounds pretty easy." I go out there and I'm doing exactly what he said. He never shook me off. I'm going, "I must be

Gene Tenace was converted to a catcher in the minor leagues and was called up by the Oakland Athletics during his fifth professional season (photography by Doug McWilliams).

doing pretty good. This is a lot easier than I thought it was gonna be." We go through the game, and I didn't realize he never shook any catcher off.

I faced Denny McLain, and I couldn't figure out how he was getting me out. I saw the ball good. He kept throwing that fastball that had a little life to it at the end. I'm going, "How am I missing this stinkin' ball?" He threw it up in the zone. It was a borderline strike. You saw it so good you couldn't lay off it.

I went 0-for-4. I was shaking my head, thinking, "You've gotta be kidding me. This guy's getting me out with that stuff?" But he got a lot of people out with that stuff. I wasn't totally concerned because I wasn't the only guy he was getting out. He was getting out veteran hitters. For a couple years, he was nasty.

In my first four starts in the big leagues, I faced four 20-game winners, and one was a Cy Young Award winner. One of the games, I was on the bench, sweating bullets. Sal Bando came down, sat next to me, and said, "Gene, are you all right?" I said, "If I keep facing these guys, I won't be here long." I was able to pull through it, survive, and end up with a decent career.

Jerry Reuss (Cardinals)

Jerry Reuss made his major league debut on September 27, 1969, with the St. Louis Cardinals. He played in 22 big league seasons. Reuss was selected to two All-Star teams.

The Cardinals contacted me and five or six of my teammates in Tulsa by letter. It was one of those registered letters, and we were asked to report after the season in St. Louis on an off-day. There was excitement with the other guys, but you couldn't celebrate too much, because there was disappointment in the eyes of some of the other guys who didn't make it.

The Cardinals just finished up a series, and when we got there, it was an off-day. We came in for a Friday game against Montreal. That was my first day in the big leagues.

I grew up in St. Louis. My parents still had a home there, and I stayed with them. That's where I put my things and hung my clothes. I was up early that morning and kept looking at the clock. Finally, around noon or one o'clock, I said, "I've gotta go." They said, "Why are you going so early?" I said, "It's my first day in the big leagues. I wanna enjoy every possible second of it."

I get inside the clubhouse, look at my locker, put on my uniform, and look at myself in that uniform, even though it was the same uniform I wore in spring training. This time, I was wearing it on my first day at the big leagues.

As we played the Expos, sitting in the home dugout, I happened to scan a group of seats that just three years earlier I was sitting in as a member of the local high school team and looking into the Cardinals dugout. I said, "I would have never guessed it would've happened like this." Sitting in those seats, becoming part of the Cardinals, and having this first day in the major leagues, some 27 months after I graduated from high school. It was at that point I remembered growing up in the suburbs. I would have conversations with other kids about playing in the big leagues, and we all seemed to have big league dreams. Everybody wanted to be a major league ballplayer, and I was one of the few that got the call.

The Cardinals were still in the hunt when we got there, even though they eventually ended in fourth place. It was the Cubs' collapse and the Mets coming on strong in the last six weeks of the season that gave them the National League East. The Cardinals had to play their best lineup against every team we faced for those two reasons.

There were some veteran players who wanted to get some more at-bats or pad their numbers for next year's contract negotiations, so you couldn't play the rookies in every game for the remainder of the season. You still wanted to be competitive. The games were important. You did try to win them, but I guess you had to walk the line to see what you had for the future and finish out the current season.

The travel, first of all, was big. It was a charter aircraft as opposed to buses. Because there were extra people traveling in September, it was difficult getting a row of seats to yourself, which was the custom for players back in those days, except the guys who played cards. I had to ask, out of respect, for permission to sit down so I wouldn't crowd some major leaguer. There were a couple of people that looked at me as if to say, "Don't even ask." Fortunately, Joe Torre was there. I asked Joe and he said, "Sure. Sit down." He helped ease the transition from minor league baseball to the major leagues.

At that time, the Cardinals were one of the few teams that allowed players to have rooms of their own. Back in those days, it was pretty much accepted that teams, in an effort to save money, would have players double up in rooms. The Cardinals were different. I guess after being in the World Series two consecutive years, Mr. Busch, as his way of saying thank you, allowed everyone to have a single room—even the rookies.

My first trip to Pittsburgh, I had a suite. I had never seen a suite, never heard of one, but I had a living room and bedroom. It was just the luck of the draw, because they didn't have enough rooms, and they said, "We'll just put him in a suite and let that be that."

The other thing, of course, was the meal money. I can't remember

1. 1960s and 1970s

what it was in the minors, $5–$10 a day, but we were now getting something way in excess of that. The meal money was given to you as cash. There were more $100 bills in that envelope than I'd ever seen before.

Once the Cardinals were mathematically eliminated, I think the final two series were against Montreal on the road, and then the Phillies at home. I was just glad I got into one game. I remember it was a cold and rainy day in Montreal. It was raining when we got to the ballpark, so there was no batting practice, and there was doubt the game was even going to be played, but there was an opening and we started the game.

I was nervous as can be. Excited and nervous for your first major league game, everyone wants to do well.

Tim McCarver was the catcher because that weekend, Ted Simmons, who would have normally started in a game like this, had military duty. McCarver caught the game, and he was the one that walked me through everything. He knew the hitters, and I pretty much went with what he wanted to do.

Somewhere around the third inning, there was a long rain delay, but Red Schoendienst stayed with me. I remember I hit a ground ball up the middle. Gary Sutherland was the second baseman. Like I said, it had been raining, and some of the water that was taken off the tarp had rolled into the outfield. Sutherland went to his right to field the ground ball. It's normally a routine play, but he stumbled a little bit, then lost a handle on the ball. I was running hard down first base, and he had no play. On the play, a run came in. It turned out to be the difference in the ball game.

Eventually, when the second rain delay occurred, I had already gone seven innings. Red said, "That's it, son. I'm not gonna have you warm up one more time." That was it for my first game in the big leagues.

On that day, not only did I pitch my first major league

Jerry Reuss was called up by his hometown St. Louis Cardinals during his third professional season (courtesy Jerry Reuss).

game, I pitched seven shutout innings, got my first win, my first base hit, and my first RBI. It was a game for me to remember.

Bobby Grich (Orioles)

Bobby Grich made his major league debut on June 29, 1970, with the Baltimore Orioles. He played in 17 big league seasons. Grich is a member of both the Orioles and Angels team Halls of Fame.

I was playing in Rochester for the Red Wings in the Baltimore Orioles organization. It was 1970, and our manager was Cal Ripken, Sr.

I was having a good year. I was almost unconscious. I was hitting .383. I was just on fire. I had a great zone of concentration, and we had a really good team. I was hitting second in the lineup, behind Tommy Shopay. Then Donny Baylor and Roger Freed were hitting behind me, with Mike Ferraro. They really couldn't pitch around me. I was getting a lot of pitches and had a good eye.

Well, Clay Dalrymple, the catcher for the Orioles, was taking a throw at home plate, and Mike Epstein with the Washington Senators slid into him in a collision and it broke his ankle. I didn't know this at the time.

I came in off the field. The clubhouse guy came over and said, "Hey, Cal wants to see you." I go, "Really, about what?" He says, "I don't know." But he had a big smile on his face, so I kinda thought, "You know what, I'm going to the big leagues." I just had that feeling when I looked at his face.

I went into his little office, and Cal said, "Hey, Bobby, sit down." Cal was a heavy smoker. He took a big puff of his Camel cigarette and blew his smoke up in the air. He said, "Well, guess what?" I said, "What's that, Cal?" He said, "You are going to the big leagues. Congratulations." I went, "That is awesome, Cal. Thank you so much. I kinda thought with the way I've been hitting lately I might get the call that first opportunity." He says, "Well, you have been on fire. They want you there tomorrow. You're probably playing in tomorrow night's game, so take the first flight out and they'll have somebody at the airport to pick you up." I said, "Okay, that's great."

I went home and packed my bags that night. I was single and rooming with three other ballplayers. Our address was 241 Benson Street, and we called it Club 241. All four of us were single, and we were just having a great time in Rochester being single ballplayers. In a way, I was kinda sorry to leave, but getting called to the big leagues was a dream come true. It was a very exciting time, and my roommates were all thrilled for me.

I didn't get much sleep that night. I was pretty anxious. I got up early in the morning, flew from Rochester to Baltimore, with a stop in the middle, and they had a fella pick me up. I went straight to the ballpark. I got in there around 3:00 in the afternoon. I had a suitcase and my baseball bag. That was it.

I got there at Memorial Stadium—a big, tall, brick, circular building—and asked an attendant where the locker room was. He pointed to a gate to go through. I made my way through the stadium and over to the area where you walk in the locker room. There was an attendant there. I said, "I'm Bobby Grich. I just got called up." He says, "Yeah, we've been expecting you. Go right down that hallway. The entrance to the locker room is right down there." I could see a door at the end of the hallway.

I took my suitcase and my baseball bag and started walking down the hallway. Just before I got to the door, there was another office on the left-hand side. I looked up and it said "Manager's Office." The door was open about six to eight inches, and I could see Earl Weaver sitting at his desk. I set my stuff down. I kinda pushed open the door a little bit and just kinda stood there in the doorway. He was writing something down at his desk, and he looked up. He said, "What do you want?!" I was shocked and taken aback. I'm just trying to catch my breath basically, and went, "I just wanna let you know I'm here." He looked at me with a blank stare and he said, "Is that all?" I said, "Yeah, that's all."

That was June 29, 1970. I don't think he talked to me again 'til like 1972. He was not a man of many words to his players. He kinda stayed aloof. It was shocking to me. I thought that he would get up and shake my hand, congratulate me, welcome me in the big leagues, ask if I got a place to stay. You know, something warm and welcoming. It was a real shock to me. I was really taken aback to be very honest with you. I was very uncomfortable from that point on for the next two years being in a Baltimore Orioles uniform, as long as the manager was concerned. It was the strangest thing. This was the first time in my life, of all the sports I had ever played, that a coach didn't immediately warm up to me or immediately welcome me. I had no experience with that. It was the most uncomfortable thing that I had experienced in my life until that point. I didn't know how to handle it.

I played that night. We took a bus ride over to Washington to play the Senators. Coincidentally, the guy on the mound was a guy named Casey Cox. He was from my high school, Wilson High School in Long Beach. I didn't really know him 'cause he was older, but that's who I was facing my first day in the big leagues—a guy from my high school. He was a tall right hander, with a sinker and slider.

I went 0-for-3 with a walk.

I come to the ballpark the next day, and there's a big white cake on the table in the center of the locker room. On the cake, it said, "Welcome to Baltimore, Bobby!" I thought, "Oh, some fan made a cake for me. That's pretty cool."

Frank Robinson and all the guys came in. He said, "Who bakes a cake for somebody who gets a walk? You didn't do anything last night. You got a walk. What's this cake all about?" He was giving me a bad time, you know. I said, "Well, come on in, guys, have a piece of cake."

Pete Richert took a piece of cake and took a bite. He goes, "Wait a minute. That's sour cream icing. Dude, smell that." I started to smell it and he goes, "No, put your nose down closer to it." I heard somebody kinda giggle. I knew right then he was gonna throw my face down into the cake if I got close enough to it.

It was a total set-up. My instincts picked up on it. I jumped away, and he tried to push me down. I think the tip of my nose hit the cake a little bit, but that was it. So he didn't get me.

Bobby Grich was called up by the Baltimore Orioles during his fourth professional season. Following his debut, teammates attempted a clubhouse prank involving a cake (Doug McWilliams / National Baseball Hall of Fame and Library).

That was the first time I'd seen that prank. Anytime we had a rookie being called up during the season, I was in on the joke from that point on. We got a bunch of rookies after that. They would go over, smell the cake, and somebody would come behind them and slam their face down into the cake. It was pretty funny.

Roe Skidmore (Cubs)

Roe Skidmore made his major league debut on September 17, 1970, with the Chicago Cubs. He played in one big league season. He is one of the few players with a perfect career batting average of 1.000.

In 1968, I had played in the Midwest League for my hometown team, the Decatur Commodores, which was in A-Ball. That winter, the Cubs drafted me out of the Giants' organization. Back then if you were drafted into another organization, you had to play one level up. When I was drafted, the Giants had already added me on the Double-A roster. I made the jump from A-Ball in 1968 to Triple-A in 1969.

In 1969 with Tacoma, we won the Pacific Coast League Championship. We had just finished the playoffs and were at a signing at Sears. It was me, two or three other guys, and Whitey Lockman, our manager. We were about finished, and Lockman called me over. He said, "Skid, I almost forgot to tell you. You've got an airplane ticket tomorrow going to Chicago. You're getting called up to finish the year with the Cubs." I was thinking about going home and eating supper, and he called me over to say, "You're going to the big leagues." What a thrill that was.

That Sunday morning, myself and Jim Dunegan got on a plane in Tacoma and flew to Chicago. I don't know what time we got there, but it must've been in the middle of the afternoon. The cabbie had the Cubs game on his radio when we were going to Wrigley Field. We got out of the cab at the players' entrance, and the guy wouldn't let us in. The game's two-thirds over, and we get there saying we're Cubs players. He's like, "Yeah, right, you are. I'm not gonna let you in this door." Finally, he went and got somebody, and they let us in.

We went into the clubhouse, and the clubhouse guy said, "You guys were supposed to be here two hours ago." He threw uniforms at both of us. I think I wore 34 pants at the time, and he gave me a 38. I tried to make it look halfway decent.

At that time, the clubhouse door was down the left field line at Wrigley Field. You had to come out of the door, way down in the left field corner. To get to the dugout, you had to walk along the bricks, inches from the fans.

I remember coming out that door, and the first thing that struck me was the noise level. You come from the minor leagues, when a good night is playing in front of 5,000 to 8,000 people. Then all of a sudden, you come out the door 30 feet from the bleacher bums. You can't hear yourself talk. Anyway, we walked down the bricks to the dugout, and took the last two seats behind the post.

Joey Amalfitano, who was one of the coaches, came up to me. He goes, "Go down in the bullpen and play catch. You're gonna go in to play first base. Ernie Banks is gonna hit during the bottom of the eighth, then you'll go in and play defense." I go down and play catch a little bit.

The inning ends, and I start going from the left field bullpen, across the field, towards first base. I got almost to the dirt near the shortstop area and looked up. Here's Willie Smith running out of the dugout with his first baseman's glove on. Wanting to be as inconspicuous as I could, I took a right turn, went back to the dugout, and sat down. Nobody said one word to me. In the top of the ninth, Willie Stargell hit one in the streets and tied the game up. We lost in extra innings.

It was about the beginning of the end for the Cubs from the time I showed up. It started going downhill quick, and the famous '69 Mets overtook them.

That was my first introduction to the big leagues. I did not get into a ballgame. I didn't pinch-run. I didn't do anything the rest of the year. I sat there till the season was over. I had a good seat for the Cubs' collapse in 1969.

I went to winter instructional league ball with the Cubs' organization. Leo Durocher was out there the whole time, sitting in the stands watching us, but he never said a word to anybody.

I went to spring training in 1970, and the first day I was standing by my locker. Leo walked up to me and said, "Skid, you're a big son of a gun. I've heard how far you can hit the baseball. You're gonna be perfect for Wrigley Field." That was probably the worst thing he could've said to me. From then on, I was up there trying to hit the ball 500 feet every time to show Leo I had some power.

In 1970, I was with Tacoma again for most of the year. As good of a year we had in 1969, 1970 was terrible. We were way behind in the league. There's about six weeks left to go in the season and Whitey Lockman, who was still the manager in Tacoma, came to myself and another player. He said, "We want you guys to go down to San Antonio. They're fighting for the pennant in Double-A. We're gonna send you two guys down to finish the year out to try to help them win, and then both of you guys are gonna go to Chicago." We're going, "Well, that's a good deal." We went down to San Antonio. They didn't win it, but it was close until the last few days.

I got called up to Chicago and I sat on the bench for almost three weeks. One rainy day in Wrigley, the Cubs were playing the Cardinals. The Cardinals were ahead, and it was a lopsided score. All of a sudden, I hear this old gruff voice from Durocher say, "Skid, get a bat." My knees started knocking, and my stomach was flipping around.

I walked up to the bat rack, and I couldn't find my bat. I'm trying not to look like a dummy rummaging through all the bats, looking for my number on the knob. I need to get in the on-deck circle. I thought, "I'm not gonna stand here any longer." There was a backup catcher named J.C. Martin. I just grabbed one of his bats and went to the on-deck circle.

Ultimately, I got my turn at bat against Jerry Reuss, a left-handed pitcher. He threw me a fastball the first pitch. I swung about an hour late and hit it down the right field line foul. I had faced Reuss in the minor leagues, so I knew he had a big overhand curveball. I thought at some point, he was gonna throw me that breaking ball. The next pitch, he hung that curveball and I hit it right on the nose to left field. It went over Joe Torre's head. He was playing third base for the Cardinals. Lou Brock fielded the ball in left field and threw it to the infield.

They threw the ball out and I thought, "Man, this is the beginning. Here we go, finally." Little did I know.

I've still got that ball. On the ball, my wife has written, "First big league hit." If I had known then what I know now, she should've written, "First and last big league hit."

Roe Skidmore was called up by the Chicago Cubs during his fourth professional season but did not appear in a major league game until the following year. He got a single in his only major league at-bat (courtesy Roe Skidmore).

I was 1-for-1 in the big leagues. I'm proud of my numbers in the minor leagues, and I'd rather talk about all my minor league hits than the one big league hit. It doesn't work that way, and I get it. There are no sour grapes involved here. I'm glad I got that big league experience, and I wouldn't trade it for anything.

Kurt Bevacqua (Indians)

Kurt Bevacqua made his major league debut June 22, 1971, with the Cleveland Indians. He played in 15 big league seasons. Bevacqua is often remembered for his strong performance in the 1984 World Series as a member of the San Diego Padres.

I remember sitting around with a few guys in A-Ball. We were talking about the guys on the team who we thought were gonna make it to the big leagues. I was very surprised to hear out of the four or five guys in the group, most of them agreed on a couple of guys that were on the team—me and Dave Concepción. I look back and I believe that was the time when I started to believe I could be a major league player, because I knew my teammates believed in me.

I was with the Reds the spring of 1971. I had had a great spring, but I was the last player cut. The year before, the Reds had won the National League Championship. They had one heck of a team. It was really the start of the Big Red Machine.

Sparky Anderson called me into his office and told me I was going down. He said, "I've got to go with the guys with experience." He was talking about Jimmy Stewart, Ty Cline, Woody Woodward, and Darrel Chaney. We had a lot of extra infielders on that team along with Tony Perez, Lee May, Dave Concepción, and Tommy Helms.

I told Sparky, "I'm ready to play in the big leagues, and I'd like to be traded."

I reported to the minor league complex and then went to Indianapolis. I was only there for a couple of weeks. Vern Rapp, who was my manager at the time, called me after a game one night and said, "We've just traded you to the Cleveland Indians." I was kind of taken aback. Even though I asked to be traded, I didn't really expect it. I don't know why. I just didn't.

I reported to Wichita, and I remember the first night in Wichita I won a $1,000 savings bond 'cause I went 5-for-5. I continued to swing the bat well, and soon Ken Aspromonte, the manager, called me in his office and told me I was being called up to the big leagues.

I flew into Boston. I remember having two or three bags and my Cleveland Indians suitcase, which I still have. That was everything that I had. I jumped in a cab. I remember being in a little traffic and getting to the ballpark. I had no idea where to go. I went to a couple of people before I finally found the player gate. I went into the locker room, and the team was already out. When I walked into the clubhouse, the only one there was the clubhouse manager. He told me where my locker was. I went over and I started getting dressed.

The reason I was called up was because a roster spot opened when Ken Harrelson retired. Harrelson was bigger than I was at the time, and they gave me his uniform. I couldn't fit in his pants.

The next thing I knew, I heard a voice say, "Get out there, kid. I want you to take a couple of swings." It was Alvin Dark, the Indians manager.

I rushed at what I was doing, not that I wasn't already rushing in the first place. I went out, and he basically cleared the starters out of the batting cage. I got in four or five swings and started that night. I made an out my first time up, and then got a base hit my second time up.

I remember the first ground ball where I had an opportunity for a double play. Carl Yastrzemski was on first, and there was a ground ball to Graig Nettles. He threw it to me, I straddled the bag, and made the throw the first. Yastrzemski came in and instead of one of the slides you used to see back in the day, he pulled up and came in easy.

I didn't realize everything that was going on and the danger I put myself in with the way I completed the double play. When Yaz got up, he said, "Next time I'm going to have to take you out." Then he just jogged away. It was his way of welcoming me by taking it easy on me.

Steve Luebber (Twins)

Steve Luebber made his major league debut on June 27, 1971, with the Minnesota Twins. He played in five big league seasons. Following his playing days, Luebber became a pitching coach.

We had a good team in Double-A with Charlotte. I was 9–1 at the time I got called up in June.

Back then you didn't have games televised all the time. You didn't have ESPN or Baseball America. You only saw *The Sporting News* about once a month. You didn't know much about what was going on in the level above you in Triple-A. Teams didn't move players up and down as fast as they do now. I knew they had a couple guys with big league time that were back in Triple-A, but I'd seen them in spring training, and I had a better spring than they had. So, knowing that type of stuff, getting chosen to go up instead of them didn't surprise me.

My manager, Harry Warner, told me. He didn't have a whole lot of detail. He said they were going to fly me to Charlotte to grab my stuff, and then I would go up that Sunday.

We were in Little Rock when Harry told me. My mom and dad had come down from Missouri to see me pitch. My parents were excited. When I was growing up, my dad was still playing men's league hardball around the region. He had played a little D-League ball before I was born. He had hoped for myself or my brother to make it.

Back then there was still the old custom where veterans weren't really hot on young players. They feared they were after their jobs. However, I was fortunate. Jim Perry and his family were very gracious to me, and we became pretty good friends. Rod Carew, Tony Oliva, Cesar Tovar, Harmon Killebrew, and all those guys were very nice to me.

The manager was Bill Rigney. He knew me from spring training, but that was about it. The pitching coach was Al Worthington, and I'd only spent about 20 days or so in spring training with him, so he didn't really know me either.

It was a week before I pitched. I was told I was going to start on that first Monday after I got there. Then they didn't tell me until about two hours before the game that I wasn't going to start.

I wanted to throw a bullpen, but they wanted me to hold off. They said, "You might pitch in relief today or tomorrow. If you don't pitch, you might throw a pen on Wednesday." That's what happened. Then they said, "You're either going to start Friday or Sunday." It was up in the air like that.

I didn't get to pitch until that Sunday. I was used to pitching every fourth day and relieving between starts. All of a sudden, I didn't pitch. I got out of my routine, and by the time I pitched, I wasn't sharp at all. I just muddled through it.

I felt like a lot of the stuff I'd done in my career prepped me, so I didn't feel intimidated. I felt like it was time to get to work. Tommy Harper was my first hitter. He could run, steal, and had some power. I was just trying to go along with what the catcher and the guys had informed me about the hitters.

I wasn't happy with the way I threw. It took me several outings to get back a little more like I was.

John D'Acquisto (Giants)

John D'Acquisto made his major league debut September 2, 1973, for the San Francisco Giants. He played in 10 big league seasons. The Sporting News *named D'Acquisto the National League Rookie Pitcher of the Year in 1974.*

I was in Phoenix. I had thrown a no-hitter and made the All-Star team. It was a very good year. From what I heard from other pitchers, the Giants gave raises to their players for making the All-Star team or throwing no-hitters. I said, "Well, I made the All-Star team, and I threw a no-hitter, so I'm gonna talk to Rosy Ryan." Ryan ran the club.

I went to talk to Rosy. Rosy was a tough negotiator. Very tough. At the time, I did not know there were financial issues going on with the San Francisco Giants, which affected the Phoenix Giants, so they weren't giving anything out. I go into Rosy's office, and he says, "What do you want?" I say, "I'd like to talk to you. I want to get a raise." He says, "What do you want a raise for?" I said, "Well, I threw a no-hitter and I made the All-Star team. Isn't that the tradition of the Giants to do that?" He says, "I don't think I can give you a raise." I said, "Oh, okay. If you're not going to give me a raise, then I'm going home."

Ethan Blackaby, who also worked for the club, was there. Ethan was trying to talk me out of it. I said, "Nope, see you guys. I'm going home." I packed up all my locker, put things in my car, and drove back to my apartment. Ethan followed me home and was trying to convince me not to go.

All of a sudden, the phone rings. Rosy goes, "All right, we'll give you your raise but you're not going to get it here." I go, "What do you mean? Did you guys trade me or something?" He goes, "No, you've gotta go to San Francisco to go get it. You've been called up. Your ticket's waiting for you at the airport."

That was a different story. That's a bigger raise, too. I had incentive bonuses at every level that I would tier up. I got the incentive bonus, which was quite a nice sum. Then I got $2,500 a month, which was quite a nice sum back then.

I got to San Francisco. I remember, I was at the airport's Holiday Inn, and Charlie Fox, the Giants manager, was waiting for me in the lobby. I go, "Hey, skip, what's up?" He goes, "Go get settled in, then I'm going to take you to dinner." I go, put all my stuff away, and come back down.

Charlie and I go to Bertolucci's. We had a great meal and a couple glasses of wine. He goes, "Oh, by the way, you should cut back on the wine a little bit." I said, "Yeah, why's that?" He says, "Because you're pitching tomorrow."

I go, "Oh, okay. Who are we playing?" He goes, "The Atlanta

John D'Acquisto was called up by the San Francisco Giants during his fourth professional season, after asking for a raise in Triple-A (Doug McWilliams / National Baseball Hall of Fame and Library).

Braves." They had three guys that hit 40 home runs that season. He said, "I'm throwing your feet in the frying pan right away. We'll see how you can do against those guys."

The next day was a doubleheader. Juan Marichal pitched the first game, and I pitched the second game. I watched the first game, and then it was my turn. I get prepped in my locker and ready to go. I walk down the long hallway at Candlestick Park and up to the mound. Marichal, Don McMahon, and a few other guys are watching me. I start warming up, and I'm throwing pretty good, but I'm nervous. My knees were shaking so bad you could have put cymbals on them, and I could have played the national anthem with the cymbals.

I get in the game, and I started off pretty good. I struck out Ralph Garr to start the game and was cruising along pretty good. The game was close, and Charlie wanted to win. He could see I was running out of steam. When I came in the dugout after the fourth inning, he asked me how I was doing. I said, "I'm doing okay." He says, "That's not the answer I'm looking for." I said, "I'm doing okay. I'm going out again."

He let me go out again. I got two outs in the fifth, and he came and got me 'cause I had men on at the time. He said, "Kid, you've had enough. You're done."

What an experience to all of a sudden be there. It happened so fast. From the negotiation with Rosy, to goin' to the big leagues, to pitching the next day was like, "Whoa, right in your face."

Jack Kucek (White Sox)

Jack Kucek made his major league debut on August 8, 1974, with the Chicago White Sox. He played in seven big league seasons. Kucek had a quick journey to the majors.

I dominated at A-Ball, and they sent me to Triple-A. I go to Triple-A, and never throw one inning. I checked into the hotel and two or three days later, I checked out and was called up to the White Sox.

The manager, Joe Sparks, has me come to the office. I think he's going to tell me when I'm starting because I'm new. He just said, "I hope you didn't unpack." I go, "Why is that?" He goes, "Because you're going to the big leagues, son. Congratulations." I went, "What?" I was in shock. I mean, six weeks in professional baseball and you're in the big leagues. I couldn't get to a pay phone fast enough. I called my mom and dad, told them, and they were just ecstatic.

I came from a small town. All of a sudden, you're in a major [league] stadium that was just huge. You go into the clubhouse and see guys like Dick Allen, Goose Gossage, Terry Forster, Bucky Dent, and Ed Herrmann. You're just in awe. You have to get used to your name being changed from "Jack" to "Rook."

First day, Chuck Tanner, my manager, said, "Jack, how you doing?" I say, "I'm great. Thanks for having me come up." He goes, "Well, it'll cost you 10 bucks." I go, "What's that for?" He goes, "It's a fine for getting to the big leagues." I go, "Well, jeez, it only took me six weeks." He says, "Well, it'll cost you another $10 for taking so long." I said, "Okay, gladly." It was kangaroo court. It's kinda fun and goes to the team kitty for a team party at the end of the year.

I go in to face my first hitter, and there were guys on base. The umpire says, "Hey, Jack. You're balking out there." I go, "Really?" He goes, "Yeah, your knees are shaking." I go, "God darn it. I'm sorry, man. I'm just scared to death."

You hear about these guys, you read about them and watch them play, and all of a sudden, you're on the mound pitching against them. It's what you dream about. Every kid that ever puts on a uniform in Little League dreams one day of playing in the big leagues. Now you're doing it. It's overwhelming. It's the greatest feeling in the world.

Jim Kern (Indians)

Jim Kern made his major league debut on September 6, 1974, with the Cleveland Indians. He played in 13 big league seasons. Kern was selected to three All-Star teams.

It was never my ambition to be a major league player.

I was never drafted, and I never got an offer to play college baseball. I got $1,000 to sign in September of 1967 as a free agent with Cleveland. That put me through one year of junior college, living at home.

I was essentially playing minor league baseball to put myself through college in the winters. I felt sad when people I played with, whose whole life's goal was to play baseball, would get released. I kind of felt guilty.

In '74, they were getting ready to send me back for my third year in Double-A. I went and told Bob Quinn, who at the time was the farm manager, that I wasn't going back to Double-A. If I had to go to Double-A, I would go back to school and finish my degree. He told me he'd give me six weeks in Triple-A.

I ended that season 17–7. I set all-time records in the American Association for strikeouts in a season with 220, and strikeouts in a game with

19. Before my last game in Triple-A, I needed 18 strikeouts to break the record for strikeouts in the American Association. In the first six innings I struck out 17, and then I struck out two in the last three innings.

After the game, Red Davis, who was the Triple-A manager, told me I was getting called up. I flew home to Michigan, spent a couple days there, and then met the club in Detroit.

It was like when I first went to the Marine Corps, walking into Parris Island, wondering what the hell was gonna happen. It was that kind of scenario. You felt a little uncomfortable walking into the clubhouse with those major leaguers.

I threw batting practice in Detroit, and I remember facing Rico Carty. He stood about three feet in front of the plate, and it kind of hurt my feelings. I said, "Do you want some fast balls? I'll throw you some fast balls. Get back in the batter's box." He said, "You just throw me the ball, kid." The first one I threw, he was about two minutes late on, and he hit it over the first base dugout. The next three, he put in the left-center field bleachers. I thought to myself, "What in the hell am I doing here?"

I'm hanging out on the team for maybe five or six days. I expect to get put into a nothing game that is out of control for my major league debut.

We ended up having a doubleheader against Baltimore in Cleveland, and we were still in contention. Ken Aspromonte, the manager, told me I was gonna start the second game. Fritz Peterson pitched the first game, and the Orioles beat Fritz, 2–0, for their fourth consecutive shutout.

That night, I threw the

Jim Kern was called up by the Cleveland Indians during his sixth professional season, after breaking strikeout records in the American Association (Doug McWilliams / National Baseball Hall of Fame and Library).

second game of the doubleheader against Baltimore, [which] was "the team" at that particular time.

In the seventh inning, I hadn't given up a run and had only given up two hits. Mark Belanger blooped one over first. Then Rich Coggins hit a double down the right field line to score Belanger. They're up, 1–0, and Ken Aspromonte came out to the mound, [assumedly] to take me out. The fans booed so hard that he left me in the game. I ended up finishing the game, losing 1–0 on a five-hitter.

I was floating on air, even though I'd lost. It was an unreal experience. Even though you've had success in the minor leagues, here you are in the majors. You weren't a high draft choice, and they pushed everybody they had money in before they pushed you. You survived seven years in the minor leagues as a non-drafted player who got $1,000 to sign. Suddenly, you've outlived the high draft choices. It's amazing when you finally get there and realize they're gonna give you a chance.

Nyls Nyman (White Sox)

Nyls Nyman made his major league debut on September 6, 1974, with the Chicago White Sox. He played in four big league seasons. Nyman had a strong start in the majors, batting .643 in September of 1974.

I was in Double-A most of the year. We had already clinched, and the Iowa Oaks in Triple-A were in a pennant race. They called me up to Iowa with just two weeks left in the minor league season. All I knew was that I was going to Triple-A.

Before the last game of the season, Joe Sparks, the Triple-A manager, called me in and said I was going to the big leagues the next day. I'm playing the last game of the season and you know the unwritten code in baseball, especially back then, if somebody gets hit, right? Well, somebody hit someone the inning before I came up to bat. I remember being on deck and thinking, "Oh my God! I'm going up to the big leagues tomorrow and this guy is going to throw at me!" Sure enough, the first or second pitch he throws at my leg. I turned on it, and it hit me flush in the thigh.

I had quite the contusion, and I limped into Comiskey Park the next day. I had a hard time walking and got treatment for about a week. The White Sox set me up with a hotel downtown and I took the L train to the ballpark. The guys found out and told me I shouldn't ride it back after night games. I would take the L to Comiskey, and somebody would drop me off at the hotel after the game. I never had a problem.

I pinch-ran late in a game against the Angels, but don't have a story there.

Ron Santo, late in his career, was the DH for the White Sox, and Chuck Tanner would platoon him. When a righty pitched, a lefty would either DH or come in for Santo. They had a pitching change, and Tanner calls Santo back. I go up and pinch-hit for my first AB. I could tell Santo was pissed. He's a future Hall of Famer, and here's a snot-nosed 20-year-old hitting for him. I hit a double. The game went into extra innings and I finished 2-for-4.

When I was called up, the whole team came up to welcome me except one person, Dick Allen. I figured he was kind of a living legend and he'd get around to it. About two weeks later, I got hit in the elbow in a game against the Angels. By this time, Allen was hurt. He would come in, get treatment, practice a little, and then get dressed and sit up in the stands. He saw what happened to me and came down into the clubhouse. I'm sitting with my elbow in a bucket of ice in the trainer's room all by myself. He walked into the trainer's room and sat down with me for a half-hour to 45 minutes as if we were friends. He went out of his way to come down and keep me company.

Nyls Nyman was called up by the Chicago White Sox during his third professional season. He pinch-hit for Ron Santo for his first at-bat (Doug McWilliams / National Baseball Hall of Fame and Library).

Randy Lerch (Phillies)

Randy Lerch made his major league debut on September 14, 1975, with the Philadelphia Phillies. He played in 11 big league seasons. Considered a good-hitting pitcher, on September 30, 1978, Lerch hit two home runs in a 10–8 win that clinched the National League East Division championship for the Phillies.

I was in Double-A with the Reading Phillies, and we made the playoffs against the Bristol Red Sox. I ended up starting and pitching 14 innings in the final playoff game. Dallas Green, the Phillies' minor league

THE PHILLIES
P. O. BOX 7575
VETERANS STADIUM
PHILADELPHIA, PA. 19101

September 12, 1975

Mr. John H. Johnson
Administrative Officer
Office of the Baseball Commissioner
75 Rockefeller Plaza
New York, N. Y. 10019

Dear John:

Enclosed are seven executed copies of the agreement whereby the Philadelphia Club selects the contract of player Randy Louis Lerch from the Reading Club under terms of the Player Development Contract.

Sincerely,

Paul Owens
Vice President
Dir. Player Personnel

PO:pm

Enc.

cc: National League

RECEIVED BY
ADMINISTRATIVE DEPARTMENT
SEP 22 1975
By

EXECUTIVE OFFICES
(215) HO 3-6000

GROUP SALES
(215) HO 3-5000

TICKETS & INFORMATION
(215) HO 3-1000

Above and following page: Randy Lerch's call-up agreement between the Reading Phillies and the Philadelphia Phillies (author's collection).

Uniform Agreement for the Assignment of a Player's Contract to or by a Major League Club

IMPORTANT NOTICE

Seven counterpart originals of this Agreement must be executed and mailed to the Secretary-Treasurer, Office of the Baseball Commissioner, accompanied by a check for the consideration. If due a National Association Club, the check shall be to the order of "The National Association of Professional Baseball Leagues"; if due a Major League Club, the check shall be to the order of that Club.

IF EXECUTED AGREEMENTS ARE NOT FILED WITH THE SECRETARY-TREASURER WITHIN 15 DAYS AFTER THE TRANSFER IS EFFECTED, HE SHALL COLLECT A PENALTY OF $50 FROM THE CLUB RESPONSIBLE, OR FROM EACH OF THE PARTIES IF BOTH CLUBS ARE RESPONSIBLE FOR THE DELAY.

This Agreement, made and entered into this 12th day of SEPTEMBER, 1975

by and between DONEL CORPORATION (Reading Baseball Club) (Party of the First Part)

and PHILADELPHIA NATIONAL LEAGUE CLUB (Party of the Second Part)

Witnesseth: The party of the first part hereby assigns to the party of the second part the contract of Player RANDY LOUIS LERCH according to the Rules adopted under the Major League Agreement and the Professional Baseball Agreement and upon the following conditions (including any provisions set forth upon the back of this Agreement):

THE PHILADELPHIA CLUB SELECTS THE CONTRACT OF ABOVE
PLAYER UNDER TERMS OF THE PLAYER DEVELOPMENT CONTRACT.

(If above space is insufficient, use back of this agreement for any additional provisions.)

In Testimony Whereof, we have subscribed hereto, through our respective Presidents or authorized agents, on the date above written:

DONEL CORP. (READING) Club   PHILADELPHIA NATIONAL LEAGUE CLUB Club

By _____ (Party of the First Part)   By _____ (Party of the Second Part)

Corporate name of Company, Club, or Association of each party should be written in first paragraph and subscribed hereto.

(OVER)

---

farm director, was in the stands and sees this 20-year-old kid go out and pitch 14 innings. I left the game, tied after 14. We lost, but after the game, Dallas said he wanted to bring me up to the big leagues when the rosters expanded. I hadn't even thought about anything like that.

He said he was going to see how they could find a spot for me on the roster. I wasn't on the 40-man roster, and he had to find a spot. I didn't know what that meant.

The season was over after that game, and he wanted me to come to Philadelphia. I remember the next Phillies game, he sat me in the VIP box, and I watched Steve Carlton pitch. I'm sitting there, and he's telling me that I'd be going down on that field and playing with those big boys. It was like a dream. By the end of the game, Dallas came to me and said the next day I was going to be on the team.

I'm a baby. The last thing I wanted to do was get into a ball game. I was just happy sitting on the bench where I was at.

We were in Chicago playing the Cubs, and the wind was blowing out about 20 miles an hour at Wrigley Field like it does that time of the year. Carlton was pitching a gem. It was the ninth inning, and the Phillies were winning, 13–2. Danny Ozark says, "Get Lerch up!" I ended up getting in the game, and by the time I got done giving up a windblown grand slam to Tim Hosley, the score was 13–7. I almost lost it for them in the ninth.

I remember Jose Cardenal threw his bat at the ball. It was way away, and I think it was a breaking ball. He hit it as the bat was coming out of his hand, just good enough to loop it over the second baseman's head. I said to myself, "If they're gonna hit them like that up here, you're in the wrong league, son."

Al Woods (Blue Jays)

Al Woods made his major league debut on April 7, 1977, with the Toronto Blue Jays. He played in seven big league seasons. Woods hit a home run in his first at-bat.

I was playing winter ball down in Ponce, Puerto Rico, and Minnesota had left me off their protected list. They were trying to slip me through. That's the story I heard from one of the scouts. I ended up getting drafted by Toronto. When I first heard, I was very disappointed because I really liked the Minnesota organization.

Cal Ermer, who was my Triple-A manager in Tacoma with the Minnesota organization, was also my manager down in Ponce, Puerto Rico. He was a little disappointed too and couldn't understand why they didn't protect me.

However, my thought going into spring training was that I was with a new franchise, and I was going to be on the team. It wasn't a matter of being cocky or anything, it was just that it was a new franchise, and I figured they didn't take me from Minnesota for nothing. That's the way I pretty much looked at it.

I was having fun in spring training. It was almost like being a kid in a candy store because you're playing against guys that you'd seen on TV and read about. We were in Dunedin, Florida, at our camp site, and I was pulled in. They had their administrative offices in little portables. I think it was Pat Gillick who told me.

Toronto was a new experience. It was not just a new city, it was a different country. It was cold—very cold—when we got up there. The city was beautiful, and we were accepted warmly.

The first game was delayed, and I didn't think we were going to play. There was two feet of snow on the ground, and it was still snowing. However, we had 45,000 people in the stands on Opening Day.

Ken Brett was the starting pitcher for the White Sox that day. Steve Bowling and I were platooning at the beginning of the year, so he started. In the fourth inning, they brought in Francisco Barrios to relieve Ken Brett. The next inning, I pinch-hit for Bowling.

Getting up there, I was just thinking, "Man, it's cold out here." I was just wanting to make contact with the ball. He threw a fast ball down the middle of the plate, and I hit it out. When I connected, I knew I'd hit it good, but I didn't see where I hit it. I didn't know it had gone out 'til I heard the roar of the crowd.

After four minor league seasons, Al Woods made the inaugural Toronto Blue Jays out of spring training in 1977. He hit a home run in his first major league at-bat (Doug McWilliams / National Baseball Hall of Fame and Library).

I didn't think about hitting one out my first at-bat. I was just running the bases and I was cold. I got around them, got home, and went in the dugout. It didn't hit me until I was in the dugout by the heater and a couple of people mentioned it.

I was fortunate one of the groundskeepers got the ball and brought it to me. I was real fortunate.

Randy McGilberry (Royals)

Randy McGilberry made his major league debut on September 6, 1977, with the Kansas City Royals. He played in two big league seasons.

We were in Omaha and Joe Burke, the general manager of the Royals, was in the stands. We knew it, but he was there to see U L Washington.

Bases are loaded with no outs, and the game's on the line. We're ahead by one or two runs. I come into the ballgame, and I had good fastball that night. I was running it up there probably 95–96 miles an hour, and that was on those day's guns. It's probably more like 98 by today's numbers. I go out there, throw nine pitches, strike out the side, and the game's over. I'm walking to the dugout, and I didn't think much about it. I'm getting the high-fives and all the good stuff.

I go in, get undressed, and shower. I'm in the shower and I'm standing there with John Sullivan, who was our manager.

He looked at me and he said, "You're going to the big leagues, kid." I looked at him, and I said, "Yep. I believe I am, too. One of these days I'm gonna be there." He said, "No, kid. You're going to the big leagues. You're flying out. You and U L are going to the big leagues. When you get through showering, get your clothes on, and go to my office. Joe Burke wants to talk to you."

I went into his office, and Burke said, "Randy?" I said, "Yes, sir, Mr. Burke." He said, "Well, we want you to go up to the big leagues. We think you can help us." I said, "Okay, that's all right with me. I think I can help you out, too." He said, "Well, you and U L are flying up in the morning. Get your bags packed and be ready to go." I said, "Yes, sir."

I don't wanna sound cocky. I believe I deserved it, but at the same time, I was like a kid in a sandbox. I mean, this is the pinnacle of my profession.

I remember telling U L when we got off the plane in KC, "Man, we have arrived." He had a toothpick in his mouth and looked at me kinda funny. He said, "Man, let's make this count." We went in and I got my locker. I had my locker right next to Freddie Patek.

I'm a little anxious, but all the guys came over. Every one of them came over, shook my hand, and said, "Welcome to the big leagues. If you need anything, just give us a holler." These guys were class acts, and we're not just talking about guys that were decent ballplayers. We're talking about guys that had careers in baseball that were notable. In my honest opinion, after all these years, I still think I played with the best Royals team that ever put on a Royals uniform.

That night they tried to loosen me up. They tried the old "Hey, kid. Go get the key to the bullpen." Naturally, I had to carry the towels out to the bullpen. That was the rookie thing, but I didn't fall for the "Go get the key for the bullpen." I told them, "If I gotta have a key to the bullpen, something's wrong."

Whitey Herzog was willing to throw me in the mix pretty quick. My first game was in Seattle, and the Seattle Mariners were a brand spanking new team. They had recruited guys that had a career behind them and ahead of them. We were pretty comfortable when I went in.

The bullpen phone rang, and they said, "McGilla, you're up. You've got the seventh and the eighth, if you do good." I went, "Okay. I guess I better do good, then, huh?" Mark Littell was laughing at me. He said, "Man, everybody throws a no-hitter in the bullpen, but when you cross that fence and go out on that ball field, it's the real deal, McGilla." I said, "Okay."

The way they had the bullpen arranged, you could pop a fastball and it echoed all over the place because the bullpen was tucked inside that fenced area. I was popping the crap out of the mitt. I was like a bull in a china closet.

They had a little Datsun B210 that would ride you out and let you out in front of the dugout, and you'd walk out to the mound. I didn't really wanna ride in the car, and I started not to. Steve Mingori stopped me and said, "Hey, kid, you better get in the car. I don't think you wanna do it your way." I said, "Okay." I got in the car and let him drive me down there.

I go out to the mound, and Whitey's already standing there. He said, "All right, kid, you've got the seventh and the eighth. Show me what you got." What I did was just what came naturally. I didn't know any of the hitters. They had charted them, and they knew who they were.

My catcher said, "Here's the way I want you to look at this, McGilla. I want you to look at it like that guy is trying to take your food off your plate, and looking at you, you ain't missed too many meals." I said, "Okay."

I was popping it pretty good that night. I couldn't tell you my stats. I just know I was on the mound, and I had a good time.

Dave Machemer (Angels)

Dave Machemer made his major league debut on June 21, 1978, with the California Angels. He played in two big league seasons. Machemer hit a home run in his first at-bat. Following his playing days, Machemer became a coach.

Before I got called up, I had been leading the entire minor league system in hitting. I was hitting over .400. It was a year of reckoning for me because I'd been playing a long time. I just got on a mission and got hot that year in the Pacific Coast League. Before you know it, my name started surfacing as possibly going to the big leagues. The thing that bothered me was I wasn't on the major league roster and had never attended a big league camp.

When I was so hot, we were in a series in Hawaii. We got a runner in a rundown. I was playing third. He slid into me, and I hurt my knee. We went home to Salt Lake, and the trainer immediately had me in the hospital and scheduled for surgery. I knew nothing about it until they came in and wanted me to sign a paper saying they were going to cut my knee. I immediately dressed and left the hospital. I would not allow them to do that.

When I got back to the ballpark that day, Deron Johnson, my manager, pretty much read me the riot act for not listening to the trainer. I went into the locker room, and he says, "You're not a doctor. He knows more than you." I said, "Deron, one of the things I can do is run." I was known as a leadoff hitter that could run. I said, "I'm not getting my knee cut on seeing it was two or three days ago when I hurt it. I need to let it settle down." This went on for almost a couple weeks.

I'd come into the locker room, and Deron would call me in the office and ask, "Hey, you ready to play yet?" It got to the point where I heard I was possibly going to the big leagues, but I didn't feel physically ready. One day I walked into his office, and at that point, my knee was feeling better. It was probably 80 to 85 percent. He goes, "Mach, I want you to be completely honest. Can you play tonight?" I go, "Deron, I'm going to be honest. It's 80 to 85 percent, but I can play." He goes, "That's all right, kid. You're going to the big leagues." I was kind of in shock because of the fact I hadn't been playing for two weeks or so. That was June 13, 1978.

I flew into Boston, where the Angels were. Then I didn't play for another eight days until my debut on June 21. I got to the ballpark and saw my name in the lineup, leading off and playing second base. Bobby Grich wasn't feeling well, so I was in the lineup.

Immediately, my stomach starts turning. My roommate from Salt Lake City, Dave Frost, had been called up a couple days before that. He kind of calmed my nerves. He said, "Hey, man. Take it easy. It's no different than what you were doing."

A weird thing about it was my bats didn't arrive from Salt Lake. I didn't have a bat, so I got one from Merv Rettenmund. When I picked it up, I said to Merv, "What in the heck? How long and how heavy is this bat?" He goes, "Oh, I like long bats, Mach." It was a 35½-inch bat and 33 ounces. I was used to 34 inches and 31 ounces, but when I picked it up, it felt good to me. I said, "I'm going to use this bat."

We were in Minnesota, and Geoff Zahn was pitching. I went up there, leading off the game. Zahn took me to 3–2. He had thrown me a fastball on the inner half on 1–2, and I checked my swing. I looked behind me at Butch Wynegar catching, and he literally juggled the ball four or five times before it dropped to the ground. It was like slow motion. I let a breath out and went, "Oh, wow. I'm still alive." After that fastball, he kept throwing me slow breaking balls away. I fouled off two or three pitches. It was at least an eight- or nine-pitch at-bat.

After a few breaking balls in a row that were in the same spot, a light bulb went off in my head. I thought, "This guy's coming back inside with his fastball." That's what he did, and I was ready for it. I knew I hit it good. I had never played in Minnesota before, but when I hit it, I thought, "That's gone."

As I'm running down the first base line, I'm watching it. I'm watching the third base umpire, because I knew it was going to be close. The next thing I knew, I saw the third base umpire circling his hand for a home run.

My nickname was Choo Choo because I made noise when I ran. The next thing I heard was Bob Clear, the first base coach, saying, "Hey, Choo Choo! Hold it! You might want to come back and touch the base!" I had run completely by first base and never touched it. I came back, touched first base, and had a floating feeling circling those bases.

I remember high-fiving John McNamara at third base, and when I came into the dugout, the first guy to pick me up was Nolan Ryan. Then they mobbed me. It was a surreal feeling at that point, like, "Wow. What just happened?" It was a good feeling.

That night, Bobby Grich took me out. We went to a Chinese steakhouse, and I had the best Chinese steak I've ever had in my life to celebrate. He goes, "Well, everybody's going to call me Wally Pipp tomorrow, Mach, but I'm going to be ready to play."

My parents were instrumental in my career and making sure I was never denied the ability to play. They were at every game growing up. Unfortunately, my father had passed at 56, two years prior to my debut. My mother, wife,

Dave Machemer was called up by the California Angels during his eighth professional season. He hit a home run in his first major league at-bat (courtesy Dave Machemer).

and a lot of my family had heard the news of my debut on a Cubs game. My mom never missed a Cubs game, and my wife was listening to it with her mom, which was ironic. Jack Brickhouse was announcing the game. I'm from Benton Harbor, Michigan, which is 100 miles from Chicago. The Cubs were playing the Pirates and Chuck Tanner, who was the Pirates' manager, had homered in his first major league at-bat. When it came across the wire that I had homered my first major league at-bat, Brickhouse announced it. He didn't pronounce my name right, but when they heard him say, "From Benton Harbor, Michigan," they figured it had to be me. So they knew before I ever called them to tell them I hit the home run, which was kind of funny.

2

1980s

The 1980s saw an evolution in the style of play. It was generally a low-scoring decade, and power numbers were noticeably down. There was a focus on "manufactured runs" through speed and stolen bases. A major reason for this was the rise of relief pitching and the role of the closer. Hitters did not face starters as often.

The 1980s were also a time of labor strife, as owners complained of rising salaries. A strike shortened the 1981 season. Major league rosters were cut from 25 to 24 players from 1986 to 1989. During this time, there was also collusion between owners in an attempt to lower free agent salaries.

There are 15 stories from the 1980s that follow.

Vance Law (Pirates)

Vance Law made his major league debut on June 1, 1980, with the Pittsburgh Pirates. He played in 11 big league seasons. Vance's father, Vern, also played in the majors with the Pirates.

I was in Triple-A and playing with Portland. We were on a short road trip up to Spokane, Washington, and I got a call early in the morning in my hotel room. I picked it up, and it was my manager, who said, "Are you sitting down?" I said, "No, but I will." I sat down and he said, "Pittsburgh just called, and they would like you there tonight. Grab a cab, go to the ballpark, and pick up your stuff."

The trainer made flight arrangements back to Portland so I could pick up some more clothing and a bigger suitcase. He said, "You'll be going up for at least two weeks because they had to put Tim Foli on the disabled list."

I called my wife, had her pack a larger suitcase, and meet me at the airport. At that point, we didn't have the security issues we do today, so she was able to pretty much meet me right off the plane. We quickly ran down to the check-in area, checked in the suitcase, and then I was back on a flight to Pittsburgh. I wasn't able to take her. At that time, we had a little one-year-old.

My dad was coaching over in Japan, so he didn't hear about it until later. I'd grown up in the Pittsburgh area, with my dad (Vern) having played there. It was a dream come true to play for the Pirates.

I remember the cab going through the Liberty Tunnel and looking down where the Golden Triangle is, where the Allegheny and Monongahela meet the Ohio. That's where Three Rivers Stadium was. The stadium was all lit up in a big circle. It almost choked me up, thinking, "Man, this is what I've wanted to do since I was five or six years old, and here's the opportunity. I'm going to go out and make the most of it."

I arrived there that night, just an hour or so before the game. I wasn't activated until the next day. I took my stuff in. There was a locker and a uniform with my name on it—all the stuff that you dream about. It was pretty exciting. I sat in the stands the first night and watched the game. I went down after the ballgame and went back into the clubhouse. Chuck Tanner said, "Be ready to go tomorrow. You'll be in the lineup."

I went back to the hotel, slept, and came to the ballpark about five hours early. I didn't have anything to do. I had no money, number one. But it was so exciting just to be in the major leagues, that I got to the ballpark very early, got dressed, went out to BP, and all that.

We were playing the Mets. I looked at the lineup card, and I was playing second base. I hadn't played second base at all through the minor leagues at that point. I was primarily a shortstop and had played a couple games at third base. I hadn't been on the right side of the infield. That was a completely different thing. Quickly, during batting practice, I took a bunch of ground balls and turned a few double plays.

I turned at least one double play. That part was very exciting in that first game.

We were facing Pete Falcone, a lefty. I remember my first at-bat, going into the batter's box, and my knees were literally shaking. I was determined not to strike out my first at-bat. I ended up hitting a fly ball to right field. I was glad I made contact.

We were beating them pretty good. I got my first hit in my fourth at-bat. I hit a line drive double down the right field line off a relief pitcher named Tom Hausman. I ended up scoring and came into the dugout. After high-fives and all that stuff, one of the players brought the baseball to me. On that ball were all kinds of curse words. I'm thinking, "I am never going to be able to show anybody this ball." I'm sure the look on my face was one of disappointment. Everybody started laughing, and they tossed me the real ball. Willie Stargell, who had great penmanship, wrote that it was my first hit, who it was against, and the whole game situation.

My father was, and still is, a very active member of the Church of Jesus Christ of Latter-day Saints, as I am. Our pitching coach, Harvey Haddix, was a teammate of his. Harvey was a fine left-handed pitcher back in those days too. I knew Harvey from my childhood days.

After we won that game, I was sitting in my locker, and I saw a pair of shoes standing down in front of me as I was taking mine off. I looked up, and Harvey was there holding a can of beer. He said, "Here, take a beer. Congratulations on your first hit." I looked up at Harvey and I said, "You know I don't drink." He looked right back at me and says, "I'm just checking, son." It's one of the things that, as a member of the LDS church, we don't believe in drinking. My dad had set the example, and Harvey was just checking to see if I followed in his footsteps.

I got to play alongside a couple of my childhood heroes. Manny

Vance Law was called up by the Pittsburgh Pirates during his third professional season. Coach Harvey Haddix tested him in the clubhouse following his debut (courtesy Vance Law).

Sanguillen was on that team, and he also played with my dad. Stargell was my dad's teammate as well. When I was a little boy, Willie used to play pepper with me out in the right field bullpen at the old Forbes Field. All of a sudden, as a young man, I'm playing right next to a guy I used to look up to as a youth.

Chris Bourjos (Giants)

Chris Bourjos made his major league debut on August 31, 1980, with the San Francisco Giants. He played in one big league season. His son, Peter, also played in the major leagues.

I was in Phoenix with the Triple-A team for the Giants. Rocky Bridges, the best guy I ever played for, was the manager. He told me an hour before a game.

He said, "You're going to the big leagues tomorrow, but I've got to play you tonight because I don't have any extra players. Normally, I'd let you sit." I didn't care. I was on cloud nine. It didn't bother me one bit.

Then at the end of the game, he said, "Don't rush. Tomorrow's an off day in the big leagues." I was rushing out of the clubhouse. My wife and I were going to pack up. We actually drove to San Francisco the next day. It's almost 800 miles.

Willie McCovey retired earlier in the year. I remember coming into the clubhouse, and after I got settled, somebody came up to me and said, "Hey, you need to chip in for McCovey's retirement watch." I'm like, "I've never played with the guy." It was $20 or something like that, but I pitched in for his retirement watch that first day.

I got called up August 28 and got into my first game as a pinch-hitter a few days later. I did not want to strike out at my first at-bat. That was always on my mind for some reason. I walked on four pitches. I didn't walk much coming up in the minor leagues. I was always up there swinging. They were probably trying to get me to chase as a young hitter.

My first weekend they had an old-timers day. A lot of ex-Giants were there, including Willie Mays. I remember everybody standing around him. I shook his hand and then went back to my locker. I remember thinking, "God, he's a little guy, and he had a lot of home runs." I said to myself, "Maybe I've got a chance." I only hit one home run. I told him that story when I ran into him at a scouts banquet years ago, and he laughed.

My short time in the big league was a blur. I tell guys no matter how long you play, you're gonna miss the game when you first get done playing.

Then it goes away. There are more important things in life, like kids and grandkids.

My son's big league call-up with the Angels was more important to me, without a doubt. When he got called up to the big leagues, we flew to Baltimore, where he played in his first game. I told my wife that was better than any day I ever played in the big leagues, just watching our son there. She agreed.

Atlee Hammaker (Royals)

Atlee Hammaker made his major league debut on August 13, 1981, with the Kansas City Royals. He played in 12 big league seasons. Hammaker is honored on the San Francisco Giants Wall of Fame.

I was in Omaha, playing for the Triple-A team with the Kansas City Royals. I started out 7–0, really hot. I started getting warned that I might be getting called up soon, but unfortunately, they went on strike that year.

Because they didn't have games, they had all the pitching coaches, the manager, and all those guys come down to watch me pitch. I think I got blitzed for six or seven runs that game. That was my first loss. They all came down to see who this guy is, and I had a horrible game. That was July 4. I told my wife, Jen, "I don't know if I'm gonna get a chance now."

The strike got resolved, and they came back to play in August.

I was still having a decent year. I think I was 10–3 or 10–4 at the time. On my wife's birthday, August 8, I got called into the manager's office. John Schuerholz was on the phone and said, "Are you ready to come up to the big leagues and help us where it counts?" I said, "Heck, yeah, I'm ready."

I went and told Jen. It was a great birthday present for her. The next morning, I joined the team at home in Kansas City. They were getting ready to go on a road trip to Baltimore.

I was in shock. Kansas City back then was a really good team with George Brett, Amos Otis, Hal McRae, Frank White, Clint Hurdle, Willie Wilson, and others. When I was in college, I remember watching Brett hitting home runs against the Yankees. Then to be there playing with these guys was crazy. It was an amazing feeling.

The manager, Jim Frey, says, "Welcome to the club. Good luck to ya. Glad to have ya." That kind of thing. Then the pitching coach, Billy Connors, goes, "We haven't seen you pitch a lot, but right now we're gonna use you out of the bullpen. Be ready every night. When the situation calls for it, you may get a chance to get in. We can't tell you when you're gonna get in, but that's why you're here. You're here to help us." I was always a starter until that point, but they put me in the bullpen when I first came up.

The first game I got in was August 13 against the Orioles at the old ballpark. I came in in relief, and my first three hitters I went one-two-three, but two balls went to the wall. I got ahead of both of those guys 0–2, so the counts were in my favor, but they hit shots to right field. Imagine if those balls would have fallen in for doubles or something.

I went back to the dugout, and they were high-fiving me. I thought I pitched horribly. When you don't have a lot of confidence and haven't established yourself yet, everything is magnified. Every pitch and at-bat was magnified in my mind more than their minds.

I was fortunate I did well. It ended up being a great debut. It helped my confidence and gave me more opportunities.

Jose Alvarez (Braves)

Jose Alvarez made his major league debut on October 1, 1981, with the Atlanta Braves. He played in four big league seasons. Alvarez's 1988 call-up is also included, as he had spent five seasons out of the majors at that time.

The first call-up was very special. I had a good year in Triple-A in my first season at that level, and my ERA was in the ones much of the season. We played the Yankees' Triple-A team in the playoffs, and I thought that I was going to get called up as soon as the season was over.

The Braves weren't very good that year and finished fourth in the first half of a strike-ridden season and fifth in the second half. Bobby Cox had seen a lot of our games because Ted Turner decided to televise our games at Richmond. When I didn't get called up, it was disappointing. I felt I proved I could play at the highest level, given the chance.

The playoffs ended, and I, along with my wife Michelle, drove from Richmond to her parents' house in Jacksonville, Florida. We had only been married since June of 1981, and we already had winter ball plans in Puerto Rico, so a couple of weeks of rest was anticipated.

We had been in Jacksonville for two or three days when we got the call. The funny part of that day is I got up early in the morning and played 36 holes of golf with my father-in-law. We came back from golf, and some of my wife's sisters and their friends were over at the house, and we played softball in the afternoon. Then that night, we all went out to dinner and bowling. It was a full day of activities.

Remember, these are pre-cell phone days. We get back from bowling and it's probably 11 o'clock at night. The phone rings at my in-laws' house, and it was my mom calling from Tampa, Florida. She says, "You're going to the big leagues!" I'm like, "What? Are you out of your mind?"

She said, "I think the Braves are calling you up." I said, "Mom, there's only a week left of the season. They're not going to call me up now." She said, "Well, this guy from the Braves front office named Pat wants you to call him collect right now, and here's his number."

She gives me the assistant general manager's phone number, and I call collect. He said, "Jose, we have an issue here. Bobby wants you up here tomorrow. We can have a first class flight ticket for you at the Jacksonville airport tomorrow morning, or you can drive. Just make sure you're here by game time tomorrow." I told him I would be there. Knowing I would never be able to sleep through the night, Michelle and I packed my baseball stuff, jumped in the car, and drove straight to Atlanta. I was dead tired but was full of adrenaline. I think we got into Atlanta about six in the morning.

We had a hotel across the street from Atlanta-Fulton County Stadium. After we checked in, I laid down for maybe an hour or two. I went over to the stadium about nine o'clock in the morning, for a 1:30 game, before they had the chance to change their minds about me.

I don't know if you've seen the movie *The Rookie* with Dennis Quaid. There's a scene when he walks into the locker room in Texas, pitching for the Rays, and looks around at all the uniforms. I remember walking in and looking at uniforms of Phil Niekro, Dale Murphy, Bob Horner, Rick Mahler, Claudell Washington, Gaylord Perry, Jerry Royster, and a whole slew of big leaguers I admired. Then in the corner of the locker room, I saw my big league uniform and number. My first number in the big leagues was 50. It was a pretty cool moment that I will always remember.

I didn't pitch the first night. The second day was October 1, and it was on that day I made my major league debut [against the Giants]. It's a cool date in my family's history because not only was it the day I made my major league debut, but five years later my son Seve was born on October 1.

I pitched two scoreless, perfect innings, and struck out two. The first guy I struck out was the pitcher, Greg Minton. Then I struck out Joe Morgan. I grew up in Tampa watching the Big Red Machine. To strike out Joe Morgan, swinging on a curve ball, and coming from being behind in the count 3-0, was an exciting debut.

Phil Niekro had started the game before being relieved by Bob Walk and Steve Bedrosian. In fact, Knucksie came up to me afterwards, even after taking the loss, and said, "Jose, congratulations on making it to the big leagues. Great debut. I hope you have a long and successful career in the major leagues. I'm really happy for you." That meant a lot to me then, and it still means a lot to me now.

In '82 I was up and down a couple times. The next five seasons, I didn't smell the big leagues—'83, '84, '85, '86, '87, all were spent in the minor leagues. During the winter of '87, I attended a conference in San Diego called PAO, Pro Athletes Outreach. It's a great conference for athletes and their wives to come and get some spiritual nourishment, grow closer together, and understand some of the challenges of professional sports in a marriage.

After dinner one of the nights, Dave Dravecky and Atlee Hammaker, two really good friends of mine, asked if I thought I could still pitch in the big leagues. I said, "Absolutely." They said, "Okay. We want you to go through a program with pitching guru Tom House." House helped transform many pitchers, including Nolan Ryan. I said, "Man, I can't go do that. It's like $3,000 to go through his program."

Dave looked at me and he goes, "Jose, if you really think that you can pitch in the big leagues, and you're willing to put in the work, because there's going to be a ton of work that Tom's going to give you.... If you're willing to do that, I will pay for it all." I, being prideful and not wanting a handout, said, "Dave, I can't ask you to do that." He goes, "No, you're not asking me. I'm telling you I'm going to do it." I really was too prideful to accept the handout, so I said, "Well, let me just think about it."

We went back to Jacksonville, Florida, after the conference, and within a day Dave called me and said, "Okay, you've got a ticket at the airport. It's this weekend. You're staying with me at my house. Atlee's coming down too. I'll see you here." What else could I say but "All right, thank you, Dave"?

I went out there, and Tom put us through a grind. Everything from changing my mechanics that would make me more efficient, to getting more movement, better control, and command of my pitches. He recognized I had an above-average breaking pitch but needed to compliment it with better control and efficiency. After a thorough analysis and prescription of exercises and drills, I had a two-inch-thick booklet that had everything I needed to get prepared for the 1988 season.

That winter I went through it faithfully. I did everything he said and then some. I went into spring training in '88 at the Braves' minor league camp in the best shape and ready to start the season. Bobby Cox was the GM at that time, and I really hoped he would bring me to big league camp, but that didn't happen.

In minor league camp, I began turning some heads as I was in such good shape, and in every scrimmage, I was dominating the hitters. Jim

Beauchamp, who was the Triple-A manager, called me over at the very end of camp and said, "Hey, they want to release you, but I'm fighting for you. You might have to start the season on the disabled list, but trust me, you're going to pitch for me, and I know that you can pitch in the big leagues." He gave me about the biggest boost of confidence any man had given me in my life.

I started the 1988 season in Richmond. I was pitching in relief behind several prospects. In fact, Atlanta called up about five pitchers in the first month of the season. John Smoltz had just come over from the Tigers in 1987, and he was on that team but still very raw and not ready for the majors. The Atlanta Braves were still not doing well, the pitchers weren't doing well, and it was like a revolving door between Atlanta and Richmond, Virginia. It seemed like every few days, they were sending somebody down and calling somebody up, except me. While holding on to hope, I admit it did get discouraging.

I think May 9, 1988, was the more exciting call-up for me. Of course, your first time's exciting, but this one was special. My career, by most opinions, was dead. I was only a franchise player that set a good example but wasn't going anywhere. On May 9, 1988, a career that was dead was about to be resurrected.

That morning, Smoltz, my father-in-law, and I went out to play golf early. On the way to the Hermitage Country Club, we're reading the newspaper, and it said that Jim Acker had some elbow problems and was likely to go on the DL. Smoltz says, "You're going to get called up." I said, "No. They're not going to call me up, John." He said, "Well, I don't know why they called up five other guys. You're our best pitcher. I don't know what they're thinking." I had to explain to this rookie that 32-year-old relief pitchers seldom get called up, and that was exactly what the front office was thinking.

We get out on the golf course, and up until this time, Smoltz had never beat me in golf. He was horrible at golf in the early days, but we get out on the course that morning and he's beating me three down through the first four holes. I think we were playing two dollars a hole. We get on the fourth hole, and he has a five-foot putt for birdie after I had just missed my 10-foot par putt.

Before he gets to putt his ball, we see this maintenance truck driving down the cart path toward the green. We're the only guys on the course. It's 7:45 in the morning. A guy gets out and says, "Is one of you guys named Jose Alvarez?" Smoltz throws his putter down and says, "Dog gone it. I knew it. You just got called up to big leagues and this was going to be the first time I've ever had a chance to beat you."

So I get in the guy's truck, and he drives me to the pro shop while John and my father-in-law kept playing golf. I called my wife, Michelle, first. She's giddy and jumping for joy. She said, "You need to call Jim Beauchamp right now. They want to know where you are." I said, "Honey, I think we're going to the big leagues. I can't see that they're going to release us, so it's either we're going to the big leagues, or we have been traded."

I called Beauchamp, and his first words were, "Shoot-fire, I told you if you stuck with me, I was going to get you back to the big leagues. I don't ever want you to come back. You need to get on a plane as soon as possible and get to Atlanta and be there for tonight's game."

I went back out and played holes number eight and nine with Smoltz and my father-in-law, and I told them the match did not count since it was an abbreviated one of only six holes. John has certainly won more than his fair share of matches since then.

My father-in-law took me to the airport in Richmond, and since we got paid on the 1st and the 15th, by the 9th, we were already out of money. I had to borrow $20 from my father-in-law so I could have enough money to pay for the cab ride from the airport to the Fulton County Stadium. I went straight to the stadium and walked in about three o'clock.

It was unbelievable walking back in the locker room. Being congratulated by Bobby Cox, Phil Niekro, and many of the guys that knew me for persevering and working hard to get back to the big leagues, and them being genuinely happy for me, was very appreciated.

I didn't get in the game on May 9, and it probably was a good thing as my feet were not even on the ground. On May 10, Tom Glavine, a future Hall of Fame pitcher, started and retired the side in order in the first inning but gave up five runs in the second inning. The bullpen phone rang. Brian Snitker, current manager of the Atlanta Braves, was the bullpen coach at the time. He said, "Jose, you're up."

I warmed up very quickly, and I came sprinting in the game with runners on second and third and two outs to face Tim Wallach. On an 0–2 pitch, he grounded out to third and left both runners stranded. I ended up pitching four and one third innings of one-hit ball. The only hit was a home run to Hubie Brooks, but I later struck him out in the sixth inning. I think the coolest part of the game was I got two at-bats and I got two hits.

That was a much more exciting call-up, and I pitched so well they didn't send me back down to the minor leagues. I finished the season being voted the Atlanta Braves Most Outstanding Pitcher in 1988.

Ron Kittle (White Sox)

Ron Kittle made his major league debut on September 2, 1982, with the Chicago White Sox. He played in 10 big league seasons. Kittle was the American League Rookie of the Year in 1983.

I was in Triple-A in the Pacific Coast League, playing in Edmonton, Canada. I had a very good year. I wound up hitting .345, hit 50 home runs, and had over 140 RBIs.

I heard that through the year, every night, they would post on the Comiskey Park scoreboard, "Ron Kittle hit a home run," or something like that. So they kept tabs of every game I played up on the scoreboard.

I finished the season, and I was really looking forward to going home, to tell you the truth. I had no idea about going to the big leagues. The manager, Gordy Lund, called me in the last day and said, "You're going to Chicago tomorrow." It was already three o'clock in the morning. I was celebrating with the guys because the season ended. I had a big apartment and good roommates. If I wasn't home, I probably would not have even known about the call.

I think I got on the first flight at six or seven o'clock in the morning. I didn't get any sleep. I just got on a plane in the morning and headed to Chicago. I get into Chicago, and I'm just dead tired. My family came up to greet me, and we all got in one car.

I was driving the wrong way down a street to get to the ballpark. The cops got in front of me and said, "You can't go this way." I said, "Well, I don't know any other way. I just got called up to the major leagues." The cops were yelling at me, "There's no way you got called up to the major leagues." I literally had to do a U-turn and go around someplace else. I was unfamiliar where the parking was, but somebody knew my name and said, "Hey, park right here."

I got to the park, got a uniform on, and was ready to play. I was really exhausted. Your adrenaline's working, but you're also human. I mean, you get tired.

Growing up as a kid, I attended a few games there with my dad and went on Little League nights. It was a massive ballpark, one of the biggest ones around. As a Little Leaguer, you said, "Boy, I'd like to play there." You never think that dream would ever become a reality, but I got there.

I take batting practice, but I'm not in the lineup. When I was not playing, it was like it was in slow motion. I wound up going in to pinch-hit in the bottom of the eighth inning, and we were losing. I hit a foul home run but got a full count, and I swung at a change-up for strike three. But I took some great swings and fouled some good pitches.

I remember after the game Charley Lau, the White Sox's hitting coach, said, "Son, you just keep swinging like that and you'll be driving Cadillacs and Mercedes the rest of your life."

Bip Roberts (Padres)

Bip Roberts made his major league debut on April 7, 1986, with the San Diego Padres. He played in 12 big league seasons. Roberts was selected to one All-Star team.

My first year in big league camp was 1985 with the Pirates, and I was on Willie Stargell's B team. I was playing very well, but one day game I had a collision with Bobby Bonilla. I hurt my shoulder to where I couldn't throw well, and I was hurt most of the season. I played in Double-A and still led the league in stolen bases, but I was considered damaged goods. Both myself and Bonilla were taken off the 40-man roster.

I thought it was the worst day of my life. I'm like, "After all this hard work to get here, now I'm off the roster. Who knows what happens now?" Well, a funny thing happened. In December, I got a call from Jack McKeon saying I'm a Rule 5 pick by the San Diego Padres.

Now, I come to Padres camp in 1986, and I'm guaranteed a spot on the team if I play well. It was an amazing journey because when you're young like that, you feel the pressure of everything. I felt pressure that entire spring training. Being a Rule 5 in San Diego that first year was tough.

Ticket stub from Bip Roberts's major league debut with the San Diego Padres in Los Angeles. He faced Dodgers pitcher Fernando Valenzuela in his debut (author's collection).

I never felt I was gonna make it because I was so nervous. I was around a team with nothing but veteran guys. This is that Padres team that had gone to the World Series in 1984.

Because Alan Wiggins was having some issues personally, they decided to draft me out of the Pirates' organization and put me in that spot. He had been a tremendous player and leadoff guy. Here I was, 22, coming up from Double-A, trying to replace Alan Wiggins. And we still had Tim Flannery and Jerry Royster playing second base. I felt like the odd man out. I just felt pressure all the time.

I started doing well in spring training, and I guess they saw I had some talent, so I was able to make the team. I was in a platoon role. Steve Boros was our manager and said, "I'm going to play you against lefties, and Tim Flannery's gonna play against righties." That's how I was starting off, but he didn't tell me I had to face people like Fernando Valenzuela.

I get to the big leagues and my first game, on Opening Day, I faced Fernando Valenzuela, and he struck me out twice. It was an eye-opening experience. I had never seen a screwball that could be thrown in the dirt or thrown for a strike. I'd never faced a guy who, when he went and threw his wind-up, looked up in the heavens and then came to the plate. He was outstanding! I thought, "If this is the big leagues, I won't be here long." There were a couple of times I dragged my bat back to the dugout, scratching my head, going, "I've never seen anything like this before."

It was a tough season, and I ended up spending two years back in Triple-A before getting the call at the end of '88 after I really earned it. The first year, Tommy Lasorda kept yelling at me from the dugout, "Hey, Roberts, you've gotta earn it! You've gotta earn it!"

Bobby Witt (Rangers)

Bobby Witt made his major league debut on April 10, 1986, with the Texas Rangers. He played in 16 big league seasons. His son, Bobby Witt, Jr., is a current major leaguer.

My journey was a little bit different. I signed in '85 and went to Tulsa in Double-A for the Rangers. It didn't go the way I wanted it to. I was 0–6, with a six-something ERA. I had never won a professional game. A lot of people don't know this. I'd never won a professional game until my first big league win.

Bobby Valentine, at the time, was going with a youth movement. I went into spring training in 1986 just looking at it as experience. I was going to go in there to see what it was all about. I remember the first guy I ever faced was George Brett, and I got him to ground out. That was the first guy I ever faced in spring training! The Royals were coming off their '85 World Championship, so it was a pretty exciting time.

I didn't know what was going to happen. I knew I was there until the end. I thought, "If I don't make it here, are they going to send me back to Double-A since I didn't have a win? Am I going to Triple-A?" I didn't know what was going on.

Bobby called me into the office and told me I was going with the club to the big leagues. This is before the cell phone era. I went to find the closest pay phone, called my dad, and told him. He was so excited.

I started the third game in Arlington against Toronto. My folks live in Massachusetts, so I didn't think they were going to come. They ended up surprising me. They came to the game, and my fiancée at the time, she came to the game as well.

One of the things that sticks out, which I think would always stick out with pitchers, is that Cecil Fielder hit a home run off me. That was pretty much the end of my game that day. It wasn't a long outing. I just remember going out there and the excitement as a 21-year-old kid, being able to start in the big leagues and having that opportunity. I was grateful.

You dream about it as a kid. When it happens and becomes a reality, it's one of those things where you're just so thankful for all the people that helped you along the way.

Bob Tewksbury (Yankees)

Bob Tewksbury made his major league debut on April 11, 1986, with the New York Yankees. He played in 13 big league seasons. Tewksbury was selected to one All-Star team.

I was a big proponent of Norman Vincent Peale and the power of positive thinking. I'd always done imagery, and as I prepared to go to my first major league spring training in my two-toned, brown 1978 Mercury Zephyr, I created an image in my mind that I was going to walk into Lou Piniella's office and have him tell me that I'd made the team. Every night before I started, I would go out on the beach with my Walkman, listen to music, and do my imagery.

I had pitched 20 consecutive scoreless innings in spring training. I was at my locker, I get a tap on my shoulder and a "Lou wants to see you." I remember walking across the navy blue Yankee carpet with the big NY in the middle.

I went into the office, and I went into my dream. I went into my visualization. He said, "Bobby, you've pitched great this spring. You're gonna get the ball the fourth game against Milwaukee at Yankee Stadium. Keep it up." It was surreal. Peale said if you see it and believe it, you can achieve it. That's how I found out. I was in a bubble mentally and mechanically.

I'm from a small town in New Hampshire, and I didn't come from a whole lot. Three of us slept in one end of a trailer, and I was the oldest. There were two other kids in there. Then we moved to a double-wide trailer after my youngest brother was born.

When we first get to New York, we have a luncheon at the Waldorf Astoria. I don't have a suit. I've never owned a suit. I don't have a sport coat. I don't have any of that. I remember I had to get something in Florida. So I went to the old Chess King store and got a gray suit, which wasn't really a suit, with a pink shirt and a thin black tie. And I had these three-quarter brown zip boots. That's what I wore to the Waldorf Astoria.

I was scared to death driving in New York. The good news is I had a shitty car. If anyone hit it, it didn't matter.

The first time I get to Yankee Stadium, the first thing I did was I went out on the mound and looked at how high the seating was. Then I remembered my high school field and just thought, "It's the same distance to the plate. It's just the environment I have to control." At that time, I was locked in, and it was pretty easy to do.

I'm staying at the team hotel in Hackensack, and I have my routine. The night before I pitch, I go on a walk, bring my Walkman, and practice my pitching. So the night before my start, I'm gonna follow the routine. I go out and start walking around the hotel area. I have a ball with me, and I start doing my imagery. Now, it's probably nine o'clock at night, I'm doing my imagery, and I'm throwing the ball against this building. A patrol car went by and saw me. He's like, "What the hell are you doing?" I'm like, "Oh, I'm Bob Tewksbury. I'm pitching tomorrow for the Yankees." He looked at me and said something like, "Yeah, right. I'm the Easter Bunny." He probably thought I was out of my mind, but I just stuck with my routine.

I was totally prepared. I wasn't that nervous. I was more excited. I think with having had so much success in spring training, I was in a bubble and locked in. I don't remember it being overwhelming.

The first pitch I threw was right down the middle. The home plate umpire peeked his head out around the chest protector and said, "Ball." You know, like, "What are you gonna do about it, kid? You're a rookie." The guys had warned me about that, so I was ready.

At the time, of course, the Brewers were in the American League. They had Robin Yount and Paul Molitor. They had a pretty good offense.

Ticket stub from Bob Tewksbury's major league debut with the New York Yankees. Owner George Steinbrenner provided him with a magnum of champagne for his outstanding debut (author's collection).

But I didn't get into a whole lot of trouble. I pitched seven and a third innings, and Rod Scurry came in and got the final five outs. The final score was 3–2.

I remember there was a magnum of champagne in my locker that was probably a couple feet tall from George Steinbrenner. I still have it in my house. It's still unopened. I remember walking out of the parking lot and feeling completely satisfied, having won my first game. It's an incredible feeling.

I remember in spring training, I came off the field, the crowd gave me a standing ovation, and I didn't acknowledge it. I'm like, "I'm a rookie. I can't do this." The guys busted my balls about it.

When I left the mound in my debut at Yankee Stadium, I got a standing ovation. I tipped my cap three ways, to the crowd in front, and then kind of right and left. They fined me in kangaroo court for overzealous hat tipping.

Later, when I played with Molitor, he used to abuse me. He'd go, "Yeah, Tewks won his first major league game. I was there. He came off, he tipped it to the front, and he turned around and tipped it to center field, and then he bowed." He just embellished the whole thing, but he was there, and it was pretty cool to share that with him as a member of the Twins.

Ed Hearn (Mets)

Ed Hearn made his major league debut on May 17, 1986, with the New York Mets. He played in three big league seasons. Hearn is the only player in professional baseball history to win a championship in A-Ball,

Double-A, Triple-A, and the major leagues in four consecutive years with the same franchise.

I was disappointed in '85 when I didn't break camp. In '86, I was really disappointed. Five weeks into the season with Tidewater, we were playing in Pawtucket. Sam Perlozzo, my manager, called my hotel room after a game. I came down because we'd often have conversations and had a pretty good player-coach relationship.

He called me in. He's like, "Yeah, man, how you doing? How are you feeling? I mean, you kind of expected to break camp." I said I was all right. He said, "Well, all this crap is done, man. After all these years, you're gone tomorrow." I'm like, "What?" It was an emotional moment for both of us. We had some good times together in the years prior to that, so it was a meaningful time.

It was probably about 11:00 or 11:30 p.m., and I called my mom and dad.

The next night, May 9, I was at Shea Stadium in a Mets uniform for a game against the Reds. My parents showed up and followed us around for a week to Houston and then to L.A., because I didn't get into a game until May 17. It was the NBC Game of the Week!

I was 2-for-2 in my first two at-bats! I remember being disappointed I had my first at-bat and it wasn't televised.

When I came up for that second at-bat, I step into the box, and Vin Scully makes note of my size, 6'3" and 215 pounds. He says, "Ed Hearn was appointed to the West Point Military Academy. He would have made an impressive general." Like on cue, I hit a rocket to left-center. It looks like the tape was cut because it was so on cue. I had a nice game at the plate. I flied out to the warning track and walked in my other appearances.

One of my biggest memories was in the fifth inning or so. The sun was straight up. I was catching and a guy fouled one up in the air. I turned, pulled my mask off, looked up, and looked dead into the sun. I couldn't see anything but purple spots. One of the tricks fans don't see is players scan the stands to see where people are looking or if they're standing or not, and you can maybe relocate the ball. Well, none of that worked. I hear steps coming at me, and I'm like, "What the hell is that?" I look up, and here's Keith Hernandez charging in. He caught the foul pop-up right inside the circle, almost in the left-hander's batter's box, flips it to me, and he goes, "I've got your back, rook."

Greg Mathews (Cardinals)

Greg Mathews made his major league debut on June 3, 1986, with the St. Louis Cardinals. He played in five big league seasons. His 11 wins in 1986 were the most by a Cardinals rookie since 1955.

It was kind of frustrating because the year prior, I was the Cardinals' number one prospect. I go to big league camp, and the last game of spring training, I popped something in my middle finger. It created inflammation. My middle finger hyper-extended straight out, and I had to go through rehab just for my stupid middle finger.

Mike Dunne was a number one draft pick, so he was a possible call-up. It was pretty much who's gonna pitch the best at that time. We were in Omaha, Nebraska, playing the Royals, and it was a doubleheader. I threw the first game, and Mike Dunne started the second game. I threw a three-hit shutout.

The next day, Jim Fregosi calls me in the office. I didn't know if I was in trouble or not, but he said, "Congratulations." I couldn't believe it. You can't put all the emotions into one moment because it was just overwhelming. I called my wife and said, "You won't believe this. I just got called up."

It's all exciting stuff, but we were so unorganized. How do we get out of Louisville? Get out of the apartment? Get a place in St. Louis? All this stuff was blowing through my head. Our son was only a year old. If I was by myself, no problem, but when you've got a family, you've gotta take responsibility for that as well. Everything was happening all at once, but it worked out.

The team was just starting a road trip to Cincinnati, so I had to get everything organized, get back to Louisville, get all my stuff, fly to St. Louis, and then join the team in Cincinnati. It was quick. They had the hotel behind the stadium. We were able to check in, get our stuff together, and then I was able to fly out to join the team in Cincinnati. It's not very far. It's only an hour flight. I was able to do that and join the team, pretty much just before game time.

Normally, in the minor leagues, everywhere was like the size of a garage. The next thing you know, it was like an auditorium in terms of the clubhouses. I walked around and looked at everybody, and I finally saw my name and my number. Everything was already in my locker. It was so cool.

It was funny because I was number 53. I guess it started with Ozzie Smith at 1 and went all the way down. They just added a number. At that time, nobody was really 53. I wasn't going to say anything. I was just happy to have a number. That made me locker mates with Willie McGee. Willie was laughing 'cause it was the same way for him originally. He was 51, but he didn't want to say anything.

I just really had time to put my uniform on and get out to the dugout before the game started.

Whitey Herzog had talked to me and let me know when my slot was. I pitched that game in Omaha, and then the next day, I got called up. They kept me on the same five-day schedule. I didn't have to wait any extended amount of time, which was cool because you kind of get in that groove of throwing every five days. That helped me.

I pitched my first game in Houston. At the Astrodome, you could hear every word everybody was saying. A good thing about it was the day before, John Tudor was pitching. I was able to sit in the stands behind home plate, charting all the pitches John threw. I was able to look at the hitters and get a good grasp on the scenario of how I was going to throw.

I did not sleep at all that night before. All I was thinking was, "Holy cow."

I was originally scheduled to pitch against Nolan Ryan, but he was scratched the last second and Jim Deshaies was put in his spot. I was more scared about hitting against Nolan Ryan than I was about pitching against him, because in the minor leagues, you don't hit. Here I am, not having swung a bat in I don't know how many years, and I've got to go to the plate against Nolan Ryan. I was afraid of being embarrassed. I was honestly relieved that I wasn't pitching against him.

The longest duration was a half an hour before the game. That is the longest time of your life. Everything was dragging, and I was like, "God, this is killing me." My heart was pounding, but by the time I walked through the lines and got on the mound, everything went away. Everything just clicked like, "All right, there's no difference between here and the minor leagues. It's the same game."

Once I threw the first pitch, I was in the ninth inning in a blink. The next thing I know, I'm getting congratulated for winning my first game. I was like, "Wow. I can't believe this is happening."

I was one out from throwing a shutout in my first start. A rookie pitcher hadn't thrown a complete game shutout on his debut in a long time. I ended up giving up one run in the ninth inning. It was close, but we still won. It was 3–1 at the end.

I remember the Houston Rockets were in the NBA postseason at the time, playing the Celtics. They interrupted the game and showed a flash of me pitching. I got some national coverage, 'cause all my friends in California sent me messages about that part too. It was a mind blower.

Ed Vosberg (Padres)

Ed Vosberg made his major league debut on September 17, 1986, with the San Diego Padres. He played in 10 big league seasons. Vosberg is the only pitcher to play in the Little League World Series, the College World Series, and the Major League World Series.

I was playing for the Las Vegas Stars. It was 1986, and our team had made the playoffs. I thought I might have a possibility of being called up when the playoffs were over. Nobody knew. They didn't tell us. However, I thought I had a realistic chance.

You don't wanna look ahead and expect anything, but I think we were thinking to ourselves, "Oh my goodness, we're losing time because we're in the playoffs. We could be in the big leagues." You hate to think that way, but I think everybody, in the back of their minds, was thinking, "Where do I really wanna be?" That's in the major leagues.

Our team won the championship, and I got called into the office. Larry Bowa called me in and said, "Congratulations."

I had a really close relationship with both my mom and dad, and I would always talk to them every couple days. I remember calling them, giving them the news, and how thrilled they were. They said they were gonna be there. It was a great thrill.

I think there were three or four of us that got the opportunity to go to San Diego. We were playing a home series against the San Francisco Giants. I remember how exciting it was. It was a great thrill, being 24 years old and getting a chance to go to the big leagues, which is every kid's dream.

I was fortunate to pitch that first series. The Giants had a bunch of great players—Will Clark, Chili Davis, Dan Gladden, and Jose Uribe. I'll never forget facing Vida Blue, who was a guy I looked up to as a kid. He was a great pitcher who won the Cy Young and MVP in 1971. I got an at-bat off him and lined out to the shortstop. It was a big thrill, just to be able to hit a ball off that guy. My family was all there, and it was a big thrill for all of us.

Over the first four innings, I gave up just one hit. In the fifth inning, Kevin McReynolds, our center fielder, dropped a routine fly ball, and it ended up costing me. I gave up three runs in the inning.

I came out of the game losing, 3–1, after five innings. We came back, and Benito Santiago hit a home run to win the game in the tenth inning.

You get called up at 24 and you think, "I'm gonna have a long career." I did get called up for a week in '87, but after '86, I didn't play in the big leagues again until 1990 with the Giants. I had a very interesting up and down career. I was very proud of the fact that many times I wanted to quit and give up out of frustration and disappointment, but I stuck it out and was very lucky to play 20 years in the game. It was a fun journey.

Mike Campbell (Mariners)

Mike Campbell made his major league debut on July 4, 1987, for the Seattle Mariners. He played in six big league seasons. Campbell was named the Pacific Coast League MVP in 1987.

I grew up in a baseball family. My dad was a huge baseball guy. Growing up with a batting cage in our backyard, my two brothers and I played baseball constantly. I threw baseballs in that batting cage all the time. In Seattle, we didn't have the weather year-round, but when the weather got good, the cage went up.

I knew I wanted to be a major league baseball player at a young age. It's what I wanted, and I just felt like I was gonna make it happen. I was a clueless kid. The odds of making it are pretty remote, but for me I just felt I was gonna make that dream come true somehow.

In 1987, I was playing for the Calgary Cannons in the PCL. I was having an extremely good year. That year I ended up being the MVP of the league, but it was late June that I got called up. Guys start talking and saying, "Hey, you're gonna get called up soon the way you're throwing the ball. It's gonna happen." One of our coaches said, "Skip wants to see you in his office." You know it's not a bad thing 'cause you're performing well. You just hope it's the call.

I go into our manager Bill Plummer's office. He said, "Sit down, Soup." That's my nickname, Soup. He goes, "Soup, you've been traded." I was like, "What?" I'm not sure of the team but I coulda swore he said to the Yankees. I grew up in Seattle. I couldn't wait to get to the big leagues in Seattle, my hometown. When I heard I got traded, my stomach dropped. He didn't wait too long, and then he finally told me, "I'm just kidding, man. You got called up to the big leagues."

I remember the first person I called was Michelle, my fiancée. Then I called my parents. It was pretty satisfying to be able to tell my parents, especially my dad. Working with us as kids with baseball and then seeing his son get there was a big deal for him.

They called me up quite a few days before I was going to pitch. They wanted to give me time. They wanted me to throw a bullpen off the Kingdome game mound after one of the games, which was kinda unique. You don't see that very often, but they wanted me to get a feel for that mound. I think it was about a week before I was going to pitch.

They told me that I was gonna be pitching on the Fourth of July in the Kingdome against the Detroit Tigers. It ended up being a huge story in Seattle, and there was a lot of media coverage because I was coming home. I was engaged to a University of Washington Husky cheerleader, and we were both doing interviews. I don't wanna sound braggy, and hopefully this is not coming across like that. It was just an exciting time.

I was up against a very good veteran hitting team, pitching against a guy that was an All-Star, and now Hall of Famer, in Jack Morris. I knew I had my hands full.

I didn't throw the kind of game I wanted to throw. I remember the first inning. Lou Whitaker flew out, and then I faced Bill Madlock second. He got on base. Then I struck out Kirk Gibson for my first strikeout, and the catcher threw out Madlock trying to steal on that pitch. So it was a strike him out, throw him out, end of the inning.

I go back to the dugout and I'm high-fiving everyone. I'm almost thinking to myself that this big league stuff isn't that big of a deal. I was just a young, green, inexperienced guy at the big league level.

Then I started to lose my location with my pitching. I started to get behind hitters. I had a big curveball, and they saw I wasn't throwing it for strikes consistently. They would just take it. They taught me a good lesson.

Triple-A hitters are great hitters, but there's a difference with the big league hitters. They're very smart. They watch, see what you're doing, and see patterns. They saw that I was not throwing the big hook for strikes consistently. They just kinda spit on it and were sitting on my fastball. It was difficult after that.

Lineup card from Mike Campbell's major league debut with the Seattle Mariners (author's collection).

That outing ended up being frustrating. I felt like I let a lot of people down. I had probably 50 people that I gave tickets to for the game.

I had one more outing and it was a little bit of the same thing. Then they sent me back to Calgary. It went from this really exciting time to this really big letdown.

I laugh about it now because I went back to Calgary, and I did what I had to do. I won my next five games and then they called me back up. From there through the rest of the season, I pitched well. My record didn't show it, but the way I pitched from there on out was pretty good for that season.

Jeff Schaefer (White Sox)

Jeff Schaefer made his major league debut April 7, 1989, with the Chicago White Sox. He played in five big league seasons.

I loved playing. I created a model for myself when I got into pro ball that whatever level I was at, that was gonna be my big leagues. I figured you do the best you can, and if something breaks from there, great.

I was fortunate to move through the Orioles organization on a timely basis to Triple-A, but Cal Ripken was up there, and Billy Ripken was coming up behind me. The design was for it to be Ripken to Ripken to Murray, not Ripken to Schaefer to Murray.

I was an organizational guy and did everything I was supposed to do. They did me a favor and sold me to the Angels. The Angels converted me from being primarily a second baseman, which I had been my whole life. They moved me over to short and things started to pop from there. I became more of a commodity because I was more versatile. I could play short and second.

From there, I got Rule Fived by the Dodgers which was nice, but I ended up back in Double-A with them before I climbed up to Triple-A for the playoffs.

The next year, '88, I signed with the White Sox. I had a good year, probably my best year.

I was married. I had one child and another one on the way. I just got to the point where I was like, "Okay, if I don't get called up at the end of this year, this is probably not gonna happen. I probably should make a decision on life and head home." I didn't get called up. I was heartbroken. I had to start to act like a man, not a boy, and make a decision.

I went home and started a limousine company in Charlotte, North Carolina. That wasn't really my home, New York was. I knew nothing about it. I got lost more times than I got people to their destinations, but I had a bottle of wine in the back for everybody so they'd get juiced up a little bit and wouldn't be mad at me.

The bats, balls, and everything were still in the house. I'd pick them up, I'd swing the bat, and I'd do whatever. The dream wasn't leaving.

Then I got a call from Terry Bevington, who was my manager in Triple-A. He got the first base coaching job with the White Sox that year. He said, "You need to come to spring training. They have some plans on making some changes with what's up the middle right now. You have a legit chance of making the big league club as a utility man." I had a conversation with Terry, who was a great advocate of mine. I said, "I'm going to get myself ready. I'll go there, but if I don't make the club, I'm coming home."

I got there and was doing everything with the big league club. I continued to survive the cuts. I was getting closer and closer to the point of going north.

Jeff Torborg, with about three days left, called me down to the right field line in Sarasota and said the golden words, "You're going north." He told me not to say a word. I said, "No problem."

I went into the dugout and called Dave Gallagher down. He was my roommate from the year before. I told him. We were in the little bathroom jumping around like, "I'm going! I'm going!" Walt Hriniak walked in the bathroom and looked at us like, "What's wrong with you guys?"

No contract was signed at that point. I was still a non-roster guy. I had heard the horror stories of teams on the last day making a trade, sending guys down, or something where you don't break with the team.

When we got on the plane to fly to Oakland, I went into the bathroom and locked the door before the plane was to take off. Jeff Torborg came on the speaker and said, "Schaef, you can come out of the bathroom. You're going north with us. Don't panic." I thought if they couldn't find me, I had to go.

We flew to Oakland the night before Opening Day and I still hadn't signed the contract. I was sweating it. I stayed up all night. I was in panic mode that something was going to happen before the next day.

I got a phone call about one o'clock the afternoon of game day to sign the contract. The whole process is almost surreal. Now I know I'm a big leaguer, but I haven't played a game yet, so am I really a big leaguer?

I walk into the clubhouse. There's my uniform hanging up, and it's a real number. I think I was wearing 56 or maybe something even higher that spring training. It was amazing. Number 15 was hanging up there. That was a thrill for me because Thurman Munson was my idol growing up, and he was 15.

As I was putting on my jersey, Carlton Fisk came down. Fisk and Munson were warriors. They respected each other, but they competed against each other to the utmost. Fisk said, "Number 15." I said, "Yeah." He knew I was from New York and was a Yankee fan. He said, "Thurman's number." I said, "Yes, sir." He said, "He was a great guy and that's a great number to wear."

I got into a game in late innings that series. I went in at second base and had one play. I also got to hit against Eric Plunk, who ended up striking me out. He threw me two curveballs I took man hacks at. I never really saw curveballs like that in Triple-A. I took the strikeout with great pride and went back to the dugout.

There's nothing like the first at-bat. There's nothing like the first play. There's nothing like the first time you see your name on the scoreboard. The firsts are incredible.

I probably savored it more than most because it did take me eight and a half years to get there. I was almost 30, and I felt like I was 12.

Greg Litton (Giants)

Greg Litton made his major league debut on May 2, 1989, with the San Francisco Giants. He played in six big league seasons. Litton played all positions except center field at the major league level.

It was really my first year as a utility player. I didn't have a position, per se. I started off in Phoenix in Triple-A, and I was playing every time at a different position.

I didn't handle it well mentally, at least offensively. Defense was never an issue for me. But when you don't have a set position or know you're going to be in the lineup the next day, it's tough not to put pressure on yourself at the plate. You feel like if you have a good game, you'll play the next day, and if not, you may not.

I had a real good first couple of games, but after three weeks, I was only hitting about .185.

I think I went 0-for-3 that night. I didn't even have a good game. I went home after the game and my roommate, John Skurla, and I were playing some old video game at the time. At about midnight, Bruce Graham, our trainer, called me and told me I needed to come to the ballpark and pack my bags. It wasn't even a coach.

I didn't believe him. I thought there were a bunch of ball players sitting around the locker room drinking beer. They were going to play a practical joke and make me think I was going to the big leagues, especially when hitting .185.

I argued with him for a few minutes, and he kept on going. I said, "All right. I'm coming."

I didn't believe it until I got there and saw it wasn't a joke. It was an incredible feeling. I wish I could put it into words how awesome it was. I had dreamed of that moment since I was probably eight years old. To finally have it happen was awesome.

I couldn't wait to drive back to my apartment and call my father. My dad was an All-Southeastern Conference baseball player at Mississippi State and had a chance to play professional baseball, but his passion was coaching. He was my coach my whole life. He was the one who taught me everything about the game. Calling him that night was pretty special because we had both put in a lot of work together.

It was a thrilling night. I didn't get much sleep and had an early flight the next morning to San Francisco. I knew it was a night game and I landed in San Francisco about noon. They said somebody with the ball club would be there to pick me up. I was looking forward to going back to the hotel, checking in, and not going to sleep, but just laying down and resting for a little bit.

About 12:30, he pulls up to the stadium. I was like, "Well, geez. I guess these big leaguers get here early for night games." I learned later that he just didn't want to go to the hotel, which was 20 minutes in the other direction, so he dropped me off at the stadium at 12:30. I wasn't complaining, 'cause I would've flown in the night before and slept in the locker room. I got to walk around the stadium before anybody really got there.

Looking back on it, I'm glad it happened that way 'cause I got to walk around the locker room and see all the names, and walk down to the dugout, which was quite a hike from the locker room in Candlestick. I got to sit in the dugout with nobody around and take it in. It was pretty cool. Time flew by, 'cause it didn't seem like I was there by myself for three hours.

I'll never forget, the first person that showed up was Brett Butler. He came over and introduced himself, and it was just awesome. He made me feel right at home. It meant a lot to me.

We were playing the Cubs, and I guess Roger Craig went with the old theory of throwing you in the fire. I started at second base that night, and Greg Maddux was on the mound for the Cubs. That was pretty cool. Growing up, there was TBS with the Braves and WGN with the Cubs. Those teams were what we grew up watching mostly.

Some young players are either cocky or just self-confident. They just think they belong there. Even though I thought I could play there, until I was actually on the field with all those guys, I don't think I truly believed it.

It was an interesting game. A lot of stuff happened.

Usually, the shortstop calls the plays in the infield. We had a shortstop, Jose Uribe, who didn't speak great English. He was a great guy and a good player, but he didn't make any calls. Before the game, Bob Lillis and I went over the other team—where to play everybody, who's going to have the bag, and all of that. He had me calling the plays, which is a big responsibility, but I don't remember ever getting nervous on defense, and I don't even remember a single play on defense.

My first at-bat off Maddux, on the first pitch I saw in the big leagues, I hit a line drive down the right field line, about three inches foul. I was like, "Oh, man." I battled but ended up striking out. I remember walking back to dugout, and I couldn't have spit if you had paid me. I had cotton mouth 'cause I was nervous. The next at-bat, I flew out to right. I just missed a pitch, hitting it real hard. Maddux was pitching a good game.

Leading off the sixth inning was Will Clark. It wasn't like one of today's shifts, but they put a little mini-shift on him. Will, being the team player that he was, pushed a bunt and just trotted to first. He probably ran about 75 percent, and he didn't even need to do that.

I still remember Maddux yelling at Will to swing the bat. You know the saying in baseball, "Don't forget about the hitter." Well, Maddux got pissed off at Will, and the first pitch to Kevin Mitchell, he hung a slider and Mitchell hit a bomb.

Then Maddux gets two quick outs, and who's up? Me.

He plunks me right in the knee. Just smokes me. It was obviously intentional. I knew he hit me intentionally. That didn't bother me. What pissed me off is he hit me right on the outside of the left knee. I went down like a log. I couldn't act like it didn't hurt. I couldn't get up because of my knee.

He's standing out there on the mound with his chest bowed out. All this stuff's going through my head like, "You can't let these guys push you around! Should you go to the mound?" I'd never charged the mound before, but all these emotions are going through my head.

Then Mark Letendre, the trainer, came out. That was the first time in my career a trainer had to come onto the field for me. That ticked me off. In my head, it made it ten times worse. I obviously didn't go to the mound, but I'll never forget the next inning. Shawon Dunston was up, and we had Big Daddy, Rick Reuschel, on the mound. On the first pitch, he knocked Dunston on his back. I would have run through a brick wall for him. As a veteran, he stood up for a rookie.

After the game, they made me ice. I had to show up early the next day. When I showed up, Mark goes, "Well, you don't even have any swelling." It hurt a little, but it wasn't an issue.

I was naïve. I didn't even know why I was called up, and I didn't really care. All I knew was I was going to the big leagues, so when I was going to San Francisco, I planned on staying there. I found out Chris Speier had hurt his back and been put on the 10-day disabled list. That is why I got called up. Of course, 10 days later, I got sent down.

It was funny because I took my golf clubs and my golf shoes, because I planned on being there. I didn't plan on going back to the minor leagues. When the guy dropped me off at the stadium, instead of the hotel, I had to walk in with golf clubs, which wasn't the best look. I put the stuff in my locker. Some of the veterans were giving me a hard time. I was like, "Well, shoot. I plan on being here all summer. I want my golf clubs with me."

After the game, I came in, and one of the veterans had taken one of my golf shoes, went around, and got all the players to sign it. Right on the tongue was Roger Craig. I'm like, "Really? You had to get the manager? You couldn't have just done the players?"

Pat Combs (Phillies)

Pat Combs made his major league debut on September 5, 1989, with the Philadelphia Phillies. He played in four big league seasons. In 1989, his first professional season, Combs reached every level of professional baseball.

I was drafted in '88 but didn't start my pro career until '89 because I was on the Olympic team, and that didn't get over until August.

I went to spring training and participated in big league camp, which was great. Of course, I knew I was gonna be sent down. I thought I was gonna go straight to Double-A. They put me in Single-A in Clearwater, and after [six] starts, they moved me to Double-A in Reading. I had a pretty good summer, but a little bit up and down.

In Double-A, the roving pitching instructor, George Culver, came into our clubhouse. This would've been middle of August in '89. He said, "We're gonna move you to Triple-A, just to get a bearing on where we wanna start you for next year."

I challenged him in the meeting and said, "Well, why wouldn't I be considered for getting called up to the big leagues this year if I finish up well?" He said, "You pitched well, but we're not projecting you to go to big leagues this year. We're thinking you'll start out at Triple-A or Double-A next year, then we'll evaluate where you are." I wouldn't say it ticked me off, but it motivated me to have a strong finish to the year.

They put me in Triple-A, and in my first starts there I threw a one-hitter and a three-hitter, so two shutouts in a row. For the third game, Lee Thomas, the general manager for the Phillies, came to see the game, and I had another good start. After the game, he talked to me about getting promoted.

It was an interesting conversation because what I remember most about him saying was because of the way I pitched in Triple-A, the Philly papers were calling for me to get promoted, and that was not his intention. He said, "With the kinda year that we've had with the big league club and the way you're pitching, you're kinda forcing our hand." I was like, "Well, I didn't mean to force your hand, but I do wanna get to the big leagues as quick as I can." So anyway, at that moment I was told I'd get the September call-up.

I think the other good news for me was there wasn't a whole lot of pressure in the call-up itself. Knowing where the Phillies were at that time in terms of rebuilding, I saw it as a tremendous opportunity. I was on a hot streak, throwing the ball well, and locked in. I felt I could go up, compete, and it would be a fun experience with less pressure to win. I could just go out there and perform the best I could.

They called us up September 1, and I had a few days to get fitted for a uniform, get in the dugout, and get acclimated to the team. I remember learning the signs and learning from the catchers how they wanted to call a game. It was a lot to soak in those few days.

I knew a little bit about the Pirates. I knew they had some tremendous players—Bobby Bonilla, Jay Bell, and some guy named Barry Bonds. But my thought going into it was, "I've got nothing to lose and everything to gain. Let's just go out and throw it."

Warming up in the bullpen felt surreal with all the emotions the guys talk about. It's the excitement, trying to control the adrenaline, and trying not to overthrow. That was the biggest thing my pitching coach, Darold Knowles, was reminding me in the bullpen. He said, "Just throw your game. Don't try to do anything different or special. What you've been doing up to this point will get big league hitters out."

It was pretty interesting. Nobody else talks to you. You go down and warm up in the bullpen, walk to the dugout, and it's complete silence in the dugout. It's not like college or high school teams with a bunch of rah-rah. It was cool I was starting at home. I had my parents, my fiancée, a lot of family, and extended family, in the stands. They flew up for the game. I also had some friends come in.

It's weird. You walk out to the mound, and it's almost like the world shuts off. All I could see was my catcher, and I couldn't hear much in terms of crowd noises. You just get locked into this zone.

I remember the nervousness of the first pitch. I threw a first-pitch strike, and all of a sudden, it's like the nerves went away. Unfortunately, the first batter hit a routine ground ball, and our shortstop, Dickie Thon, threw it in the dugout. So right off the start, I've got a man on second, no outs. It's not the start you envision, but I gave up the one run in the first inning, and that was it.

I had a couple big strikeouts in the game, including striking out Bonilla on a split-finger pitch. There were certain key moments that just never leave your mind. Thirty years later, I can still envision certain pitches of that game that are stuck in my brain.

I remember walking off the mound, and we had a 2–1 lead in the sixth inning. I felt good. I felt like I did my job and put us in a position to win it. Jeff Parrett, who was having a tremendous year as a middle guy, was brought in for the seventh inning, and things didn't go well.

Obviously, I was disappointed I didn't get the win, but the team won. You have to put aside those selfish ambitions and goals because if the team does well and we win the game, there's a lot to celebrate.

One of the funny things was my mom was a very vocal fan. She was vocal that night, and the Phillies fans loved it. They were kinda having fun with her. There were certain times in the game when I wasn't so locked in, and I could hear my mom's voice.

The next day in the paper, I think it was the Philly *Daily News*, said, "Combs and Mom Defeat Pirates." It was kinda funny, but I walked into the clubhouse and just got hammered by my teammates. That next Saturday, we had kangaroo court and I got fined for having a loud mom. I had to have a conversation with my mom to say, "Hey, Mom, this is not like college and high school. You've gotta keep it down a little bit in the stands."

There's a trivia question about my call-up. I was the first player in major league history, in my first professional year, to go from Single-A, to Double-A, to Triple-A, and to the big leagues. I touched all levels in the minors and got called up in September. It usually comes up as a trivia question on somewhere like ESPN. It's kinda funny because people will start texting me, saying, "Hey, you're on ESPN again."

3

1990s

The 1990s were another decade of expansion, with the growth from 26 to 30 teams. Central divisions were developed. The Milwaukee Brewers moved from the American League to the National League.

The influence of money on baseball grew in the decade. The 1994 strike saw the World Series cancelled for the first time since 1904. Interleague play was introduced. Playoffs were expanded with the additional division winners and wild card teams.

While scoring and power numbers were low in the 1980s, they increased dramatically in the 1990s, enhanced by the use of steroids.

Rules for the disabled list were modified, impacting the frequency of roster changes at the major league level.

The 42 players whose stories follow debuted during the decade.

Bill Sampen (Expos)

Bill Sampen made his major league debut on April 10, 1990, with the Montreal Expos. He played in five big league seasons. Sampen led the Expos with 12 wins during his rookie season.

I was playing winter ball in the Dominican and was with Pittsburgh at the time. When I was down there, I was told I was taken in the winter Rule 5 draft by the Expos. I didn't know what that was, but the one thing I gathered from it was I was gonna go to big league camp, which was my first opportunity. At that point, I didn't know what would come of it.

It was late in camp. The numbers were dwindling, and obviously my odds were increasing as people were getting shipped to Triple-A. I don't remember the exact moment, but it was literally just a couple days before we broke camp that I was informed they were going to keep me.

I had an advantage that year too. They expanded rosters because of the lockout. It made it a little bit easier for them to keep me. It was lower risk for them with the expanded rosters.

I got into the second game of the season, and the one word that comes to mind is surreal.

I had grown up a Cardinals fan. I lived two to two-and-a-half hours from Busch Stadium and had been there a number of times throughout my childhood. I had listened to the Cardinals on the radio about every night. We didn't have games on TV all the time back then.

I show up in St. Louis and there's Ozzie Smith, Terry Pendleton, Willie McGee, and Vince Coleman. Those were my guys. They were kinda my heroes. It was a bit odd and nerve-wracking. First, that I was even on the same field. Then when warming up in the bullpen, to think, "Okay. Now I'm gonna have to go pitch against these guys. This can't be real."

Brett Gideon tweaked something, so that was what led to me being put in. I had already been out in the pen warming up, so it was kind of a normal entry. I don't know if I got any extra pitches, but I had time to prepare in the bullpen. From that standpoint, I was ready. I'm not sure I was ready mentally, but physically, I was ready.

The first guy I faced was Tom Brunansky. He lined a single to right field. That was kind of a wakeup call, like, "Okay. This is real. This is now a competition. This is work." Fortunately, he didn't line it over the wall. He just lined it into right for a single for a more subtle wakeup call.

Kip Gross (Reds)

Kip Gross made his major league debut on April 21, 1990, for the Cincinnati Reds. He played in six big league seasons. Gross also played five seasons in Japan.

I was with the Mets for three years in their minor league system. I got traded over to the Reds and went to spring training in '90. I got a big league invite, but that was the year they had the lockout, so it was a limited spring training.

I did well at spring training. At the end of camp, it was the strangest way how they handled this, but they didn't call individuals into the office. They called the entire group that was getting sent down into the office. I'd never seen it before or after.

After the meeting was over, Lou Piniella stops me and says, "I just want to let you know, you should be on this team, but we need to carry three catchers."

I start the season in Nashville, and I'm pitching well. We go to

Oklahoma City. I can't remember if we got rained out, or what it was, but we didn't play that first night's game. Pete Mackanin was our manager. He takes us to an indoor batting cage so the hitters can hit. There really isn't anything for the pitchers to do, but we all go.

We're in this facility, and guys are having fun hitting balls. Over on the side, there's a basketball court. Most of the pitchers are over there. I was never that guy who really wanted to play basketball much, but I thought, "What the hell, I'm gonna go over and play a little bit." I go over, get the ball, and I start playing for about 30 seconds.

Mackanin calls me over. He goes, "I don't want you playing basketball." I said, "I know I'm not very good, Pete, but I'm just hanging out with the guys shooting some hoops." He goes, "No. I gotta tell you right now. Don't say a word to anybody, but you're going to Cincinnati in the morning, so you can't play. The press doesn't know anything about this. You can't tell anybody."

I'm sitting there with the best news I've ever heard in my entire life, and I can't tell a soul until the morning.

My roommate was Donnie Scott, the catcher. I'm sitting in this room with him that night, and I'm looking at him like, "Dude, I gotta tell you something right now, but I can't." I wasn't gonna tell a soul. That morning, I wake up early. Donnie's like, "What in the hell are you doing?" I said, "Dude, I got called up." I knew Donnie quite a bit and he was happy for me. He'd already played in the big leagues and was a switch-hitting catcher.

I get on a plane and go to Cincinnati, where they're playing the Braves. I go in the clubhouse, and I already know everybody 'cause I'd been playing with them through spring training. Barry Larkin was the first guy to come over, say hi, and congratulate me. He was always awesome to me.

Then Norm Charlton comes over to congratulate me. I knew Norm pretty well from spring training. Every clubhouse has a place where you can put your personal items, so you don't have to keep them in your locker. He takes me over, opens this drawer, and it's full of cash. He goes, "You're new here. You probably don't have very much money, so if you ever need some, it's right here. If you need it, take it. Just return it." It was an honor system with the team. It was wide open; there wasn't even a key. The team was so close that everybody had an eye on what was going on. I don't think anybody knew about it other than the players.

I go out for the game that day, and it's raining. I'm just sitting there watching, and nothing's happening. I'm on the bench, and I do not want to leave that dugout. They ended up calling the game. They didn't even play. I was sitting up there like, "Man, my first day in the big leagues, and I don't even get to see a game played."

At that time, the Reds had won eight straight to start out the season. The next day, Lou tells me to get up for the ninth inning. I go in for the ninth inning, and my first hitter is Dale Murphy. I'm thinking, "Holy shit! I've gotta face Dale Murphy for my first hitter!"

I get on to the mound. I swear to God, I couldn't have thrown my first pitch more down the middle of the plate in the strike zone. But it was ball one. I'm thinking, "Okay, here's this rookie thing I heard about." The next pitch I throw is low and away. Third pitch is up and in a little bit, so I'm 3–0 on Dale Murphy.

Next pitch I throw right down the middle again. It's now 3–1, and I throw the next pitch right down the middle also. He grounds out to Barry Larkin for out number one. Then I get Ernie Whitt on a fly ball and Jeff Blauser on a pop-up to second base. Game's over, and I shake our catcher's, Joe Oliver's, hand.

I found out that night it was a record for the Reds starting out a season at 9–0. That was the year we went wire to wire and then swept the World Series.

I didn't stick around long that year, but it was really cool how it all transpired. They came out with a video at the end of the season, and the video starts off with me throwing the last pitch of that ninth game and shaking Joe Oliver's hand.

Joe Grahe (Angels)

Joe Grahe made his major league debut on August 4, 1990, with the California Angels. He played in seven big league seasons. In 1992, Grahe led the Angels with 21 saves.

We had just gotten into Las Vegas to play that night, and for any guy that plays in the PCL, that's kind of the highlight of the whole season.

I think I was due to pitch the third night we were there. I was doing my routine and had just got done running some sprints. The pitching coach, Chuck Hernandez, came out and asked me, "How you feeling?" I said, "I'm fine." He said, "Well, make believe you're pitching tomorrow night instead of two nights from now." That's about all he said.

I'm out there, and my mind starts going. I do what all self-respecting players do, consult the Bazooka Joe fortunes on the bubblegum wrappers. It said, "You have an unexpected trip coming up."

The whole game, I'm in the dugout and my mind's racing. Then after the game, it happened. But it didn't happen right after the game. I'd showered and everything. I'm standing there going, "What's going on here?" Then they called me in, and our manager, Max Olivares, told me. It was surreal. He said, "You're pitching in Anaheim tomorrow night." I'm like, "Okay."

I didn't know the circumstances of why I was called up. They didn't give me any background. Bert Blyleven and his family were in a car accident, so they needed me for a spot start. I didn't know at the time of my call-up it was just for one start.

I had no idea where the Angels were at the time or who they were playing. I'm like, "Who are they playing?" They go, "The Oakland A's." I'm like, "Oh, boy." A year earlier, I was in the College World Series, and now I'm facing the defending World Champions tomorrow night.

I catch a flight in the morning, out of Vegas to Orange County. It was a whirlwind. It wasn't one of those call-ups when you can hang around for a day and then pitch. You're gonna fly over in the morning, and you're starting that night with 50,000-plus people there. Anaheim Stadium back then was huge. They still had all the football bleachers. It was neat, but it was scary at the same time.

I didn't have time to sit around and stew on the gravity of the situation. It may have been a blessing in disguise. It was just go-go-go. Get out on the mound and pitch.

The hard part about the whole thing was I didn't know any of the big league players. A lot of times, the guys that are considered prospects, per se, get to go to a big league camp to get some exposure. I was due to go to big league camp that spring, but it didn't happen because of the labor situation. There was a lockout that spring, and they got a late start. The non-roster guys got shut out because they had to hurry to get everybody ready.

I'd never been in a big league clubhouse. There were a lot of walking baseball cards in that clubhouse—guys that I'd collected. It was a very veteran team. I'm like, "What the heck am I doing here? Do I belong here?" That's the main thing rookies have to overcome—the feeling of belonging or not belonging.

My first impression when I got on the mound was, "Holy cow. It is bright out here." I had never been on a field where all the lights were on the mound. There were no shadows. I was used to fields with shadows, but it wasn't like that there because they had so many lights coming from different angles.

Then I look in there, and there's Rickey Henderson. I went after him. My first pitch was just off the plate, and the umpire called, "Ball." I'm like, "All right. The umpire's testing me." I tried not to show any emotion. I

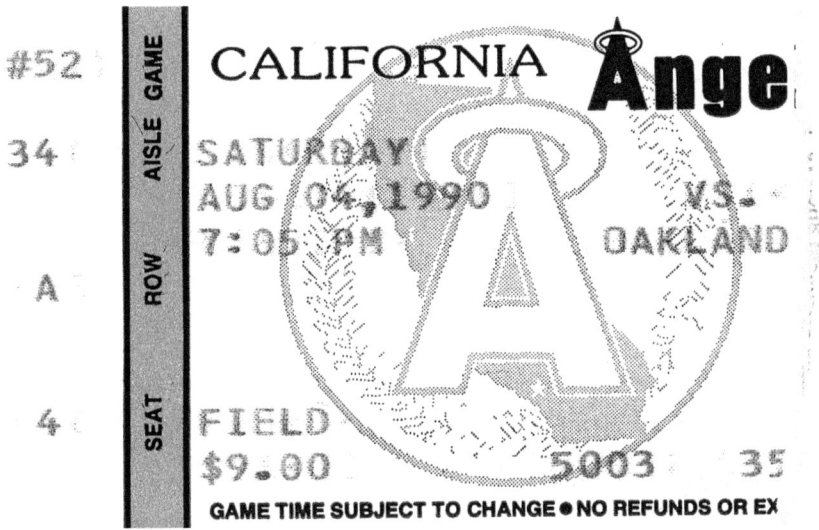

Ticket stub from Joe Grahe's major league debut with the California Angels. The first batter he faced was the A's Rickey Henderson (author's collection).

ended up walking him on four straight pitches I thought were pretty good. That's just the way it goes with rookies and debuts.

There were a few rocky points, but it went pretty well. I got my first strikeout with Jose Canseco, and then I was able to get Dave Henderson, who was a fantastic hitter in his own right, out with a strikeout. Nobody really turned me around that night, so I was like, "Wow. I might be able to do this."

When I was done, I was completely spent. All the emotion had just gone out of me. I don't think I slept the night before, and with the hype and nervous energy all day, I felt like going and taking a nap. That much emotion had just fallen out of me.

We won the game in extra innings, and I had done fairly well.

I got to the ballpark the next day, and they called me in before we went out to batting practice. They said, "Good job. You helped us win a ballgame last night." Then they explained what was going on with Blyleven, that he'd be back, and that I was going back to Triple-A. It was all positive. I got it and was grateful for the opportunity. They said, "You'll be back. Be ready."

It was fun watching the game that day. It was a Sunday day game. I already knew I was going down, but they said, "You're gonna stay for this game, and then we've got you going out Monday morning." It was like I wasn't even sitting in the dugout. I was still floating.

John Briscoe (Athletics)

John Briscoe made his major league debut on April 18, 1991, with the Oakland Athletics. He played in six big league seasons.

We began the season on a road trip. I was with Huntsville in Double-A. We started off on the Orlando and Jacksonville swing right out of spring training. We played in Orlando and started to play in Jacksonville. At about 3:30 in the morning, I got a call. Me and a few other guys were in the room playing Nintendo, 'cause that's what ballplayers do when they can't sleep after a game. I thought it was a prank call and was about to hang up.

It was Harvey Dorfman, who was our team's traveling psychologist, so to speak. I valued Harvey and had been around him since rookie ball in '88. I had a pretty good relationship with him.

Harvey said, "Yeah, John, they want you in Anaheim tomorrow night." I'm like, "Who is this?" I flat out didn't believe him, and I was about to hang up. I was mad. Then he was like, "This is Harvey." It didn't sound like him.

I had a 7:00 flight and started freaking out. We couldn't find the equipment guy to open the place up to get my stuff in Jacksonville, so I went with no equipment. I didn't have my own glove, shoes, jock, anything. I had to borrow that stuff when I got to Anaheim.

It was neat 'cause I got to fly through Dallas, where I lived at the time, and I got to meet my family on the layover on my way to Anaheim.

I got out there right at 6:00 p.m. and hurried to get to the game. I didn't feel like I fit in. I was like, "Man, I've been watching these guys on TV." I had about ten innings in my career in Double-A, and I'm in the big leagues all of a sudden. I had never been to a big league camp yet, so I didn't know anybody other than the guys that were in the minor leagues.

Tony LaRussa let me know, "I'm not going to throw you in anything crazy. You're not going into tie ballgames or anything like that. I want you to get your feet wet before anything else." It didn't start sinking in till the phone rang and they said, "Bris, get up." We were on ESPN that night. I didn't get in the game, but I got in the next night.

I could have run through a wall. I felt like Superman. It was like, "Man, I am here. I've been wanting this my whole life."

I hadn't even been in a pitchers/catchers meeting where they go over the reports on guys. I was pretty much just going by what the catcher was calling. I had no idea about those guys. I just followed whatever he told me to do. It was like, "I'll do it as well as I can do it."

I got my first big league strikeout that night looking, which surprised me because young guys don't get too many strikes right off. Ken Kaiser was behind the plate. He was also very intimidating. I spoke to him twice, and he just looked at me. I was like, "Okay, I'm going to shut up."

The first night I faced Dave Parker, who I watched as a kid on TV. That was one of the first guys I had to face. I was like, "Man, he looks a lot bigger in person." I was thinking, "Boy, I don't want to make a mistake to this guy because he can hit it out of sight." He ended up hitting a fly ball to the outfield and making an out, which I was pleased about.

I was in a fog over the deal. It was surreal because I hadn't slept for basically about 36 hours from when I got the call until I finally sat down after pitching. I was like, "Okay, what's going on? I've traveled across the country, and I am not in the minor leagues anymore."

John Briscoe was called up by the Oakland Athletics during his fourth professional season. He used borrowed equipment for his debut (photography by Doug McWilliams).

I honestly could have cared less about the equipment issue. I used Kirk Dressendorfer's glove and Bob Welch's shoes that were two sizes too big. I'm standing around going, "Man, I'm wearing Bob Welch's shoes. Are you kidding me?" I loved him as a kid when he was with the Dodgers.

Jeff Nelson (Mariners)

Jeff Nelson made his major league debut on April 16, 1992, with the Seattle Mariners. He played in 15 big league seasons. Nelson was selected to one All-Star team.

I got drafted by the Dodgers as a starter, and my first three years, I never won a game.

Then I was a Rule 5 pick by Seattle. At first in the minor leagues with the Mariners, I still started. About halfway through the 1990 season in Double-A, I got sent back to Single-A. My pitching coach, Ross Grimsley, went to me and said, "We're gonna make you a reliever."

I was throwing over the top then, and I closed for the rest of the year. I went to my first big league camp in 1991 and then I went back to Double-A.

I was throwing a bullpen in Jacksonville, Florida, and I started throwing three-quarters. My slider got bigger, and my balls started moving. My catcher, Jim Campanis, Jr., said, "Don't ever change." I went to Triple-A for half the year. Then I went to winter ball and led winter ball in saves. That pretty much turned the corner for me.

I went to big league camp in '92 and thought I had a good chance. I thought maybe I was gonna make the team, but during the last cuts, I got sent down to Triple-A Calgary.

There was a save situation. I'm waiting and expecting the call. I didn't get the call in the ninth inning, and I was like, "You've got to be kidding me. What's going on?" We wind up winning the game and I go into the clubhouse. Keith Bodie, the manager, calls me in, and he says, "One of the relievers got hurt on the big league team. You're going to meet them on the road."

I got lucky because we weren't going to have a very good year, and I think they knew that from the start. A lot of times when guys get called to the big leagues, whether you're a position player or a pitcher, you have the stress of thinking, "If I don't have a good game, am I going back to the minor leagues?" When I got there, Dan Warthen, the pitching coach, came to me and he said, "Listen. I want you to relax. You're going to have your ups and downs, but you're going to be here the whole year. Don't worry about getting sent down." I was like, "Wow. All right." Mike Schooler was our closer, and I was going to pitch the seventh and eighth innings.

I didn't throw at all during the first series.

We went to Chicago, and I got into a game for the seventh and eighth innings. That's when the White Sox got good crowds, and they had the sound meter going. I come in, and I'm used to small minor league stadiums that seat 2,500 to 3,500 people. It was a little overwhelming, but I don't remember putting a lot of pressure on myself or being overly nervous. I was never afraid.

The first hitter I faced was Steve Sax. Then shortly afterwards, Frank Thomas. I actually had to step off the mound. I was like, "Oh, my God. There is nobody in the minor leagues that is as big as this guy. This guy's a monster." It's funny, he wound up being one of the guys I probably faced the most and also one of the guys I had the most success against.

It was a close game. We wound up losing, but I pitched two shutout innings.

Ever since you were a little kid, you've got the dream that you were going to play in the major leagues. Then you spend all that time in the minors as a starter going back and forth, and you're questioning if you're ever going to make it. Once I became a reliever, I gained a lot of confidence.

Jeff Reboulet (Twins)

Jeff Reboulet made his major league debut on May 12, 1992, with the Minnesota Twins. He played in 12 big league seasons.

In '92, I didn't go to big league camp because I had an injury in the off-season. I came back and started off well in Portland, Triple-A for the Twins. I was hitting over .300, and my hitting had always been the question mark. I had always played good defense.

We were traveling to Edmonton for a game. It was snowing when we were getting ready to land.

My roommate on the road was Chip Hale. He had been in the big leagues before, and we were buddies. He's "Mr. Optimistic," and he was telling everybody we were going to play. Everybody knew we were not going to play.

We went to the hotel, and I got a message from Scott Ullger, the Triple-A manager, on the hotel phone. He said, "Hey, I need to see you in my hotel room." Chip said, "Hey, don't forget to ask him if we're playing or not." I'm like, "Okay." I figured Scott was setting something up where they'd have me say they're making us clear the field, but it really wouldn't happen. We'd play a trick on Chip.

I go to the room, knock on the door, and Ullger's there with my roommate at home in Portland, Jim Kahmann, who was the trainer. I thought it was odd he would be in the room.

Scott's like, "Hey, I've got some bad news. You didn't pass your drug test." I looked at him, used a few choice words, and said, "I'll piss right now!" They chuckled and said, "No, you're going to the big leagues."

I went back to my room, and Chip was there, of course. He goes, "What did they want?" I said, "Well, I'm getting called up." He was excited for me. A couple minutes go by and Chip's like, "Hey, did you ask him if we're playing today?" That was typical Chip.

The next day I flew out from Edmonton. I'd never been to the

Metrodome and didn't know much about what was going on. I had played with a few of the younger guys, but the team was very veteran-oriented. They had won the World Series the year before, and it was very businesslike.

Andy MacPhail was the GM, and they decided to go with me because I was a defensive guy. I'm in his office to sign my contract. He says, "We're glad to have you." He hands me the contract and slides the pen over. I go to sign the paperwork and pick up the pen. It flops out of my hand and hits the table. I picked it up and go, "Oh, sorry about that." He goes, "It's okay. Just don't let it happen on the field." That's when you realize it's a little serious here.

I ended up playing that first evening. I pinch-hit for Randy Bush. Tom Bolton was pitching for the Red Sox. Randy's a lefty, and Tom was tough on lefties. Tom Kelly sends me up there. It's the seventh inning, and we were winning by a few runs. I'm just pinch-hitting and I'm nervous as heck.

I didn't have a helmet. I had a regular Portland helmet, which had a double ear flap. So I went up there with my double ear flap helmet.

Bolton's got a good curveball. The first pitch he throws me is a curveball, and I think I swung when it was halfway there like I was expecting a fastball. I missed it by a mile. Then they threw me a fastball up, and I fouled it back.

The next pitch, he threw me another curveball. He bounced it, and I think it barely caught dirt in front of the Minnesota turf. It was probably a 55-footer. It didn't even make it close to the plate. Of course, I swung again. It was so bad that it bounced over Tony Pena's head. I struck out but ran to first and made it to first base on a punch-out.

Our first base coach's name was Wayne Terwilliger. He was a much older guy, but a super positive, awesome guy, and a great coach. I get to first base, and he's excited. He's going, "Man, that was great." I'm going, "Twig, I struck out." He goes, "Reb, anybody can get a hit or even a home run in their first at-bat. I guarantee you in the history of the game, nobody's ever gotten on first after a strikeout." The first baseman looks at me like, "He's probably right."

I was embarrassed more than anything that I swung at pitches like that. I didn't strike out a whole lot. I was clearly very nervous.

Kurt Knudsen (Tigers)

Kurt Knudsen made his major league debut on May 16, 1992, with the Detroit Tigers. He played in three big league seasons.

After a game, we go back to the hotel and watch ESPN. We were on the road playing the Syracuse Blue Jays at the time. While watching ESPN, I saw that Alan Trammell and Bill Gullickson got hurt.

Right then my roommate looked at me and he goes, "Somebody's goin' up, and I have a feeling it's gonna be you." I was doing well. I was a relief pitcher, and they had already called up a starter a few days prior. I didn't think anything of it and went to bed.

It was a getaway day, so we were getting up at six o'clock in the morning to catch a flight. As I was walking down the hallway with my luggage, one of the assistant coaches, Kevin Bradshaw, came up to me and says, "Skip wants to see you in the restaurant."

The skipper was Joe Sparks. It's either good news or bad news when an assistant coach comes up to you, and I was having a great year. So I knew I wasn't going down. I went into the restaurant, sat down, and Sparks goes, "Hey! Congratulations, kid. You're going to meet the big boys in Kansas City. We'll get your flight when we get to the airport."

This was kind of funny, because they have a rule that if you get called up to the big leagues, you have to fly first class. They bumped me up to first class, and I flew with my Toledo Mud Hens team to Pittsburgh and ended up switching planes there. I was in first class, and the rest of the team had to go and sit back in the other seats. I caught a little flack about that.

I ended up meeting the Tigers on the road in Kansas City, playing the Royals.

I land in Kansas City, sometime probably around 10 or 11 o'clock. I had to go to a mall and find some clothes to wear because they had a dress code. I got to the park early, got my uniform and my locker.

The bullpen was behind the left field fence, and they had part of it cut out so you

Kurt Knudsen was called up by the Detroit Tigers during his fifth professional season (author's collection).

could see what's going on. I was down there, watching the game, kind of soaking everything up.

All of a sudden, the phone rings. Mike Munoz looks at me and he goes, "Knudy, you're up." I probably jumped three feet, took off my jacket, got my glove, and started warming up. All of a sudden, the phone rang again, and they said, "You're going in."

The bullpen door opened, and I don't remember getting from the bullpen to the mound. I can't remember what happened until I got to the mound. I was very excited and probably hyperventilating a little bit.

I get out of the inning and go back out for another. I had a ball hit into right-center field. My center fielder and right fielder collided, and the ball dropped. I thought to myself, "Wow. It's my major league debut and this happens to me?" I ended up giving up one unearned run.

Lineup card from Kurt Knudsen's major league debut with the Detroit Tigers (author's collection).

This might sound kind of confusing, but my brother-in-law's brother-in-law lived in Kansas City. My brother-in-law and sister called him from my brother's house, where there was a speaker phone. My parents didn't have a speaker phone, but the phone in Kansas City was put up to the television set so my parents and everyone could listen to the game.

Growing up, there were two things I wanted to do in my life. I wanted to play professional baseball, and when professional baseball was over, I wanted to be a police officer. I got those two and am very happy with the way my life went.

Eric Fox (Athletics)

Eric Fox made his major league debut on July 7, 1992, with the Oakland Athletics. He played in four big league seasons. Following his playing days, Fox became a coach.

I had some injuries before I made it to the big leagues. I had major knee surgery in college when I was on the USA team, and then when I got to Triple-A with Oakland, I had another major knee surgery. However, that didn't detract from my thinking I would ever play in the big leagues. I never lost that train of thought.

I went down to Puerto Rico and did well. I was told if I did that, I might get an invite to big league camp in 1992. I got invited to major league camp, had a really good spring training, and made the All-Star team for the Cactus League. I opened some eyes, but unfortunately, I didn't make the team.

They sent me down to Triple-A, and a month later, they sent me back to Double-A. Being 28 years old, after two major knee surgeries, I was going backwards. I had some reservations and the thought of quitting slipped into my mind.

I went back to Huntsville, played for two months, and that's when I got the call.

I was a good friend of Troy Neel. He had just hit his first big league home run. I had a piece of paper with his phone number, because I was going to give him a call. I remember showering up after the game and the clubhouse guy said, "Hey, they want to see you in the coach's office." Keith Lieppman and some front office people with Oakland were at the game. I walked in, and I had the piece of paper. They said, "What's that?" I said, "Well, it's Troy Neel's phone number. I'm going to give him a call to congratulate him for his first home run." They looked at me and said, "Well, why don't you tell him in person?"

It was right before the All-Star break. I think Jose Canseco and Dave Henderson

Eric Fox was called up by the Oakland Athletics during his seventh professional season. He overcame multiple injuries in the minors (photography by Doug McWilliams).

were on the disabled list and Rickey Henderson had a slight hammy twinge. They said, "We're gonna fly you to Detroit but we don't know if you're going to be activated or not. If Rickey can play, then we're going to send you back to Memphis." That's where the team was going to be.

I called a couple people, but I really couldn't get too excited. I went to the old Detroit stadium, but my bag was still packed. I had heard horror stories of guys getting called up but never getting activated.

The guys come in from batting practice. Rickey Henderson's laughing and sweating, and I was just thinking, "This really sucks not knowing." Rickey got in the shower, suited up, and I remember watching him walk up the stairs to get to the ground level.

As soon as he disappeared, Tony LaRussa looked behind the wall and said, "Hey, rookie, come on in and sign your contract." That's when it hit me.

I got into my first game against the Detroit Tigers as a pinch-runner in the ninth inning. I got thrown out on a pitch-out at second base. Chad Kreuter, my roommate from Puerto Rico, was the catcher and knew I was a runner. I was given the steal sign. Unfortunately, they picked a great pitch to pitch out on, and Chad threw me out. LaRussa was pissed he called it. I don't think he knew the catcher was a buddy of mine.

Jeff Frye (Rangers)

Jeff Frye made his major league debut on July 9, 1992, with the Texas Rangers. He played in eight big league seasons. Frye hit for the cycle while with the Toronto Blue Jays in 2001.

I was playing with Oklahoma City in Triple-A. I had played the first 87 games of the year without one day off. I was doing really well and hitting .300.

I was in Louisville, Kentucky, playing against the Louisville team, and I had just found out I'd made the Triple-A All-Star team. They had the American Association, the Pacific Coast League, and the International League all combined. I had made that team, which was a huge honor.

I was asleep in my hotel room, and my roommate at the time was Bobby Brower. He had been in the big leagues and was a great guy. All of a sudden, the room phone rings about 9:00 in the morning, which was unusual. Usually, we'd take our phone off the hook because we basically slept until we woke up. Our games would be over at 10:00, and by the time we got back to the hotel, it would be 11:00 or 12:00. By the time we'd wind down, it was 1:00 or 2:00 in the morning. Unless we had a day game or something, we were sleeping in.

So the phone rings at 9:00 a.m., I pick up the phone, and it's our manager, Tommy Thompson. He was a quirky, fun guy. I say, "What's up, Tommy?" He goes, "You're not going to the Triple-A All-Star Game." I say, "I'm not?" He goes, "Nope. You're going to another level. Come up to my room, big boy." I looked across the room at my roommate, and I didn't say a word. Bobby looks at me and goes, "You're going to the big leagues, and you're not coming back, either."

I go up to Tommy's room. He tells me they're calling me up to the big leagues, that the Rangers had just fired Bobby Valentine, that me and Brian Bohanon were getting called up to the big leagues together, and that Toby Harrah was going to be the interim manager.

I had to go to the stadium in Louisville with the equipment manager. They don't go to the field that early, generally, so I had to get someone to meet Brian Bohanon and me there, pack up all our stuff, head to the airport, and get on a flight. We landed at DFW at 5:00, and the game was at 7:00.

The Rangers send a car to pick us up, and we go to the stadium. I hear all the details about Bobby Valentine's last official act as manager was to call me and Brian Bohanon up, and that Toby Harrah, who was the bench coach, was gonna be the new manager.

We get to the stadium about 5:30 and I see Joe Macko, the legendary equipment manager, who'd been there forever. He goes, "I've got your locker in there with your uniform." I go in there and see Frye, number 51. He goes, "Go check out the lineup." I walk over to the board, look at the lineup, and there I am, number 51, leading off and playing second base. I look down at the bottom, and Nolan Ryan's pitching for us! Right into the fire! The game starts in an hour and a half, and he says, "If you hurry up, you can get out in time for BP." I was like, "I've got no chance. BP's over in 15 minutes." I hadn't even unpacked my stuff, so I'm like, "I'm just going to try to get ready and go take infield."

I go take infield at about 6:10, come back in, and they give me a little scouting report. We were facing Scott Scudder, who I didn't know much about. I was definitely nervous, but I didn't have enough time to sit and think about it, which was probably a blessing in disguise.

I got two base hits, a walk, and a sac fly. I ended up going 2-for-3 with three runs scored and an RBI my first big league game.

My first at-bat, I'm shaking in my shoes in the batter's box, but the dude walks me. My next at-bat, I came up and hit a line drive to left field, a sinking liner that Albert Belle tried to make a sliding catch on. It bounced past him, so for my first official at-bat in the big leagues, I got a triple.

Later, I get to first and the guy hitting behind me hits a double play ball to third. They throw it to Carlos Baerga at second, and I took him out. I knocked him on the ground. Back then that's what you were supposed to do. I come back to the dugout, and I'm getting high-fives and all that stuff.

A couple of innings later, Albert Belle is on first base. A ball's hit, they throw it to me, and Albert Belle is running directly at me. He doesn't even slide. He runs directly through the base without sliding.

It was like a blur because everything was happening so fast. We had some pretty good players on our team, and there I was, thrust right into the leadoff spot, playing second, my first game.

Bret Boone (Mariners)

Bret Boone made his major league debut on August 19, 1992, with the Seattle Mariners. He played in 14 big league seasons. He was the first third-generation major league player.

I never thought of anything else. It was never a question in my mind since I was five years old. Once you get there, you've gone through the trials and the tribulations, and you're 30 years old looking back at that young kid, you can laugh at yourself. I was very naïve, but it played as an advantage for me. It's fun to look back and laugh.

I was in Calgary, Canada, and it was anticipated the whole year, but I figured they were going to wait 'til September to call me up. It was out of nowhere. I had no idea.

I remember I was hitting, and I got a base hit to right field. I rounded the bag, came back to first, and gave a fist bump to the first base coach. A guy comes out to run for me. I say, "What are you doing? You're not running for me!" He goes, "That's what skip said."

Keith Bodie was our manager, and he starts coming out. He was this New York tough guy. He had that personality, and I really liked Keith. He comes out of the dugout, and he's serious. He goes, "Are you the manager or am I the manager?" I said, "You're the manager." He goes, "Get out of the game. He's running for you." I said, "No, he's not. For what?" He goes, "You didn't hustle out of the box."

We started getting heated. He's screaming at me and I'm screaming at him going, "I always hustle out of the box! That's bullshit!" I think I took my helmet off and threw it. He's playing the part well, and I'm pissed.

I get to the dugout and he's chasing me to the dugout like we're gonna fight. He looked at me, and he starts laughing. He goes, "Kid, you're going to the big leagues." I was in shock. I didn't know what to say.

At the time, the third-generation thing was kind of a big deal. That had never been done. We didn't have internet or any of that stuff, but the local news company had come out. They were hiding behind the dugout, and they followed me off the field.

I remember going home and calling my dad and my grandpa. I told them I had a flight in the morning to Baltimore. I couldn't sleep. I got my apartment packed and just sat there and played solitaire all night.

I got on the plane, and it was my first first-class experience. Back then I looked really young for my age. I looked like a little kid. I was so excited. I was just looking around, waiting for people to ask me where I was going so I could tell 'em. Finally, a guy asks me, "Where are you headed?" I said, "I'm going to Baltimore." He asked, "What are you doing in Baltimore?" I said, "I'm playing against the Orioles tonight." He goes, "No, come on." I said, "Yep. Want to come to the game?" He said, "I can't go to the game, but I'll be watching." He asked me, "What are you gonna do your first at-bat?" I said, "I don't know what the result's gonna be, but I'm gonna hit something hard somewhere."

Again, I hadn't slept all night. I was just going on adrenaline into the park, and I got there late, right at the beginning of batting practice. They said, "You're in group two."

I had a ton of reporters around asking me questions while I was getting dressed, and then the next thing I know, it's game time.

My first at-bat was against Arthur Rhodes, who was also my first at-bat in my minor league debut. I hit a double off him my first minor league at-bat, and then for my first big league at-bat, I got a base hit up the middle and an RBI.

The first baseman for the Orioles threw the ball in, looked at me, and said, "Kid, you've got 2,999 to go." I remember looking at him and saying thanks, but I was thinking to myself, "I'm gonna get way more hits than that." That's the naivety I talked about. I really thought I was gonna get 4,000 hits.

Fast forward six weeks. I'm sitting at my locker having a beer and thinking, "The big leagues is really hard."

I got through the minor leagues quick. I got the call-up, and the big leagues were very humbling for me at the beginning. It wasn't like Triple-A.

The day I got called up, I was just so sure of myself. I remember a couple teammates wanted me to sign a bat for 'em. I was leaving and I remember thinking to myself, and I might have even said it sarcastically to someone, "I'll never see the minor leagues again." I was the heir apparent to Harold Reynolds at the time in Seattle. In my brain in mid–August of '92, I thought I'd never see the minor leagues again. Well, little did I know.

In '93, Lou Piniella was my manager, and man, he was tough on me. He sent me up and down three times. Appropriately enough, I got a lot of crap from my teammates that next year about saying I'd never go back to the minor leagues again. I deserved it, but I laughed it off.

Jimmy Campanis [another third-generation professional player who nearly reached the big leagues] and I have a lot of history together. We played together at USC, then A-Ball, and then Double-A. I had a decent amount of time logged with Jimmy. I said, "He ain't gonna beat me to the big leagues." He bet me a car. Jimmy was a cheap guy. When I got there, he sent me a Matchbox version of the car—a BMW.

We had a good time in the minor leagues, and it was a friendly rivalry, but I never really thought about it. The last thing on my mind in the minor leagues was the third-generation thing. I didn't give a shit, and as a matter of fact, I resented it.

I remember in Triple-A, everybody wanted to talk about this big anticipation. I love my dad to death and had an unbelievable relationship with my grandfather, but as a young "house on fire" player, I didn't want to hear about it. They did what they did, but that had no bearing on me. I wanted to talk about what I was doing right then, not if I had big shoes to fill. I never felt like that for one second.

There was never any pressure or anything like that. I wanted to get there and play in the big leagues for a living. It had nothing to do with my family. I appreciated and respected what they had done before me, but that had no bearing on what I was gonna be.

Fast forward 30 years, and now I'm sitting here with a 21-year-old son that's gonna be a pro soon. As a father, I look at it much differently. It's not from a pressure standpoint, but more of "Wow, if Jake was able to get through and be good enough to make it, that would be unbelievable!" But that's the father in me, and that's probably not what he's thinking.

Mike Trombley (Twins)

Mike Trombley made his major league debut on August 19, 1992, with the Minnesota Twins. He played in 11 big league seasons. In 1999, Trombley led the Twins with 24 saves.

I was with Portland in Triple-A at the time in '92. That day we were in Calgary, Canada, playing the Calgary Cannons. I wasn't pitching that day and actually played golf with my pitching coach and the coach on the Calgary team.

We got back, went to the ballpark, and Scott Ullger, our manager, told me I was getting called up. My flight was later that evening, and I was to meet the team in Cleveland.

I was very excited for the fact I was gonna become a major league baseball player but had some reservations about my talent. I was never a hard thrower. I threw mid– to high 80s. I had some pretty good breaking stuff. I was always wondering how long it was gonna last. I figured, "I better get off to a good start in order to stay here."

I met the team in Cleveland. The next day, I headed to old Municipal Stadium. I don't care if everybody sarcastically says, "What a first stadium to play in." For me, it was the greatest thing ever, because it was a major league stadium. I was a big baseball and football fan, so I knew about the Indians and Browns. My college roommate at Duke was Greg Torborg, and his father managed the Indians in the '70s.

Tom Kelly was good about letting guys feel comfortable about being part of the situation before being thrown in the fire. I didn't pitch that first day. I just sat and watched. Jose Mesa was pitching for the Indians against the Twins. We got beat, 8–1, and Mesa struck out Kirby Puckett three times that night. I remember thinking, "Golly, I couldn't get Kirby Puckett out at all. What am I doing here?"

I remember warming up in the bullpen the next day. My heart was pounding out of my chest. At the old ballparks, you'd warm up down the line, so everybody was seeing every pitch you'd throw. I was extremely nervous. I took the mound for the first time, and I remember thinking my leg was shaking so hard I was gonna balk. An out-of-body experience is the best way I can explain it. It was really hazy.

The first batter I faced was Junior Ortiz. He hit a soft line drive to second base, and thank God it was an out. I don't know what kind of stuff I had that day. I don't know where I was locating it. I was just lucky to get three outs.

Matt Walbeck (Cubs)

Matt Walbeck made his major league debut on April 7, 1993, with the Chicago Cubs. He played in 11 big league seasons. Following his playing days, Walbeck became a coach.

The previous season, '92, I was in Double-A in Charlotte and had a good year. They invited me to spring training, and I was on fire. Everything I was hitting was falling. I just felt lucky, confident, humbled, everything. Pretty soon, I'm standing there with a week or so to go before Opening Day. People are starting to say, "I think he might make the team." I'd never played Triple-A.

Ryne Sandberg got injured. He broke his hand, so it opened a spot on the roster. Then they started saying, "Now your chances are even greater." But they had Steve Lake and Rick Wilkins, so I would be a third catcher.

A couple days before Opening Day, I was in right field, on one of the back fields at Hohokam. Jim Lefebvre, the Cubs' manager, came over with Larry Hines, the GM, and tapped me on my shoulder. They brought me over to the foul line in right field and said, "Congratulations, you're goin' to the big leagues. You made the team." I was like, "Wow."

It was a great, unbelievable experience, knowin' that I made the team outta spring training. My mom and dad were both there. They weren't expecting it, so that was very special for me. It was a special moment. It was a dream come true. I was in complete euphoria. It was something I'd wanted my whole life, and all of a sudden, it's happening.

I started the third game of the season against the Braves on April 7. It was at Wrigley, and there wasn't even ivy on the walls. It was raining, misty, and cold. I recall the wind was not blowing very hard that day. It was just a cold, dreary, damp day. Everything looked big. You look up and you see the double-decker, and it was just awe-inspiring.

I'll never forget running out on the field. When they called the team out, I screamed at the top of my lungs.

It turned out to be an amazing game. Steve Avery was on the mound for the Braves. In my first at-bat, I flew out to center. I was so nervous, my legs were shaking at the plate. My heart was thumping and felt like it was gonna pop out of my chest.

I ended up gettin' my first hit that game. I drove in Sammy Sosa to tie the

After six minor league seasons, Matt Walbeck made the Chicago Cubs out of spring training in 1993. He made his debut in the third game of the season against the Atlanta Braves (courtesy Matt Walbeck).

game late with a swinging bunt down the third base line. Kent Mercker was pitching. He slid and couldn't come up with it, so my first hit was a swinging bunt infield single with an RBI. I can still feel it. Unfortunately, we lost the game and that was disappointing, but the experience was wonderful.

I've gotta tell ya, playing for the Chicago Cubs, in front of the Cubs fans, there's nothing like it. It's the mystique there. It was awesome.

Dave McCarty (Twins)

Dave McCarty made his major league debut on May 17, 1993, with the Minnesota Twins. He played in 11 big league seasons. McCarty was an oddity for a position player in that he batted right-handed and threw left-handed.

We were in Portland, where the Triple-A team was for the Twins. Scott Ullger, our manager, called me into the office and said, "Hey, one of the guys got hurt up there and went on the DL. You're getting called up."

I was thrilled. The first call was to my wife and then, right after, I called my parents.

I was on a flight that next morning, and I can't remember if I went to the hotel first or straight to the field. It's a little overwhelming. There were guys like Kent Hrbek and Kirby Puckett there. I got to know those guys a little bit in spring training, but doing it for real was exciting and somewhat intimidating. Coming up through high school and then college, you know a lot of the names. You're thinking, "Wow, a year or two ago I was watching this guy on TV, and now I'm gonna be playing with him or against him!" You've got to get over that quickly to be able to focus on playing ball and do what you need to do.

I remember grounding out my first at-bat and then getting a hit, a single, my third, and just being thrilled to get that first hit out of the way quickly.

To dream of being a big league ball player and then accomplishing it was a real high point.

Tim Worrell (Padres)

Tim Worrell made his major league debut on June 25, 1993, with the San Diego Padres. He played in 14 big league seasons. Tim's older brother, Todd, also pitched in the majors.

I was with Las Vegas, and we were on the road. Our manager was Russ Nixon, and the pitching coach was John Cumberland. They called me into Russ's hotel room and told me the news.

The same day, they also called up Frank Seminara, who had a great second half of '92, to start the first game after we arrived. However, they were sending him back right after. Frank and I were friends, but it was a little awkward sittin' on a plane next to each other, knowing he's gonna start the game and fly back to Vegas, and I'm stayin'.

I was excited, but I wasn't super overwhelmed.

Even though I was scheduled for a start, they put me in the bullpen the first two days I was there. They basically put me in the bullpen instead of having me throw a side bullpen. The first night, I'm only supposed to get in the game if it's an extreme situation. Nothing happens. The second night, I'm thinking, "This is gonna have to be a super extreme situation if I get in this game." I was only a few days away from my start.

Well, I'm sitting down there and early in the game, Wally Whitehurst took a line drive off his leg. They pulled him out and yelled down for me. You wanna talk about someone not prepared for that moment at all? I jumped up, had trouble finding my glove, and jogged in to warm up. I didn't get any bullpen warmups because it was an injury.

I remember being in such a rush, the home plate umpire walked out and said, "Son, you've got all the time you need." That's how fast I was throwing. I looked at him and I said, "I'm ready. A couple more and I'm good to go." I wasn't.

I walked Hal Morris and then Kevin Mitchell hit a bomb off me. Mitchell hit a ball around his neck. He hit it hard, don't get me wrong, but off his bat it looked like it went straight up. I wasn't thinking home run. It kept goin' and goin'. In old Jack Murphy Stadium, they had space between the fence and the wall where the stands were. It came down there.

After that, I thought, "It can't get any worse than it just did." As soon as that home run happened, I relaxed and was able to continue.

Wally got the loss. For the rest of my career, he gave me crap about him laying on the table hurt, and while the trainers were workin' on him, I come in, give up a bomb, and he's the pitcher on record because he had a runner on base. If you hear Wally tell the story, he'll tell you I punched out everyone after the home run, which is not true.

Jerry Spradlin (Reds)

Jerry Spradlin made his major league debut on July 2, 1993, with the Cincinnati Reds. He played in seven big league seasons. In 1999, while with the San Francisco Giants, he became the first pitcher in franchise history to strike out four batters in an inning.

I was in Des Moines, Iowa, and we were playing the Iowa Cubs.

Marc Bombard was my manager. The funny thing was, I had just pitched that night and didn't do that great. He calls me into the office after the game and tells me to shut the door behind me. I'm like, "Great, they are either going to release me or they are going to send me down." He's like, "Well, I just wanted to let you know they are calling you up." I was like, "Well, I just did horribly." He's like, "Well, one bad outing doesn't make a season."

It was only for two or three days. I didn't even get to pitch and got sent back. Joe Oliver had a freak accident. He accidentally stabbed himself reaching into the dishwasher. They needed to call up another catcher. He was only down for a couple days, maybe even just a day, so it wasn't that serious.

I went back and I was bummed. You're there in the Reds dugout, and then you've gotta go back to the old Bush Stadium in Indianapolis, which was horrible. I think I had a day to travel back, and I technically didn't have to report until the following day. I put my stuff in my locker and was just sitting there, watching a couple innings. I told one of my teammates, "I'll see you guys tomorrow. I'll just go get some dinner and go home."

Literally, the next morning, I get a call from my pitching coach, Mike Griffin, who says, "You're going back. You need to come to the field and get your stuff." I got the call because Bip Roberts went on the disabled list. I drive back to the field, get my stuff, and then drive back to Cincinnati.

At the time, I was only making $1,800 a month. When I got the first call, I drove there and got the money for the plane fare for driving, a week's worth of meal money, and I got put in a hotel. Two or three days later, I got sent back and got the plane fare for driving back. Then when I got called back up, I got the plane fare for going back. I was like, "Man, I've got all kinds of cash right now." It was more money than I made in a month at Triple-A.

We were playing Pittsburgh. I got in that night. It was a start of a new inning, so they didn't put me in with runners on. I pitched two scoreless innings.

The initial thought going through my head, for a brief moment, was, "Whoa, I'm actually here." Then I'm like, "Okay, focus on the glove, forget the stands, forget the people, focus on the game, focus on the catcher." I knew if I focused on my surroundings, I wasn't gonna be effective. Then after they took me out, I started taking it all in.

I remember, after one of the games from the first call-up, I was at a sports bar grabbing a bite. I was sitting there watching ESPN, and they were showing highlights of games. They show our game and I'm thinking, "Wow. I was just there."

Scott Sanders (Padres)

Scott Sanders made his major league debut on August 6, 1993, with the San Diego Padres. He played in seven big league seasons. Sanders also played one season in Japan.

I was at a hotel in Tacoma, Washington. I was with the Las Vegas Stars, and I was going to be pitching against the Tacoma Rainiers that night. I was laying in bed, just kind of relaxing, around 10:30, 11:00 o'clock in the morning. This was pre–cell phone days, and my hotel phone rang, which hardly ever happened. I lean over, pick it up, and it's Randy Smith, the general manager of the Padres.

For a little back story, Randy Smith was previously the scouting director. He and Kevin Towers, my area scout, were basically the two guys who signed me out of Nicholls State in the first round in 1990.

The first thing Randy said was, "Hey, Scott, you're not pitching tonight in Tacoma." The first thing that comes out of me as a competitor was, "What? Why not?" He's like, "Because you're going to pitch tomorrow night in Jack Murphy Stadium against the Colorado Rockies." I think I jumped up and hit my head on the ceiling.

When he said that, I was like, "Wait, what?" He said, "Yeah. We have a doubleheader that just got scheduled. You're pitching the second game of the doubleheader against the Colorado Rockies tomorrow night." He said, "Pack your bags. We'll be getting you a plane ticket and you'll be down here tonight."

I was obviously excited. I ran downstairs, grabbed a *USA Today* paper, started looking at the Rockies' lineup, and all that stuff. Then I packed my bags and headed to San Diego.

When I got drafted, I got to work out with the Padres for about a week. I'd already been in the clubhouse and met some of the guys. I knew a few guys from spring training, so I felt comfortable there. But when you walk in with your bag knowing that you're going to be putting on the big league uniform, it is a different feeling. I was really excited. All your life, you dream of pitching in the major leagues, and it was coming to fruition.

The tricky thing was I wasn't going to be put on the roster until after game one of the doubleheader. For game one of the doubleheader,

I couldn't sit in the dugout. I had to stay in the clubhouse. I stayed in the video room, and I watched the game on TV.

Game one was over, and we had about a 45-minute break. I got myself ready, went out, got loose, and got ready for the game. The amazing thing about my debut was that at the time, Tony Gwynn had 1,999 hits. He was going for hit number 2,000, which is obviously a huge milestone for anybody's career. He went on to hit over 3,000 obviously, but at that point, it was a huge deal.

At the time, the Padres weren't really a top-notch team. They were in the middle of a fire sale and selling off some of the big names. The crowds weren't usually that big. Well, that day, since Tony was going for hit number 2,000, there was almost 45,000 people there. It was a ridiculous amount of people. They all wanted to see Tony Gwynn. It was also towel night, when they gave out beach towels, so it was a double whammy.

I went out and pitched six-plus innings. They scored five runs for me in the first inning, which obviously made it very easy for me to settle in and not press. I won my major league debut, which is always a blessing. On top of it, Tony Gwynn got his 2,000th hit in my debut, which made it even better.

Scott Sanders was called up by the San Diego Padres during his fourth professional season. Tony Gwynn collected his 2,000th career hit during Sanders's debut (courtesy Scott Sanders).

It's funny. I went through my pre-game ritual, and everything was great. When I sat on the bench, I started getting antsy. I was ready to go, and I ran out to the mound. I warmed up and when that first batter walked up, Eric Young, all of a sudden, I had butterflies in my stomach. I couldn't remember the last time I pitched and had butterflies in my stomach. It had been a long time. The first pitch was a ball. I got to a 3–2 count, and I walked him. But after the first pitch, my butterflies kind of went away. That first pitch, my legs were kind of jelly-legged, and it was a weird feeling. Once he got to first base, I settled in. I got out of the inning with no runs, and then, like I said, they went out and scored five for me in the bottom of the first inning.

I walked off the mound after six and two-thirds, and when I was walking off the field, everybody was giving me a standing ovation. At that point, I looked up and all I saw were towels waving. I was like, "Geez, there's a lot of people here tonight."

After, we went to dinner. I brought my whole family and a bunch of friends. I sat down and I said, "Man, they had a lot of people in the stands tonight." My dad said, "Yeah, I think there were 50,000 people." I said, "That's amazing. I had no clue how many people were in the stands until I walked off, tipped my hat, and looked around. When I was out there pitching, I had no clue if there was anybody in the stands." When you get locked in and focused, you really don't see your surroundings. My dad looked at me like, "Scott, you're BSing." I was like, "Dad, I'm serious. I had no clue how many people were in those stands until I walked off and saw those towels waving." I get chills just thinking about it.

Steve Trachsel (Cubs)

Steve Trachsel made his major league debut on September 19, 1993, with the Chicago Cubs. He played in 16 big league seasons. Trachsel was selected to one All-Star team.

I was in Des Moines, Iowa. We were in the playoffs. I had just pitched, and won, game six to get us to game seven. I showed up to the ballpark and started putting my stuff together because, either way, I figured we were going home.

The manager was Marv Foley, and the pitching coach was Bill Earley. It was probably an hour or so before batting practice. They called me into Marv's office and said, "Hey, we've got great news for you. After the game, you're going up to the big leagues." They were like, "Obviously, we don't want you to tell anybody. One, because we're playing game seven and we wanna win that, but two, there's eight other guys going with you too. They're calling up nine players."

Basically, I had to sit all through batting practice and the entire championship game, knowing I was going to Chicago the next morning, and I couldn't tell anybody.

We win the championship and have the huge celebration. They were pulling the other guys in during the celebration in the clubhouse. The celebration went till about 3:00 in the morning. I rushed back to my apartment, packed everything in my truck, and probably by 2:00 p.m., I drove to Chicago.

I had a small Ford Ranger truck with a little shelf thingy on it, and I packed it to the gills. I pulled up to the Westin on Michigan Avenue and basically parked it there for the next three and a half weeks.

The first time walking into Wrigley, I had my Iowa Cubs bag. I'm walking down the stairs, and Jim Lefebvre was at the bottom of the stairs. We had never met. I wasn't in big league camp or any of that stuff. I'd never been to Wrigley before. He just kinda points at me and asks, "Trachsel?" I said, "Yeah." He was like, "I'm Jim Lefebvre. It's about fucking time you got here. I wanted you here three months ago." I was like, "That's the first I heard about it." I wasn't a roster guy, so I got a good chuckle out of it.

He told me I'd be pitching four or five days later. He said, "Just enjoy it and take a couple days to get yourself acclimated. Welcome to the big leagues."

My debut was against the Marlins. Matt Walbeck caught that first game since he knew me. We had been in instructional league, Double-A, and Triple-A together, so we knew each other well.

Ticket stub from Steve Trachsel's major league debut with the Chicago Cubs (author's collection).

I was nervous as could be. I think the day before, they had introduced all the guys on the Triple-A championship team on the field before the game. That was cool. It gave me a judgment of how many people were gonna be there. I just prepared like I normally had been doing all year. I didn't really have any reports on any of the guys to go through. It was kind of short notice, and they didn't have as much of that as they do now.

I remember the first hitter I faced was Chuck Carr. I worked him to a 3–2 count, and I was known as a control guy that didn't walk anybody. I'm like, "Well, I'm not walking my first big league hitter." I grooved a fastball down the middle, and he flew out to center for my first out. The next hitter was Bret Barberie. He rolled over a split for my second out. Then I got behind in the count to Jeff Conine. He ended up hitting a solo homer to left field. The fourth hitter was Orestes Destrade. I got him out to end the inning.

I lost on a squeeze. I was kinda shocked by that and wasn't expecting that the first game.

I got a base hit that game, on the first pitch I saw. Chris Hammond was pitching against me, and I got a base hit to left. They take the baseball and fake like they threw it in the crowd. They doctor it up, and you get the ball at the end of the game. Everything on it's spelled incorrectly. The dates are wrong. It's a gag ball. Of course, I was naïve enough to fall for it for a couple minutes.

Ray Holbert (Padres)

Ray Holbert made his major league debut on May 2, 1994, with the San Diego Padres. He played in five big league seasons. Ray's brother, Aaron, also played in the majors.

I had a good spring training and thought I was gonna make the team but went to Triple-A and was awful. I was so bad that I considered retiring there in Triple-A that year.

I remember getting the call from Russ Nixon, the manager. He said, "They need you to take off. You're going to the big leagues." There was a brawl the night before, and they thought they were going to be short players. That was the reason why I went up. It wasn't because of my play; it was because I was already on the 40-man roster.

When you get that call, it's pretty cool. It's something you've been waiting for your whole life. It's a little helter-skelter. You're obviously trying to get ready really quick to go be with the team. I went to the mall and bought a suit, because I didn't have a jacket to wear on the plane, and that was a mandatory thing.

The next day I was on a plane, and I was headed to Montreal. My call-up was a little different, 'cause the first time I went up, I went through Canada. I had the chance to fly first class for the first time, which was cool. I had a chance to come through customs for the first time, which was cool. But one of the things that I'll never forget is my $50 cab ride from the airport to the ballpark. I still don't think I got paid back for that.

Walking into the clubhouse, I can remember trying not to smile. You're trying to act like you've been there before, even though you haven't.

I remember getting there early and seeing the spread. There's a big difference between the spreads in the minor leagues and the big leagues. There were all kinds of things you could eat. I remember thinking, "Wow! Look at all this food!"

As you're walking in, the guys are congratulating you. Bruce Bochy was there, called me in, and congratulated me. It was more surreal than anything. When I talked to Bochy, he said he was going to try to get me in for a pinch-hit appearance or something, to get the butterflies and nerves out. I went in, I believe, the second day with the team, when we were in Philadelphia.

My first at-bat was off Danny Jackson. I remember going in because he was a left-hander, and they needed a right-handed pinch-hitter. I went up there and worked the count good. I fouled off some pitches but ended up punching out.

It really didn't matter at that point. I was trying to hold back a smile because that was my first big league at-bat, and I had just got into a big league ballgame.

One of the cool things is Tony Gwynn and I grew up in the same area, so I'd had a chance to get to know him throughout the years. We had a pretty good relationship. He had taken me under his wing. Every spring he would take care of me and make sure I was okay. When I went up, it was more like a big brother thing, so I wasn't in awe of Tony. It was more like, "Hey, I get to see my big brother again, and he's gonna take care of me." When I was up there, I think the coolest thing was getting to see Tony work every day. At spring training, obviously the younger guys like me were on separate fields. We weren't working out with the star players. To be able to see him work every day, see what he did, and how he prepared was ultimately one of the biggest benefits for my career.

Andy Carter (Phillies)

Andy Carter made his major league debut on May 3, 1994, with the Philadelphia Phillies. He played in two big league seasons. Carter had the unique distinction of being ejected from his major league debut.

I was in my eighth year with the Phillies' organization. I was in Triple-A and having a good start of the year, but I wasn't even paying attention. I was at the point where I was like, "Whatever happens, happens."

Before batting practice, me and some guys used to go out and shoot behind the stadium in the woods. We were out there shooting, and we come back to the yard at 3:00. The manager, Mike Quade, calls me in. He's like, "There's a sheriff here. You're gonna be arrested for shooting." I'm like, "You've gotta be kidding me." He's like, "Nah, you're going to Philadelphia."

I was born and raised in Philadelphia, so it was a dream come true.

The first day I got there, I got there early, 'cause I had to take all my stuff. My first initiation was in the food room of the clubhouse. I go in there, and Dave Hollins is sitting at the table. I got some food and sat down. I knew his brother in the minor leagues. I say, "Hey. How ya doing? Andy Carter." He looks at me, doesn't say a word. I go, "How's your brother doing?" He looks at me again, takes his food, throws it in the trash, and walks off. I'm like, "Okay? Well, that's nice. I guess that's the initiation."

They had the Macho Row there with Dykstra, Daulton, Incaviglia, and so on. Larry Andersen was there, and he was one of the nicest guys in the world. He goes, "Just don't go down there and bother with them. They do their thing down there." I'm like, "All right, no problem." It was good advice at that time.

I knew a couple of guys that were already up there that I played with earlier in the year, so that was kinda nice. Nobody was mean or anything like that. They just always had to win, and I understood that. It was a serious clubhouse.

Shortly after I got called up, we were either in San Diego or San Francisco. Curt Schilling was in the locker room and he's like, "Meet me down in the hotel lobby at 9:00 a.m." There was a dress code. You're required to dress nice. I think I had one suit, a pair of slacks, and dress shoes. He took me and another guy, Toby Borland, out. We went to a custom suit shop. I think he spent at least $7,000 on clothes, shoes, belts, custom suits, shirts, and stuff. Mariano Duncan did the same thing!

Another time, we were out to dinner with Randy Ready, Larry Andersen, and a couple other veteran guys. They took three of us who just got called up out to an Italian restaurant. I think the bill that night was 4,500 bucks. They were ordering custom wines and all that stuff. I'm like, "Wow. This is unbelievable. That wine bottle was like 2,000 bucks!" At the end of the night, they threw their credit cards in a hat, and they shook it up. I think Larry Andersen had to pay that one.

A lot of those guys were super good guys and helped the young guys get accustomed to stuff. They'd say, "When you get to the hotel, this is how you tip these guys. Each guy gets this amount. Don't give them more than that. That's all they get." Everybody has to tip, so you always have to have one hundred $5 bills on you at all times. Everybody's tipping everybody, it seems like. I'm like, "Wow. That's a lot of tips."

I was there for about two weeks. I didn't even get up in the bullpen for the first week or 10 days. I was waiting and anxious to get in there.

The night before I got in, we had a brawl with the Padres. Early in the year, I guess somebody threw high and tight on Tony Gwynn. Andy Ashby, who had played with us for years and I knew well, pitched that night for the Padres. He threw up and in on Mariano Duncan twice. The second time, the benches cleared, and I was in the pile. I grabbed Ashby. I'm like, "Dude. Don't start swinging, man. It's me, Andy." He's like, "All right, man!" I'm like, "I don't know what the hell's going on. You all right?" He's like, "Yeah, I'm fine." After a bunch of run-around, the brawl got over with.

The next night was when I got called in a game. From not pitching or doing anything the first two weeks, I was like, "Man, I can't wait to get in the game." The anxiety was off the charts.

The first guy I faced was Brad Ausmus. I played against him when he was in the Yankees' organization. I'd done well against him before, so I was hyped up. I went in there and felt good. I got two quick strikes on him, and I go, "I'm gonna knock him down." However, I hit him right in the back, so that wasn't good.

The next batter I got out. Then I threw a slider to the next guy, down and in, and I hit the guy in the back of the foot or the knee or something.

There were no warnings because they had the brawl the night before. I got thrown out after eight pitches. Jim Quick was the home plate umpire. As soon as I hit him, he was like, "You're gone." I'm like, "For what?" He's like, "What do you think, 'for what?' You hit him."

Jim Fregosi, our manager, comes out to argue and goes, "What the hell?!" I go, "I didn't throw either one of those on purpose." He thought I did because it was the night after the brawl. I was just so amped up, I was just letting it rip. He's like, "All right, but you're paying my fine too." I ended up paying my fine and his fine too.

Some of the guys on the team were like, "Dude, you're crazy." I go, "No, I'm not. I didn't do it on purpose. Trust me."

It was an interesting, different debut for sure.

Jeff Cirillo (Brewers)

Jeff Cirillo made his major league debut on May 11, 1994, for the Milwaukee Brewers. He played in 14 big league seasons. Cirillo is honored on the Milwaukee Brewers Wall of Honor.

We were in New Orleans, and we had just been rained out. My wife and I were having dinner on the skinny. Like any good Triple-A baseball player making $1,400 a month, we were taking advantage of a coupon to either TGI Fridays or Hooters.

Cell phones were just coming out. I had a cell phone, and the Triple-A manager, Chris Bando, called me and asked, "How are you swinging?" I said, "I'm doing okay." He's like, "Well, you're going to be swinging tomorrow in Boston."

I flew out to Boston the next day, and I got into the game that night as a defensive replacement late in the game. We were getting beat, and I went in the seventh inning but didn't get to bat. So there's not really a story there.

However, the next day Roger Clemens was pitching. Jose Valentin's wife went into labor, so he had to leave. I was thrust into the starting lineup. I went to USC as a pitcher, and as a kid my favorite pitchers were Tom Seaver and Roger Clemens. I remember above my bed, I had a poster of Roger Clemens holding a mini rocket in his hand. It took me back like, "Wow! I had a poster of this guy above my bed, and in about an hour I'm gonna be facing him." The whole thing was surreal.

I remember looking up in center field, and it was the first time I'd seen my face on a jumbotron. Everything was very new. I'd say, it's kind of like a dream and reality hitting all at once. You're facing the pitcher that you idolized as a kid.

I struck out my first at-bat. At Fenway, the dugout is farther than any other dugout from home plate, and I ran back to the dugout.

Greg Vaughn, who was a great role model and veteran, sat down next to me. He goes, "First major league at-bat against Roger Clemens. You'll never forget it. Can you do me a favor?" I was like, "Yeah. Sure. No problem. What?" He goes, "When you strike out, we don't run back to the dugout in the big leagues." I'm like, "Noted. Got it."

My second at-bat, which was a better at-bat, also ended in a strikeout. I walked back to the dugout, put my helmet away, and kind of slammed my bat into the rack. I sat down, he looked over at me on the bench, and gave me two thumbs up.

Mark Acre (Athletics)

Mark Acre made his major league debut on May 13, 1994, with the Oakland Athletics. He played in four big league seasons. Acre also played one season in Japan.

It was May 12, 1994, and I was playing for the Tacoma Tigers. It was a closing situation, just like any other day, and I was closing up there. They got somebody else up in the pen. At that point, everybody was like, "Ah, shit, man! You're getting called up!" I was like, "You think so?" They were all like, "Yeah!"

The game's over and we go to the locker room. Casey Parsons, the manager, calls me into his office and starts yelling at me! He's like, "Mark, you've gotta start throwing that fuckin' fork ball, man! If you go to the big leagues, you can't rely on your fire and your fast ball. The players are too good! You've gotta work on your fork ball, your split." I was like, "I will, man. I will." He kept harping on me. I was like, "Fuck, man. Get off my ass. I will, for sure. Jesus Christ!" He goes, "You're going to need it because you're going to Kansas City tomorrow morning." I was like, "Oh!"

I gave him a big hug. They opened the door and said, "Hey, the kid's going to the big leagues!" Then everybody was hugging me and all that good stuff.

I went back to my apartment, and Eric Fox was my roommate at the time. He had already been to the big leagues, so I was asking him all kinds of questions. I go, "Do I take everything?" He goes, "You're not coming back, are ya?" I'm like, "Fuck no!" He goes, "Take everything!"

Then I got on the phone, and I called my mom. I'm like, "Mom, I just got called up! I'm going to Kansas City tomorrow!" She's like, "Oh my God!" She was going crazy and telling my stepfather. At that exact moment, when I was holding that phone telling her, I was giving Eric Fox's girlfriend a thumbs-up. Eric Fox's girlfriend lived with us. That picture's on a coffee mug in my office this very day. The other side of it is from the next morning, when I had my suit on and I had my luggage. She took a picture of me before I left. So she got a picture of me when I was telling my mother and the next morning when I was leaving. She put them on a coffee mug and gave it to me when I was in Oakland. So that was super cool.

I didn't sleep all night. I went to Tacoma and flew to Kansas City first class. I grew up very humbly and never flew first class. I'm flying and I'm telling the flight attendants, "I'm going to Kansas City! I'm going to Kansas City!"

I was on cloud nine, obviously. It was early. I think it was around noon or maybe 1:00 p.m., so I went to the hotel first. It was the Ritz Carlton in Kansas City. I get in the cab and I'm like, "Ritz Carlton." Once again, I grew up very humbly. I walked in, checked in, and went up to my room. I'm like "Oh my God! This is just unbelievable!" I couldn't believe it!

I was counting the minutes. I knew there was an early bus. I went downstairs, and the first person I saw was Ron Darling. Darling is like, "Oh, what's up, man? You got called up?" He goes, "All right!" He was fired up! Then I saw Bobby Witt, who treated me like gold. He was like, "The big kid! Ya gonna throw the potata?!" He was excited. I got on the bus, and then we all headed to the field. Tony LaRussa welcomed me and said, "Take care of business."

I got to my locker. My jersey's there with my name on it, with number 55. I'm like, "Holy shit! I'm here!" I was right next to the SLUSH PUPPiE machine. It was like a convenience store in there—all the food you want to eat! I'll never forget the SLUSH PUPPiE machine right next to my locker. I must have had 20 SLUSH PUPPiEs before I got on the field.

Kauffman's a beautiful stadium with the water fountains and everything. I remember the sound of the ball off a bat in the stadium, rather than a minor league field. It's music to your ears, even if you are a pitcher.

It was Friday the 13th and George Brett weekend. He had retired the year before. Brett was in a Corvette, riding around the field. I got to meet him, and that was the first autograph I got in the big leagues. I had him sign a ball that's in my office to this day.

We were getting killed that game. Dennis Eckersley was pitching, just throwing a mop-up inning. I was warming up in the bullpen because I was going to throw the eighth. A guy hit a home run, and I'm not kidding you, it hit the grass and rolled right to me in the bullpen.

I was shitting my pants going in. I remember running out there excited, and Tony handing me the ball. I wanted to see what I looked like on the big screen, of

Mark Acre was called up by the Oakland Athletics during his fourth professional season. He pitched a scoreless inning against the Kansas City Royals in his debut (photography by Doug McWilliams).

course. I threw a couple pitches, turned around and looked up, kicking the dirt a little bit.

I threw one inning. I walked the first hitter I faced but struck out Vince Coleman that inning.

I was only supposed to stay there for a week because Rickey Henderson had pulled a hamstring and they needed another arm. Well, they ended up releasing somebody and kept me. I was up there for almost two years.

It was such an honor to be there with the A's, because I grew up watching them and my grandparents had season tickets. It was surreal.

Marty Cordova (Twins)

Marty Cordova made his major league debut on April 26, 1995, with the Minnesota Twins. He played in the nine big leagues seasons. Cordova was the American League Rookie of the Year in 1995.

In '94 I was playing in Triple-A and had a really good season. I would have been in the major leagues that year as a September call-up, but we went on strike. Then the next season, we started on strike, and they had replacement players for '95 at the beginning.

I knew I was gonna get an opportunity to make the team if we got back to playing ball. Once we finally settled the strike, Tom Kelly played me every inning of every game that entire spring training. Nobody ever does that to somebody because it's a grueling season, but he just wanted to make sure I had the ability to play.

I was fortunate. Because of the strike, Shane Mack, who was a starting left fielder, went to Japan. It opened left field. If there wasn't a strike, he may have just stayed in the United States, but he wanted to make money and leave. That was fortunate for me.

I kinda knew I was gonna make the team because the position was open by default, and I had a good spring training. I probably hit .320 or maybe even higher, but Kelly waited till the last minute. It might have been a couple of days before we broke for the season that he called me in the office and said, "You're gonna make the team."

The way it worked out was the schedule was already made for the season, even though it was a strike-shortened season. When we went back, it just went to where the schedule was. We had one game on the road in Boston for the first game, then we went back home after that.

I remember that I was really nervous, like, crazy nervous.

Boston was a good team that year. We ended up getting beat,

9–0. Scott Erickson didn't pitch very well, and we didn't hit very well at all.

During my second at-bat, I had a 1–1 count and I swung. I was so nervous the bat flew out of my hands and went into the stands. They were booing because I went to get my bat. I'm like, "You've gotta give me the bat back." They passed it down, but they were all booing. Then the next pitch, I struck out. Walking back to the dugout, and it's a long walk there in Boston, the fans were brutal, yelling at me.

I remember in the outfield, and it only happened this game and never happened to me again, I was so nervous my eyes wouldn't stop twitching. I had trouble seeing.

It's nice that I was Rookie of the Year because that's something only one person was. That's a unique thing people will talk about, ask questions about, or get your autograph for.

Again, it was a strike-shortened season, and I was there the whole year. Garret Anderson missed a month and a half or so. That was really the reason. If he had been there the whole year, he probably would have won. It was a close race. I didn't win by much.

They had the media votes for the Rookie of the Year and then the players' vote for Rookie of the Year. I didn't really care what the media thought. That didn't matter to me much, but the players voted me as the Rookie of the Year as well. It's more meaningful when your peers think you're the best player for that year. Then again, it really was because I was there the whole year. Garret had a great year.

Gary Wilson (Pirates)

Gary Wilson made his major league debut on April 28, 1995, with the Pittsburgh Pirates. He played in one big league season.

I had a great year in '94 and was put on the major league 40-man roster in the off-season. However, the huge disappointment was we couldn't go to camp. They had replacement players. I was basically sitting back here in Sacramento, unable to go to my first major league spring training.

Once they got things ironed out with the collective bargaining agreement, I flew immediately to Bradenton, Florida, and started an abbreviated spring training. I went in there with eyes wide open, trying to impress. I came out against the Phillies and pitched really well. Then it just kept building. All of a sudden, I had eight or nine scoreless innings, and the press was starting to talk to me like it was a realistic possibility. At the same time, I knew that for your first camp, you're most likely not going to make the team.

I had a shaky outing later in camp, but we had a couple guys injured. Then I reeled off another good outing. It went to the last few days before we were going to fly to Pittsburgh to start the season. Eventually, someone tapped me on the shoulder and said, "Skip wants to see you." I went into the office there in Bradenton at McKechnie Field. Jim Leyland, the manager, and Cam Bonifay, the general manager, were in there and told me they were taking me to Pittsburgh.

We worked out in Pittsburgh before opening night against the Expos. I got goosebumps walking through the tunnel, stepping onto the turf, and looking around the old Three Rivers Stadium, a stadium I'd seen on TV. It was an amazing feeling.

There's so many more things kids get now, whether it's a baseball card, their name on a glove, or their name on the back of a jersey. Back then it was never like that. You dreamt of what it was like to have a baseball card or your name sewn on a glove or the back of your jersey. Seeing that jersey that's got your name embroidered on there was just amazing.

I didn't get in the first few days. I got in my first game in Philly. The fans were just brutal. I remember getting hit by coins and things coming from the deck when in the bullpen.

My style was to pull my hat down so I could just see the catcher and go. I wish I would have taken it in a little bit more. I remember getting strike one. Then I threw a curveball down and in that Jim Eisenreich hit for a home run. It was a slap in the face wake-up call. He was the same guy I had gotten out in spring training just two weeks earlier. It was just a different vibe in a major league stadium.

It was a rocky first outing for sure. I threw a wild pitch and even got hit by a line drive that ricocheted off me to short. Everything happened so fast. I wasn't happy. Once that happened in Philly, I wanted to get back out there to prove I could do better than giving up a couple runs my first inning out.

I didn't stay in the majors long. It was only about 45 days, but it's very special to me and I have a great appreciation for it.

Jim Mecir (Mariners)

Jim Mecir made his major league debut on September 4, 1995, with the Seattle Mariners. He played in 11 big league seasons. Mecir is notable for having overcome club feet to become an effective pitcher as well as for regularly throwing a screwball.

I was coming off the mound the last game of the season in Edmonton. I had closed out the game, and my manager, Steve Smith, came out.

He said, "Congratulations, good job." Then he said, matter-of-factly, "All right, you're going to the big leagues."

It was shocking. I wasn't even in the dugout yet. I'm like, "What are you talking about? Are you kidding?" I wasn't sure what was going on.

I went to the clubhouse, but I didn't leave with the team. I sat in the whirlpool just thinking about it. I don't remember a lot because my mind was spinning so much. It was a blur.

I remember getting up that next day, and I had to go to Baltimore. At the time, Lou Piniella was manager, and you had to wear slacks and a collared shirt on the road, no matter where you were going. It wasn't just to the plane.

I had to go to Brooks Brothers. I had a credit card and spent money on clothes that was more than I made half the year in Triple-A. I was like, "How the heck am I going to afford this?"

The first four days, I didn't pitch. I hardly slept or ate. I was nervous as hell about getting that major league debut. My first game was pretty much the dream you have as a child. I couldn't have scripted it any better. I grew up a Yankees fan, and one of my favorite players was Don Mattingly. It was '95, so it was the last month of his career. I look around Yankee Stadium. I see the façade, the monuments, and everything I remembered as a kid. It was an unbelievable experience.

I knew in the first inning it might be the day. It wasn't going well. We were getting destroyed. In the second inning I got that call to start warming up. I was down in that bullpen, throwing the ball all over the place. I was bouncing it, hitting the cage, hitting the fence. I was unbelievably nervous.

When I got the call, we were down, 8–2. They opened that gate, and I walked out on the field. It was unbelievable seeing Yankee Stadium from that perspective. For some reason, the nervousness kind of went away. It was like, "Holy cow! I'm here! I did it!" I got on that mound, and I started throwing my pitches.

I pitched extremely well because I just said, "Screw it. Do I even deserve to be here?" It was almost like I pitched as a fan. I was just thinking, "Oh my God. This is unbelievable."

I pitched three and two-thirds innings without giving up an earned run, in front of friends and family. I went on to pitch 10 more years, but that's probably my greatest memory.

Shawn Estes (Giants)

Shawn Estes made his major league debut on September 16, 1995, with the San Francisco Giants. He played in 13 big league seasons. Estes is honored on the San Francisco Giants Wall of Fame.

3. 1990s

I started to believe I could be a big league player when I was in high school, probably my senior year. Scouts were telling me I could potentially get drafted in the first round. At different points in your life, you have a lot of confidence, and then you fail, and you start to doubt a little bit.

I struggled in the minor leagues, doubted myself, and got hurt. Then I had to go through a whole transformation. Everybody has their own path, and they more than likely doubt themselves at some point due to failure or injuries.

In high school, if you're a high draft pick, you probably dominate wherever you are. You don't fail a lot, so your confidence is off the charts. Then most guys get humbled like I did. You have to figure out what it really takes. What it comes down to is obviously determination, your straight will, and how competitive you really are. That's when you find out what you're made of.

I was drafted by Seattle in the first round in 1991, and I was traded to the Giants in April of '95. I had made two starts in the minor leagues with the Mariners' Low-A team in Wisconsin, the Wisconsin Timber Rattlers. It had been my third consecutive year in Appleton, Wisconsin. But that was the first year I came into spring training where I felt like I had turned a corner.

The off-season before, I figured some things out physically with my mechanics. Mentally, I was meeting with a guy named Gary Mack with the Mariners, and he helped with the mental side of the game. A lot of guys have too much pride to think they need help mentally, but I felt at that point, I needed help. The Mariners set it up for me to where I was meeting with him, and his assistant, a couple times a week out in Arizona. Not only was I feeling good about myself physically because my mechanics were in tune with where I wanted them to be, but mentally I was starting to think the right way.

The reason I'm saying this is because I was going to the same Low-A ball team for my third consecutive year, but mentally, it was the first time I felt I was going to start heading in the right direction. I was heading toward the path to the big leagues, like I expected all along.

The Mariners were trying to win their division that year and trying to get their stadium built. They needed to win, so they traded a lot of their minor leaguers away for some guys that could help them at the big league level.

After two games in Wisconsin, I got traded to the Giants. I was ecstatic because I grew up a Giants fan. My family are all Giants fans. I grew up in northern Nevada, so that's who you root for. I was pumped.

Even after two starts in the minor leagues that year, I had a lot of confidence that it was going to be a big year for me, and it was a change of scenery for me, which I probably needed.

The Giants sent me to Low-A, and I made four starts there. I got sent up to High-A in San Jose and pitched maybe a month and a half there. Then I got called up to Double-A and pitched a month and a half there. We ended up winning the Texas League that year and played a little bit longer into September.

It was a whirlwind year. I made four different stops, and I was pretty content on going home and looking forward to the next year, where I thought I potentially could start in Triple-A. I celebrated the Texas League championship that night in Shreveport with my team, and I was going home the next day.

I was staying with a host mom, a lady named Gayle, and she lived by herself. She would host players every year. I stayed with her for the month and a half that I was in Shreveport.

I went to bed that night, and I got a knock at my door. I can't remember what time it was, but it was late 'cause we had won the Texas League and we were celebrating. I had got back to Gayle's house, was going to hit the hay, and get ready for my flight the next day.

She knocked on my door, and I could tell she had this look in her eyes. It was pre-cell phones, so they called her home. She had this look on her face with this big smile, because I think she knew exactly what was going on.

Bobby Evans, who ran the minor leagues at that point for the Giants, was on the other line. Maybe they had talked prior to me getting the phone, but I was kind of confused why he would be calling at that point.

I get on the phone and Bobby says, "You had a great season. We traded for you, but we don't know much about you. Obviously, you pitched your butt off in the minor leagues this year, but we want to give you an opportunity to see what you can do at the big league level."

I was shocked. I didn't see it coming. If you're in Double-A or Triple-A and you're having a good year, during the season there's talk that you could be called up. You read your name in the paper, and you get a feel for what the organization's thinking. There was none of that. I didn't hear a word about potentially making my debut the same year I got traded and started at Low-A ball.

I couldn't sleep that night, obviously. I called my mom and dad and everybody I knew that would be awake and told them the news. I flew out to St. Louis the next day and made my debut a couple of days later in Pittsburgh.

We had some pretty big names on that team. Guys I grew up watching—Matt Williams, Robby Thompson, Royce Clayton, Kirt Manwaring, and obviously Barry Bonds. Even Deion Sanders was on that team in '95.

Looking around the clubhouse, there was a lot of star power. As a rookie, I was a bit awed. I was already in shock that I got called up to the big leagues, and then I was in awe that I'm in the same clubhouse as all these guys that I, at least in high school, ended up becoming a big fan of.

I got there and it was kind of funny 'cause the team really wasn't in it at that point. There were only a couple of weeks left in the season, and they were going to give me three starts. Like I said, I'd just been traded to the organization that year, so no one really knew me or what I featured. They wanted to see what they had. I could see the standings and see that the Giants weren't in any danger to win the NL West that year, so I knew they didn't bring me up to make that push.

I remember sitting next to William Van Landingham right before my first start in Pittsburgh. Dusty Baker says to William and I, "All right, I just want to let you guys know we need these next couple games, so we need you guys to go out and pitch well." No pressure, right? I'm making my major league debut, and I know there's not a whole lot at stake team-wise, but for Dusty to come up and tell me, "Hey, we need these games." I'm thinking, "For what? So we're seven games out instead of nine?" But it locked me in.

I didn't know much about Dusty at that point, what a competitor he was as a manager, and that he was trying to win every game. He wanted everybody to go out there and be motivated to win. Dusty and I ended up having a great relationship for the six-plus years I was a Giant. He was a motivator. That was his main attribute as a manager—his ability to motivate players and get the most of their abilities. He was just trying to see what I was made of.

I was extremely nervous, as I think anybody making their debut would tell you. I was just trying to keep it all together mentally and control the adrenaline.

I remember running to the mound from the dugout at Three Rivers and not really being able to feel my legs. It was turf. I almost felt like I wasn't touching the ground. It was a surreal moment.

I had this rush of adrenaline overcome me. Warming up, I was just hoping that I could get it to the catcher's area. I was throwing to an area. I wasn't trying to hit my spots. I was just trying to find a way to control my heartbeat. I was having a little bit of an out-of-body experience. I didn't want to throw one 30 feet or over the backstop. I just wanted to try to get it in the area of the catcher, Kirt Manwaring.

At that point, it was all instinctual, just reaching back, letting it go, and seeing what happens. There's really no touch and feel at that point. There's no feel for what you're doing. You trust what you know how to do, and you hope for the best. Whatever sign the catcher throws down, that's the pitch you're going to throw. You're not shaking at that point.

I remember the first inning, and then, after that, it was kind of a blur.

That first inning went well. I struck out Jacob Brumfield to lead the game off. Then I struck out Jay Bell, the second hitter. Then I got Orlando Merced to pop up for the third out. I went in the dugout thinking, "Wow. That was pretty awesome. That was a cool way to start this thing."

I may, at that point, have relaxed too much. I was like, "Okay, I'm here in the big leagues and I just had a pretty good first inning." Then after that, it didn't go as well. I got knocked out in the sixth inning that day. When I look back on it, the numbers were a lot worse than I threw. I left the game with the bases loaded, and Mark Dewey came in after me. He gave up a single, a walk, and a sac fly. All those runners scored, so they got tagged on my line.

I think the only thing that would have been better, would have been if I was able to make my debut in San Francisco at Candlestick, one of the few places I'd watched a major league game. Then obviously, all my family and friends would have been able to be there. Because we were in Pittsburgh, I didn't have anybody there. Then again, that might have been better for me, because I didn't feel as much pressure as if I had people there.

While you're playing, you're surrounded by guys that are all really good. I think you lose a little perspective of how small a percentage of people that play baseball make it to the major leagues and how difficult it is to not just get to the big leagues but stay there. Getting to the big leagues is definitely something to be proud of. Staying there is something I'm most proud of.

Jason Kendall (Pirates)

Jason Kendall made his major league debut on April 1, 1996, with the Pittsburgh Pirates. He played in 15 big league seasons. Kendall was selected to three All-Star teams. Jason's father, Fred, also played in the majors.

The previous year, we won the league championship when I was in Double-A. I got the MVP of the league, and I knew I had a shot because they didn't have an everyday catcher.

I can honestly tell you, I don't know how I heard the news that I'd made the team. In the off-season, I was told, "You're going to big league camp, and you have a shot to make the team." I'm like, "I'm making it." My first manager was Jim Leyland, so at some point he had to call me in and say, "Hey, you made the team."

Roger Wilson was our equipment manager then, and he's like a second dad to me. I had number 52 when I found out I was making the team. My dad wore 18, 16, and 5. Five was taken, so I said, "Hey, can I wear 18?" Well, Andy Van Slyke had worn 18. A lot of these clubhouse guys won't just offer up someone's number. I asked for 18, and he was like, "You know, Van Slyke wore that." I said, "I don't give a fuck about Van Slyke." He goes, "That is exactly why you're going to get number 18."

We opened against Florida. Paul Wagner's pitching for us, and it was at Joe Robbie Stadium. The Marlins don't draw very well, but on Opening Day, everybody draws well.

I was obviously nervous. I was nervous before every game that I ever played. If I didn't have that feeling, shit, I wouldn't have been playing. But it was a good nervous. Obviously, for your first big league game, you're pretty much shitting yourself.

I was hitting eighth, and Kevin Brown was pitching for the Marlins, throwing like 98 with unbelievable sink.

Carlos Garcia hits a triple off the wall, and it's the first time somebody really put a bat on the ball. Then I get my first at-bat. I took the first pitch. It was like 98, a fricking outside heavy two-seamer, strike one. I step out and I'm like, "Oh shit, all right." I'm thinking to myself, "Fuck!" Next one was the same pitch and I hit a line drive foul ball that almost killed their manager. I remember I stepped out and I'm like, "Holy fucking shit. If every big league pitcher is like this, I have zero chance in this game."

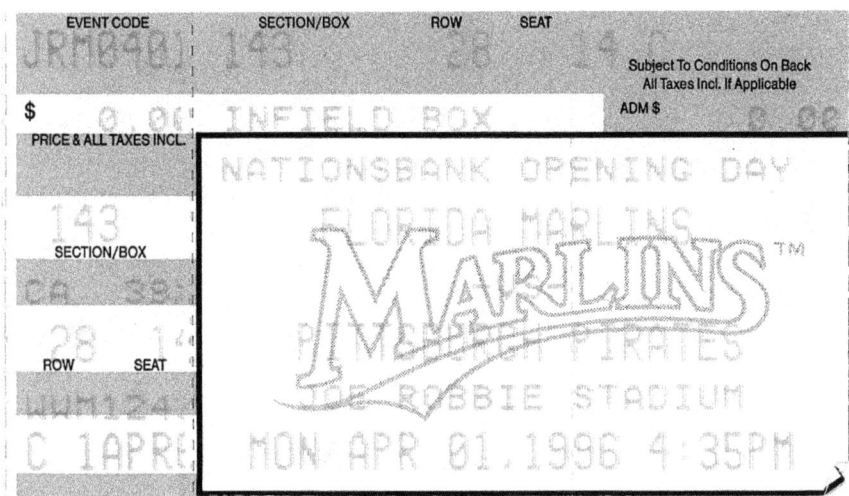

Ticket stub from Jason Kendall's major league debut with the Pittsburgh Pirates in Florida (author's collection).

The next pitch was the same pitch and a ball. I step out and I'm like, "How the fuck am I going to hit this son of a bitch?" The dude hangs a slider and I hit a line drive up the middle. We went up, 1–0.

After I hit, I go back to catching. Frank Pulli was the umpire. He goes, "I liked your daddy, kid. Don't think you'll ever get a fucking 'nother [pitch]." I'm like, "Mr. Pulli, I appreciate that." He gave me that third pitch, that one on the outside. He could've rung me up.

I went 3-for-4 that day and we won the game. I ended up having great stats against Kevin Brown, but he was right there on top of the filthiest pitchers I ever faced.

It was probably the only game in the big leagues I ever played where I felt 100 percent physically. Mentally, you feel like you can jump out of the stadium. Then when you're done with your first big league game, your body starts hurting because you've got to do it the next day.

Jason Hardtke (Mets)

Jason Hardtke made his major league debut on September 8, 1996, with the New York Mets. He played in three big league seasons. Hardtke also played one season in Japan.

I bounced around a lot. Two years into being with the team that drafted me in the third round, Cleveland, they traded me to the Padres. That kinda turned me sideways. It was definitely an eye-opener. I played a few years with the Padres' organization and had some injuries.

I got traded for a big leaguer when I went from Cleveland to San Diego, and then I went from San Diego to the New York Mets in the Rule 5 draft. Every time I changed organizations, it was because people were wanting me. It wasn't because I was getting released.

Progressing through those organizations, I never really worried about who was below me or ahead of me. I just figured if I take care of what I'm doing and do my best, good things were going to happen. I had to prove myself going into each organization, but it worked out.

I had a great year in 1996 playing with the Norfolk Tide. I was hitting well and playing good defense. We had a good team, and over half the guys already had some sort of big league experience. We went to the playoffs and ended up losing to the Columbus Clippers, the Yankees' Triple-A team.

Steve Phillips was our assistant GM at the time. He was calling people in after the game and letting them know they got called up. I knew I had a good year, but I didn't know if it was going to happen. I was the last one to get called in.

I was on the phone late at night calling people. I remember calling my dad and talking to him. I could hear him getting choked up. It was super emotional, but super exciting. I'll never forget that.

I think we took the first flight out of Columbus to Atlanta, then went straight to the ballpark. There were three or four of us going up together.

When I show up, I go find my locker to see what number they gave me. I was born in Wisconsin, so my family followed the Brewers. I was a big Brewers fan growing up, and my favorite player was Robin Yount. I look in my locker and see "Hardtke number 19." I couldn't believe it.

Bobby Valentine was the manager. I knew him because he had started that year in Triple-A. When they fired Dallas Green, Bobby got the big league job. I got to the locker room and Bobby said, "When you get situated, come on in." I go in and he says, "Congratulations. How'd it go?" I said, "I was up all night talking to people. It was kinda crazy." He goes, "What are you telling me? Are you too tired to play?" I said, "No, I'm not too tired at all." He goes, "Well, good, because you're in there batting second and playing second."

I was between Lance Johnson, who led the world in triples that season, and Bernard Gilkey, who set the Mets' record for RBIs that season. Then there was Todd Hundley, who broke the home run record for catchers that season. There was a lot of good stuff going on, and I was thrown in the middle of it, which was pretty cool.

Greg Maddux was pitching for the Braves. I was nervous and my legs were a little shaky, but for the most part, I was pretty good. My first at-bat, I go up there and I get two strikes. I'm like, "Whatever you do, you just can't strike out your first at-bat." As a hitter, that's not something you want to think. I ended up popping up to the second baseman, Mark Lemke. I remember hitting first base, looping around, and thinking, "Thank God!" That was probably the happiest I've been hitting an infield popup, which was a little weird.

I settled in a little, got a couple ground balls in the field, and felt I could relax and play. I faced Maddux my next two at-bats also. I ended up hitting a double into right-center field and then another double into left-center field. It was pretty special to get my first couple hits off him. I could sit down and go, "Oh man, I just went 2-for-3 off Greg Maddux with two doubles." Everything he did in the game was amazing.

I had ups and downs my whole career, but at that point, I had played in the big leagues and got hits in the big leagues. No one could take that away from me. It was a sigh of relief.

Scott Spiezio (Athletics)

Scott Spiezio made his major league debut on September 14, 1996, with the Oakland Athletics. He played in 12 big league seasons. Scott's father, Ed, also played in the majors.

I was playing for the Edmonton Trappers in the Triple-A Coast League. We had a really good team. I ended up hitting 20 homers in the regular season and had 91 RBIs. I had a good year and I thought I proved I should get a call-up. I was on the 40-man roster at the time and felt I put in my dues.

We made the playoffs, and I was happy that we made the playoffs, but at the same time, I'm like, "Crap, they might not call me up now." We go into the playoffs, and I caught fire. We ended up winning the league championship.

We were at a hotel, with a bar at the bottom. After we won, we went to that bar. I wasn't a big drinker at the time, and I hardly ever went out, but I figured there were some big league guys there and they were buying. I had four or five beers, which was a lot for me then. It closed down, and we all went back to our rooms.

I see a light flashing on the phone, and I wonder what it is. I pick it up, and I hear somebody that sounds like Gary Jones, our manager. He's like, "Hey, Speez, this is Jonesy. Congratulations, man. You're getting called up."

Right away, I'm thinking this is one of the guys. Mark Acre used to do a Jonesy impression, and so did a lot of other guys. I figured just when I get back to my room, they're going to call me at two in the morning and act like Jonesy. They used to call me up on the road and be like, "Hey, Speez, this is Jonesy, do you have any toothpaste? I brought my toothbrush, but I've got no toothpaste."

I'm like, "Very funny, guys." He's like, "No, seriously. This is Jonesy." I was like, "Oh, really?" He's like, "Yeah, man. You've got a flight going to Cleveland. You've got to be at the airport at like five in the morning."

Now, it's Friday the 13th at two in the morning and it's an hour from the ballpark to the airport in Edmonton. I was trying to figure out how I was going to get back to the clubhouse to get my stuff. I had like five bags. It was a pain in the butt to get a cab, but somehow, we worked it out. I get to the park, get my stuff, get to the airport, and check all the bags.

I get on the plane, and it's a dinky little prop plane. It's the 13th, I'm a little superstitious, and we're flying through thunderstorms going towards Cleveland.

We land in Cleveland, and I'd never been to Cleveland. I get my bags and a cab and say, "Take me to the park." I go straight to the park. I get to the front of the park, and I don't know where I'm supposed to go. I just had him drop me off out front.

I've got five bags there, and I'm supposed to go to the visiting clubhouse. I'm there pretty early, and I'm looking for a way to get in. I'm walking all around the stadium until I find somebody. I say, "Hey, I just got here from Triple-A. How do I get to the visiting clubhouse?" They showed me, and I went in.

You've got all these emotions going on, and you're like, "Holy cow, this is big time." I'm in the clubhouse, and I see everybody's locker with all these big names—Mark McGwire, Jason Giambi, Terry Steinbach, Mike Bordick, and Scott Brosius.

Then I see my name. It says Spiezio, and it has number 13 on it. It's Friday the 13th, and I never liked the number 13. I liked numbers with sevens in them. I look at our clubhouse guy and I'm like, "Man, 13." He's like, "That's what we had left." I'm like, "Okay."

I go and talk to Art Howe and see I'm in the lineup at third base, playing against arguably one of the best-hitting teams that has ever played. So I'm right in the game, with no sleep, and it's raining. I know their first three guys are fast and can bunt. I'm going to be on a wet field, playing against these guys. Then you've got huge sluggers that could kill you down at third base too.

Anyway, the game got rained out before it started. So I did not play on the 13th, and I begged and pleaded to get a number divisible by seven. I got 21 the next day.

The next day, we had a doubleheader. I was thinking I was going to start the first game, but I didn't. The whole game I'm watching and I'm thinking, "Am I ever going to get in?" I didn't get in. The second game, I got to play. The assistant coach for my high school team and my dad both got there before the game, and that settled me down a little bit.

Chad Ogea was pitching against us. I had gone on a recruiting trip to LSU, and he was one of the guys that took me out. I didn't know him super well, but I knew him at least. That helped a little bit too, knowing it wasn't someone like Roger Clemens that I was facing for my first at-bat.

I got up there for my first at-bat, and I hit a line shot to right field. I hit it hard, and it took one bounce. Manny Ramirez was out there and cut it off. If it wasn't wet and soggy from all the rain the night before and earlier that day, it would have been into the corner. I would have at least got a double, possibly a triple.

I got to first and they threw the ball into Barry Weinberg, our athletic trainer. He would write it up real nice with the date, who it was off of, and all that stuff. Well, the inning ended, and I came in. Everybody's giving me high-fives, and then McGwire says to me, "You know, there's nowhere to go but down now." I'm thinking, "I guess he's right. I can't hit 1.000 my whole career."

Then Barry Weinberg throws me a ball that looks like a first grader took a pen to it. I'm like, "Oh my God! Is this really it?" They're all like, "Yeah, do you like it?" They were messing with me, but they let me think about that for a whole inning while I was out there on the field. When I came back in, Barry showed me an example of what he'd done and let me know he'd take his time. I'm like, "Thank God. I didn't want to show that to my kids and grandkids someday."

I later heard they weren't planning on calling me up, but I had such a good playoffs, they felt I deserved it. Looking back, it's a good thing we made the playoffs, 'cause I might've been at home, disappointed. Instead, I got all that experience, and I think that led to me making the team the next year.

Scott Spiezio was called up by the Oakland Athletics during his fourth professional season, following a strong playoffs performance in Triple-A (photography by Doug McWilliams).

Josh Booty (Marlins)

Josh Booty made his major league debut on September 24, 1996, with the Florida Marlins. He played in three big league seasons. Following his baseball career, he played in the National Football League.

I was probably a bigger football recruit than I was at baseball, and I was a top baseball recruit. My senior year, I concentrated on football when it was football season and then baseball when it was baseball season. I knew if I had a good senior year, I was gonna go high, and I could get paid. That's what I was thinking.

3. 1990s

I had a great agent, Jeff Moorad, who was with Leigh Steinberg, and they were really the first true mega-agents. Moorad had a lot of big-named guys like Will Clark, Matt Williams, and Manny Ramirez, so I chose him. Will Clark was always my favorite player growing up. So I chose Moorad, and he got me drafted. We positioned me to get drafted by Florida at fifth in the first round of the 1994 draft because they were a new franchise. They didn't really have anybody in the minor league system at third base, and we knew that Wayne Huizenga was very wealthy and could pay the type of money that would take me away from going to play baseball and football at LSU. I wanted to play in the big leagues early and get paid, so I went to the Marlins' organization.

When I got to the minor leagues, there was no one ahead of me, and in that contract, I had big league call-ups starting in 1996. That's one of the reasons I chose to go with baseball out of high school. I had big league spring training invites, 40-man roster, and big league call-ups for September, so I knew I was gonna get called up. I didn't know if I'd get any at-bats, but I knew I was gonna get called up and I was their first-round pick, so they wanted to get me at-bats in the right situation.

I went from A-Ball to the big leagues in '96. In A-Ball, I hit 21 home runs, which was the team's franchise record, but I struck out 195 times, which was also a franchise record. I was hitting homers or striking out. I didn't have much plate discipline. The day after my last minor league game, I went straight to the Marlins.

In '96, we weren't in a playoff run or anything. I got called up in September, and they gave me my first at-bat against the Braves, who were dominating at that time, with John Smoltz, Steve Avery, Tom Glavine, Greg Maddux, and all those guys.

I was with the team for three weeks

Ticket stub from Josh Booty's major league debut with the Florida Marlins. His contract included call-ups starting in 1996 (author's collection).

before I got that at-bat, and I can remember how nervous I was. I dreamed about that stuff. I'm like, "Oh my God! I'm in the big leagues!"

My first at-bat was against a guy named Kevin Lomon. I remember getting in the on-deck circle at Joe Robbie Stadium, and instead of putting one donut on my bat, I put two donuts on 'cause I hadn't swung in a while against a live pitcher. Everybody's laughing, but I'm like, "Oh man, I ain't hit in three weeks!"

I singled in that plate appearance. I took a fastball to right field for a base hit, between first and second. I was happy.

Micah Franklin (Cardinals)

Micah Franklin made his major league debut on May 13, 1997, for the St. Louis Cardinals. He played in one big league season. Franklin also played two seasons in Japan.

The night before, they sent someone down and made the transaction at the big league level. Willie McGee and Dmitri Young called me that night and said, "Hey! You're coming up."

Well, I went to the ballpark the next day, and I hadn't been officially called up yet. The manager, Gaylen Pitts, mentioned that guys were going down, but he didn't tell me I was going up. Sometimes when people get called up, they won't play in the game, but I was playing in the game. I'm like, "Man, maybe they changed their mind."

I had a decent game that day. After the game, Gaylen Pitts walked by me a couple of times. I'm like, "Man, they're not calling me up." Finally, about the third time he walked by, he said, "Hey, Micah, come on in the office."

It was right to the point. I walked in and he said, "Congratulations! You're going up."

I ran outside to my wife, Lisa, and told her. At that point, we had our oldest daughter. My mom and dad happened to be in town too. We were jumping up and down and couldn't believe it.

I'm in Louisville, and they give me a flight from Louisville to Philly. My wife, daughter, and my mom and dad got on another flight. My grandmother and grandfather drove to Philly from New York.

You hear stories about guys getting first-class seats to go to the big leagues. Well, I was on a little plane that had one seat on each side. There were no first-class seats, and I'm in the back of this plane, which was about a 15-seater, flying into Philly.

We're going down for our landing, and all of a sudden, we're going back up in the air. We didn't make the first landing. We had to go back up, circle around, and do it again. I'm like, "Man, I finally get called up to the major leagues and I'm not gonna make it. I'm gonna die in this airplane."

I got into Philly, took a cab to the hotel, and got ahold of Willie McGee. We took a cab over to the Vet. I introduced myself to Tony LaRussa and then the whole coaching staff. I saw my name on a locker, which was always a dream. From that point on, it was like a flash. It was so fast. All of a sudden, we took batting practice. That was amazing. It was a great experience, being on a major league field, taking batting practice.

I was in there the first day. It was almost a "dream come true" day. It turned into a nightmare.

My first at-bat, on the first pitch I saw, I barreled it up and I hit it down the first baseline. Rico Brogna jumps up and snow cones the ball. He robbed me of a double. The next at-bat, we had guys on first and second. I hit a ball down the right field line into the bleachers, foul. It was long enough to be a home run, but I ended up striking out. Then I struck out my last at-bat. I could have been 2-for-3 with a double and a home run, but I ended up 0-for-3 with two strikeouts.

I owe so much to Willie McGee. I met him when I was 19 years old, and he took me in and mentored me. I hit with him every day in the off-season, and it was a dream come true, just to be there with him and drive him crazy. I remember after Rico Brogna snow-coned that catch, I walked right up to Willie and joked, "Man, this league is going to be too easy." That was the kind of relationship we had. He was awesome. Being able to experience it with him was one of the best memories I'll ever have.

Rick DeHart (Expos)

Rick DeHart made his major league debut on July 16, 1997, with the Montreal Expos. He played in four big league seasons. DeHart also played one season in Japan.

I didn't get drafted out of college. I had a whole year off after school. I just kept telling myself, "Man, this can't be over." After your senior year, if you don't get drafted, you're pretty much done.

Well, about a year goes by, and I'm goin' to work the third shift. Every Sunday I'd stop at the Kwik Shop, and they had the *Baseball Weekly* magazine. In the back of the paper, they always had ads for selling equipment, buying equipment, and even umpire school. I told myself, "If I can't play, I'll try to stay in baseball somehow."

One night, technically morning, I opened it up and there was a work ad that said, "Wanted: Baseball players for new league in Taiwan. Tryouts in Fort Lauderdale." I'm like, "You've gotta be kidding me."

It was like 2:00 in the morning. I called this number, and the guy that answered was pissed, 'cause I called at 2:00 in the morning. I wanted to see how legit it was. He was like, "Call me back tomorrow morning."

Right at 7:00 a.m., I called him, and he gave me the rundown. He was like, "Yeah, we're gonna have a week-long tryout for a new league in Taiwan. There's gonna be a couple scouts for the league there. It's an open tryout."

You had to pay $400 for the tryout, but they took care of the hotel and the rides back and forth from the hotel to the field. They also fed you.

I'm still living at home. I told my dad and my family about it. Everybody raised about 500 bucks. They put in $20 here and $20 there and got me a bus ticket—not an airplane ticket, but a frickin' bus ticket from Topeka, Kansas, to Fort Lauderdale. This is before iPods, iPads, and all that stuff. I think I had a Walkman cassette player and a bunch of magazines for entertainment.

I get there, try out, and end up getting signed by a team. However, a Montreal scout was there too. He was like, "Do you really wanna go to Taiwan?" I'm like, "Hell, yeah, man. I took a Greyhound bus for three days." He goes, "If I can get you an opportunity to play here in the States, do you want to play for a team here?" I'm like, "Yeah."

I packed up my bags, he took me an hour away, and dropped me off at a hotel. This is already in the middle of spring training, so teams are almost being set. Players were pissed, thinking, "Who's this new guy coming in? Now they'll have to reshuffle."

Anyways, the Expos end up signing me and putting me [on a] low A-Ball team. This was 1992.

Let's fast forward from '92 to '97. I'm in Triple-A, playing in Ottawa, Canada. I'm making the minimum, which was like 1,200 bucks a month, and I'm paying taxes in both Canada and in the States. I was having a decent summer. My velocity was up and, as a lefty, that was getting a lot of attention from the front office.

I was sitting in the clubhouse, and my roommate, Geoff Blum, was sitting next to me. We get our paychecks. I look at it, and I was like, "Blum, I don't know if I'm gonna be able to pay rent this month." He looks at me and is like, "Yeah, man, I don't know what to do."

I remember taking my paycheck, wadding it up, and throwing it in my locker. I start cussing like, "I'm fucking quitting, man. I'm just gonna work at McDonald's. I'll probably make more doing that."

We had a doubleheader that day. They gave us our checks after the first game, and then about 10 minutes before the next game gets ready to start, I get a tap on the shoulder. It was my manager, Pat Kelly. He's like, "Hey, step in the office." I'm like, "Aw, man, he probably heard me cussing and yelling about quitting." He goes, "Sit down. We need to talk."

Pat and Bo McLaughlin, the pitching coach, sat me down in the office. Pat goes, "We heard you in there yelling and cussing. We're gonna have to get rid of you, man." I'm like, "Yeah, I figured. I probably deserve it." He goes, "Pack your bags. You've gotta meet the team in Philly tomorrow morning."

I fell out of my chair onto the floor. They had to pick me up. They knew all the tribulations and trials I went through, and they teared up.

I'd never been on the 40-man roster. It was a matter of being there at the right time, being a pitcher, and being a lefty. Lee Smith, who was a closer for a lot of teams and is now in the Hall of Fame, was ending his career, which opened a spot for me.

This is before cellphones. I remember going back to the hotel and trying to call my family. I couldn't get ahold of anybody. I finally got ahold of my grandma, and she was like, "Oh, I thought you were already in the big leagues." She didn't know pro baseball. She thought Triple-A was the same. It kind of took the wind out of my sail. I'm like, "Grandma, no. I'm getting called up to the big leagues." She never really understood.

The next day I flew out to Philly. I never was in big league camp, so I didn't know any of the coaches, the manager, nobody. Montreal was a small-market team, but we did have a couple superstars in the making with Vladimir Guerrero and Pedro Martinez. I got in the hotel, and I had a phone call from Pedro Martinez to meet him in the lobby. He took me out for lunch and to get a suit. I didn't have a suit at the time, just some khakis.

The old Philadelphia stadium was a dump. But of course, I'm still in awe. Don't get me wrong.

I'm sitting in the bullpen, and they had plexiglass. I remember you could barely even see the game. There was so much spit, chew, and gum all over the plexiglass. I'm like, "Man, some of the Triple-A stadiums are in better condition than this place."

I didn't think I was gonna get in the game that day, but of course, I get in. It's late innings, and my name is called. I remember jogging from the bullpen to the pitching mound. I happen to look up at the scoreboard. They had a tron up there, and they had me running. I almost freaked out. I was like, "Don't fall. Don't trip." I'm sure people were giving me shit like, "Dude, he's watching himself on the tron right now."

I come in, and I'd never thrown to the catcher. He had never even heard of me. He goes, "I've never seen you throw. What do you have?" I go, "Fastball, curveball.... Let's just stick with that."

There was one out and men on first and second. Rico Brogna swings at the very first pitch and hits a weak ground ball to second base. The second baseman flips it to our shortstop, Mark Grudzielanek, who steps on the bag and starts walking toward the dugout. He thought there were three outs, but it was only two outs. He didn't throw the ball to first base.

Now, I've got a guy on third and first with two outs. The next pitch was a fastball inside, and I threw a wild pitch. The runner ends up scoring. I'm already thinking, "God, I'm gonna get sent down after the game." That's how my mind was working. I walk the batter, and the guy after that gets a hit.

Then the highlight I had was Curt Schilling came up to bat. I'm like, "No way, dude. I just watched this guy on TV last summer. Now, I'm facing him." I ended up striking him out, 'cause he took a fastball looking. It's over, and I walk back to the dugout.

My debut went from a one-pitch double play to a wild pitch, walk, and base hit, but I ended up staying up for about a month.

Mike Misuraca (Brewers)

Mike Misuraca made his major league debut on July 27, 1997, with the Milwaukee Brewers. He played in one big league season.

I was moving along, and when I got to Double-A in '93, I started coming into my own a little bit. That's when the Twins were starting to recognize me as a prospect, and I thought, "You know what, I'm gonna pitch in the big leagues." I got hurt that year, and that derailed things a little bit. But I always kept that belief. Even though I was a non-drafted free agent, that didn't deter me.

I had a lot of close calls, but it didn't pan out until '97 with the Brewers' organization. Even the way that happened, it wasn't like, "I'm throwing so well, they're gonna call me up any minute." I had no clue.

We were on a road trip in Tacoma. I'd been throwing well up until that point, but I wasn't getting my hopes up or anything. Bob Mariano, our interim manager, called me in the office with the pitching coach, Mark Littell. When they called me in the office, I just had a feeling that's what they were gonna tell me.

I was starting at that point, but they said, "Hey, do you have any problem pitching out of the bullpen?" Well, I knew they weren't talking about taking me out of the Triple-A rotation and putting me in the bullpen. I knew what they were talking about. I said, "Shoot, I could do that. No problem." They said, "Well, you're going to Detroit tomorrow to make your debut. You're going to the big leagues." I was numb. I couldn't believe it.

The first thing I did, of course, was call my parents. Cell phones were basically in their infancy. I remember going outside the locker room in Tacoma and calling my parents on the pay phone. My mom answered, and I said, "Mom, get Pop and put him on the phone. I've got something to tell you guys." My dad got on the phone, and I told them. It was a big moment for our family.

My dad and I were pretty close, and that was a big dream of his. Now, being a dad, I can only imagine how proud he must have been. At the time, I kinda took it for granted, like it was no big deal. But calling him was very memorable.

That night, I went out and bought myself a sports coat. The next morning, they gave me a first-class ticket, and I flew in to Detroit. First, I dropped my bags off at the hotel. Then I took a taxi over to the stadium. I don't know if they were expecting me, but the guy just opened the gate right up for me.

It was an unbelievable feeling. I can't really explain it. It was something that you'd thought about your whole life and now you're actually walking into a stadium as a big league ballplayer. It was obviously one of the biggest highlights of my life.

I went into the locker room, and I saw my jersey there. The pitchers and catchers were having their meeting. They were going over the scouting reports. I joined and was listening in. I was on cloud nine. It was like I was on a field trip. It was an unbelievable experience.

I didn't pitch the first two nights. I got in on the third day. It was a Sunday. Cal Eldred started, and it was a close game.

I remember the bullpen phone ringing, and Billy Castro said, "Mizz, you're up." Those butterflies were real. I looked up on the big stadium board there, and it said, "Warming up in the bullpen, Mike Misuraca." Then when I came in, it said, "Mike Misuraca, making his major league debut."

When I started warming up, I was rapid-firing. Billy stopped me. He slowed me down. He said, "Look, before I made my debut, I couldn't even feel my feet." I said, "Well, I can feel mine, 'cause they're shaking." He started laughing. He said, "Just take a couple of deep breaths. It's the same game." I calmed down.

Matt Walbeck was the first big league hitter I faced. I split the plate on the first pitch. I threw a nice pitch and centered it low. I knew he wouldn't be swinging because they hadn't seen me yet. So I was gonna get a quick strike, and that's exactly what I did. That took a lot of weight off my shoulders, so to speak. Then with the next pitch, I threw him a change-up and he rolled it over to the second baseman.

I had a good, one-two-three first inning. I remember walking off the mound and passing the first base coach for Detroit, Jerry White. He was a former Twins coach, so we knew each other pretty well. He said, "Mizz, man, you don't know how happy I am for you right now. Congratulations." I looked at him, nodded, kind of smiled a little bit, and went into the dugout.

I struck out Travis Fryman to start the next inning. It was only a two-run game at the time. Then I hung a 3–2 change-up to Bobby Higginson. In Triple-A, they woulda let it go for ball four, but in the big leagues, he decided to hit it up on the roof.

That was it, and they brought in somebody. But we ended up winning that ball game. It was a great debut and very memorable.

A funny story about my debut was that my friend Rob flew up. He goes, "I'm gonna see your debut." He flew to Detroit and met me there. He's a buddy that I grew up with. We played Little League together, and he's actually married to my cousin. He's like 6'6", chiseled out, and he looks like a major leaguer. I remember going to the big league hotel, and there's always fans there, you know, autograph seekers. I can remember walking in with Rob. They all went running towards him, and I just walked right on by. He thought that was so great. He's like, "I've never signed autographs." I said, "Just go with it." He's sitting there signing autographs, and I just walked right by everybody 'cause the last thing I looked like was a big league ballplayer.

Being a scout now and knowing how many good baseball players don't get to the big leagues, or Double-A, or Triple-A, for that matter, there isn't a day that goes by that I don't appreciate it. I'm very proud of it.

Obviously, I didn't have a big career up there, but I can tell guys how to grind it out. I played every level in the minor leagues and obviously wasn't a bonus baby. Every promotion I ever got was because I earned it. It wasn't because they had a couple hundred thousand dollars invested in me and they had to keep moving me along. They had no money invested in me—absolutely nothing. There was no reason to keep me around, other than I was holding my own.

Steve Woodard (Brewers)

Steve Woodard made his major league debut on July 28, 1997, with the Milwaukee Brewers. He played in seven big league seasons. In his debut, Woodard outdueled Roger Clemens.

Mike Caldwell was my pitching coach in A-Ball and Double-A. He had pitched in the big leagues and was like a dad to me.

I was 14–3 in Double-A and went up to Triple-A for one start before I went to the big leagues. Mike kinda knew before it all happened. When I had my last start in Double-A, he didn't tell me too much, but he told me, "Just be expecting it. You might be up in the big leagues pretty soon."

I got called up to Triple-A, and I made a start in Salt Lake City. I threw seven innings without allowing a run. The next day, we traveled to Tacoma, and I found out there that I was going to the big leagues.

The manager got Mike Caldwell on the phone, and they told me. It was a cool moment. It was just surreal. Mike was still there in Double-A, but with him being around me most of my career in the minor leagues, I think it was just one of those things where they wanted him in on it. He was part of everything that was going on.

The first people I called were my parents. My parents were with me every step of the way. I wouldn't have done anything without them. They made sure I was here and there, had everything I ever needed, and supported me. My dad had always coached me all the way up.

I rushed to get packed and on a plane. I flew out the next morning and met the team in Detroit, at the old Tiger Stadium. They were already playing the game when I got to the ballpark, got dressed, and went down to sit in the dugout. Nobody knew who I was.

I'll never forget, I went and sat in the dugout, and it was about the seventh inning of the game. Bob Wickman was pitching. He comes in off the field and goes, "Who are you, man?" But Bob ended up being the guy that took care of me for the next several years, and he and I actually got traded to Cleveland together.

We were there for one more day, so the next day I was there for batting practice and everything. I got a chance to sit and talk with Doug Jones. Jones sat me down in the clubhouse and told me the things you do and things you don't do. When a veteran guy's telling you that, it's a cool moment.

I was already kind of put in the rotation. They already knew when I was going to start, but they didn't tell me until I was in Detroit, the day before I was going to pitch. There was a doubleheader scheduled back in Milwaukee against the Toronto Blue Jays because of snow. They told me I was going to throw the first game of that doubleheader against the Blue Jays. At that point in time, I realized I was going to be pitching against Roger Clemens. Roger Clemens was somebody that I'd idolized, grew up watching, and wanted to be like. It was a weird feeling being able to pitch against your idol.

We flew into Milwaukee the night after the last game in Detroit. My parents were already in town. It was one of those nights where you don't sleep, getting ready for the next day.

Back in '97, we didn't have the cameras, video, and everything like we do now. They didn't have great scouting reports and didn't know a lot about me. It was an advantage for me as the pitcher. The first batter of the game was Otis Nixon. I'll never live it down because I do a lot of stuff with Otis now. He led off the game with a double, right off the bat, down the left field line. But it was the only hit I gave up that day.

I got the next guy to fly out. Then my first big league strikeout was Joe Carter. Carlos Delgado was up next, and I was able to strike him out too.

From that point on, it was like I was in a dream world. I could never have expected the day to end up like it did, going eight shutout innings, striking out 12 guys, and only giving up that one hit to the first batter of the game. I don't think I could write that script, especially with Bob Uecker doing the game. I've got video, and his voice doing it.

It was amazing, sitting there watching Roger Clemens pitch. I'm pitching against him, and matching him, inning for inning. He won the Cy Young Award that year also.

Roger was real cool about everything. After the game, he came over to

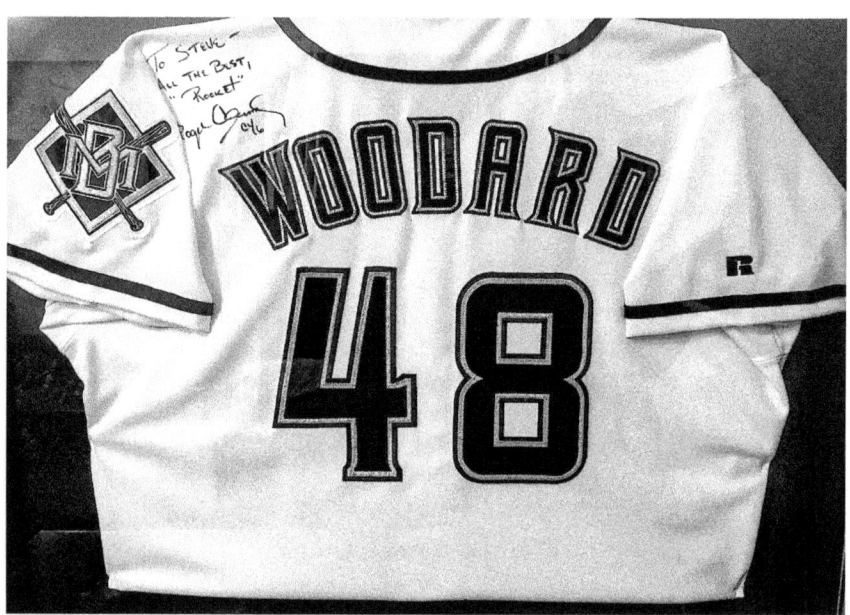

Jersey from Steve Woodard's major league debut with the Milwaukee Brewers, signed by opposing pitcher Roger Clemens. (Courtesy of Steve Woodard.)

the clubhouse. I walked out, and he introduced himself. He told me, "Kid, go back in there and get your jersey." I went back in there, got my jersey, and he signed it for me.

I've got that jersey hanging up at home. It's something I will cherish for the rest of my life.

Sean Lowe (Cardinals)

Sean Lowe made his major league debut on August 29, 1997, with the St. Louis Cardinals. He played in seven big league seasons.

I'd had a good year and it was my second season in Triple-A. It wasn't necessarily a September call-up, but it kinda was.

I was playing in Louisville. We were at home, and I'd just got done throwing my bullpen 'cause I was gonna start August 29. I got done throwing the pen and went into the locker room.

I remember my manager calling me in the office, sitting down, and talking about how my bullpen went. I said, "I feel good. I wish the season wasn't gonna be over." He goes, "Well, I don't think you're gonna throw very good here because you're gonna be throwing in Kansas City." Todd Stottlemyre had a sore arm, and they were gonna rest him.

I get outside, go to the pay phone, and call my parents.

It was a long time coming in my opinion, but the Cardinals at that time had a veteran team. My first thoughts were, "All right, Kansas City. They don't have big crowds and they're a young team." However, my first start was the first interleague game in Kansas City between the Cardinals and Royals. It was near a sellout.

I got there the day before my start. I got to go out on the field before the game for BP and all that stuff, but then I watched that first game in the clubhouse. I couldn't sit on the bench because I wasn't on the active roster. They weren't gonna make the move until the next day.

I actually watched that game in the clubhouse with Dennis Eckersley. I didn't really talk to him. There was a lot of respect there. It was different back then. He'd been up there so long, and I was a scared little rabbit. If I had talked to him, he'd been fine, but he wasn't gonna say much to me. He wasn't a jerk about it. That's just the way it was.

It was great I got to start. It's easier to prepare. If I had to sit down in the bullpen not knowing when I was gonna throw, I probably would have been throwing up everywhere. Knowing I was starting, I was kinda able to ease myself into it.

I got to the clubhouse as early as I could because I couldn't wait. I kinda stayed to myself. Around 5:00 or 5:30, Dave Duncan, the pitching coach, comes and says, "We're gonna do a meeting with the catchers and go over the hitters. Make sure to bring up what you've got." A good thing about it was a handful of the guys on Kansas City I had played against in the minor leagues. I knew some of the hitters more than I would have if it'd been a different team. When the meeting was over, the nervousness started setting in because I started thinking about the hitters more.

Once I got the ball in my hand and started warming up in the outfield, everything turned into the same thing. The nervous energy was there, but the competition, fight, and focus on what you've gotta do took over that nervous energy a bit. You know you've gotta go out there, take the ball, and be a big boy.

I went four and a third innings. The first couple innings were really good. When they came back through the order, that's when I had some issues. Tony LaRussa didn't stick with me that long afterwards, but we won the game that day. I was happy we won but felt I could've done better. It wasn't the greatest debut, but I felt I did good enough to help the team win.

Kevin Millar (Marlins)

Kevin Millar made his major league debut on April 11, 1998, with the Florida Marlins. He played in 12 big league seasons. Following his playing days, Millar became a host on MLB Network.

It was interesting. In 1998 I got a chance to go to big league camp for the first time. That was the year the Marlins disabled the World Series team of 1997 in the off-season. They were gonna go young, and they got rid of all their big boys. I had a chance to go to spring training that year because I was Player of the Year in the minor leagues in '97 in Portland, Maine. However, I didn't make the club and got sent down.

Literally seven days into the season, I got a phone call from our farm director, who said, "You're going to the big leagues." I remember going, "What?" 'cause they had just started the season.

I immediately called my grandfather and my dad and told them I was going to the big leagues. That call is something you wait your entire life to make. The odds are against you. It was immediate tears of happiness and joy. Now that I'm a dad, I understand it. I didn't understand it at that point.

They were on the road, in Philadelphia. I jumped on a plane that evening and headed to Philadelphia. I'll never forget being at the hotel that next morning, waking up, and being ready to get to the field. When I woke up, I wanted to get over there.

When I got in the cab, and the cab driver asked me, "Where are you going?" and I said, "Veterans Stadium," that is when it hit home, like, "Wow! I'm going to a big league stadium." I'll never forget that moment. You're going to a major league field at 12 o'clock, the guy looks at you and goes, "Are you a player?" and you say, "Yes, I am."

You walk into that place and see your jersey hanging there. Your shoes are perfect, and everything's polished up. It was something that I'd never been a part of and obviously had never seen. You walk in, the head clubhouse guy greets you, shows you your locker, and then there's Jim Leyland, the big dog. It was pretty awesome to get that "Hey, congratulations, kid." There's nothing like it.

I knew I wasn't playing that night and I didn't get into a ball game there. I had the nerves of trying to get that first at-bat under my belt. My first at-bat was on a double-switch in Pittsburgh. I came in the sixth inning and ended up walking in my first at-bat. My first at-bat was against Francisco Cordova. He was a nasty sinkerball pitcher. I had a good at-bat off him and walked.

My next at-bat was a base hit up the middle against the closer for the Pirates, Rich Loiselle. I ended up scoring, and the game went into extra innings.

All the hard work, not being drafted, and I proved everybody wrong. When I put on the uniform, I kind of had that mentality at that point. It finally happened. It's tough when you're not a drafted player. You have to pass a lot of guys that have a lot more opportunity because the team's got a lot more money invested in them. There are a lot of obstacles to do that.

Geoff Jenkins (Brewers)

Geoff Jenkins made his major league debut on April 24, 1998, with the Milwaukee Brewers. He played in 11 big league seasons. Jenkins is honored on both the Milwaukee Brewers Wall of Honor and American Family Field Walk of Fame.

I got called up from Louisville, in Triple-A. John Jaha was playing first base for the Brewers, and he got injured. That created an opportunity for them to call me up.

My Triple-A manager called me in and told me. I remember going back to my locker after he told me. I just sat in my chair and was almost breathing heavy, like, "Oh my gosh, this is happening." It's a very emotional moment.

It was incredible. Not only did they call me up, but they called me up when they were playing at Candlestick Park against the Giants, a team I grew up watching in Rancho Cordova.

You're going through a whirlwind of emotions. Since you were five years old, playing whiffle ball on your front lawn with your brother, it's all come full circle. You're getting on a plane and going to the big leagues. It's the thing that you've been working your whole life for, putting in those 100–150 swings a day, taking fly balls, doing your workouts, having the work ethic that you need to get to this point. You finally get to the big leagues, and not only was it a call-up, but for me it was really special walking into Candlestick Park, going, "Oh my gosh, I'm walking in here to play a baseball game in the big leagues."

I would say the coolest thing for a big leaguer is to see his name on his jersey in the locker room for the first time. I got there early. I beat everybody to the park, of course. I see my name on the back of the jersey, and I have this moment. It jolts you back. You think, "All the hard work I've put in has finally come to fruition." Then you realize, "Okay, I'm here, but I've gotta keep working. It's great that I'm here, but I wanna stay here." It's a joyous occasion for you to see that jersey, but then you realize, "I've gotta stay here."

They put me in the lineup the first day. I'm facing Orel Hershiser. At USC, I used to go to Dodger Stadium and watch him pitch. All of a sudden, I'm facing him.

I came out to early batting practice and saw Dusty Baker behind the cage. Barry Bonds was hitting and launching balls. I'm there going, "This is crazy. I grew up watching this guy and now I'm playing against him." And I grew up going to Dusty's baseball camps. Dusty turns, looks at me, and goes, "I cannot believe that you're in a big league game right now against me." That was really cool.

I vividly remember being excited nervous, but not scared nervous. If you're scared to death in that game, you won't make it. I got out there about 45 minutes before the game and started running sprints, just trying to calm myself. When you get in the game, you just kind of let the switch go off. You clear your head, and you just go hit.

The first at-bat, I lined a single to center. Then my third at-bat, I hit a home run to right-center.

It was awesome. I had two busloads of people come down to watch me play, including my grandmother. She had to be in her mid– to late 80s. She was sitting down the left field line. She had this guy in front of her, and the guy knew I was in the game because she told him. I hit the home run,

Geoff Jenkins was called up by the Milwaukee Brewers during his fourth professional season. He hit a home run in his debut (author's collection).

and the guy stands up and he's going nuts. He's cheering, and he turns to my grandmother and he's like, "Hey, Grandma, did you see your grandson just hit a home run?" She's like, "I could have seen it if you weren't standing up right in front of me."

It was a special moment after the game. I didn't know how many people were at the game. There were probably 150 people, and almost all of them were waiting after the game to congratulate me as I came out of the clubhouse. It was a pretty neat moment for me.

We all have moments in our lives where we can vividly remember sights, smells, and senses. For me, that's one of those days where I can remember how the wind was and what the smells were in the park. Even right now, I'm getting the chills just thinking about it. It's one of those days etched in stone.

Bob Howry (White Sox)

Bob Howry made his major league debut on June 21, 1998, with the Chicago White Sox. He played in 13 big league seasons.

We were in Calgary and had a home game. Our clubhouse was in left field, and our bullpen was right by the clubhouse, but our dugout was on the first baseline.

We're sittin' down in the bullpen, and in the middle innings of the game, we see the pitching coach walk across the field and head into the locker room. I wouldn't have thought anything of it, but one of the guys in the bullpen, Mike Heathcott, goes, "Somebody's gettin' called up."

After the game that night, we went in the clubhouse. The manager called me into his office and said, "You're going up. You're flying out in the morning to Chicago. They have a 1:00 game." He said they just needed someone to fill in for a couple days. The Calgary team was going on the road for about a week. He's like, "You're gonna go up and help out, then you'll probably meet us back on the road in a few days."

The whole thing was kinda crazy. I think I got up and left Calgary about 4:00 in the morning. I land in Chicago about 12:00 for a 1:00 game. The assistant GM picks me up and gets me to the field. It was about 1:00 when I walked in the clubhouse.

It's five minutes before the game starts, and everyone's out there. The first thing I see is Frank Thomas stretched out on the couch in a full uni and spikes, and my locker is right down by that couch. He looks up at me and he's like, "Another rookie, huh?" At that time, they were going young.

I unpack what I needed, get my uni on, and they took me to the bullpen through the tunnels. By the time I could walk out to the bullpen, shake hands with the guys, and get settled in, it was the second or third inning.

They call down no sooner than I could say hi to these guys and say, "Get up!" There was no time for anything. I got ready, the inning ended, and they said, "You're in the game."

I think that was for the best. There was no time to sit, think about it, and wonder when I was going to get in. There was no time to get nervous.

I remember going through the gate and jogging onto the field. You look up and see how big the stadium is. You're used to playing in a place that holds 2,000–5,000 people, and now you're running in the middle of a huge stadium.

The first hitter I faced was Ron Coomer, but to be honest, I didn't even think about who the hitter was. The catcher walks out and asks what I throw. I don't know any of the hitters. Whatever he threw down is what I was throwing. I threw two innings and faced six hitters. I couldn't have asked for a better debut.

The manager in Triple-A said I'd probably meet them back on the road. I never went back. The next time I saw the minor leagues was when I got hurt in 2003.

Creighton Gubanich (Red Sox)

Creighton Gubanich made his major league debut on April 16, 1999, with the Boston Red Sox. He played in one big league season. Two weeks after his debut, Gubanich became only the fourth player in history to hit a grand slam as their first career hit.

In '99, as a minor league free agent, I got a token big league invite with the Boston Red Sox. Going in there, I know Jason Varitek's there, Scott Hatteberg's there, and Mandy Romero is the third catcher in line. Then they had a bunch of young guys.

In spring training, all these guys are playing and I'm sitting down. In nine years, I've established myself as a hitting catcher. I can catch, throw guys out, and call a good game. But I wasn't getting any playing time in spring training.

I ended up getting an at-bat against Boston College when we had a game against them. I hit a bases-clearing triple late in the game. I'm like, "Okay, maybe this will open up their eyes a little bit and they'll let me play a little more." I sat for the next week and didn't get a shot.

I don't know what the hell made me do this, but I walked to Jimmy Williams's office and knocked on the door. I go, "Hey, you got a minute?" I just told him like it was. I said, "You don't know me from a hole in the wall. I'm a minor league free agent. I got my token big league invite. But here's what I can tell you. When I look around this clubhouse, I know that I can help you out. I know what you have as a backup here in case somebody gets hurt. I can hit better, and I can catch better. All I'm asking for is a chance."

He's like, "All right, we'll get you in a B game tomorrow and have you catch." I was 3-for-4, threw a couple of guys out, and blocked a couple balls in the B game. Then I picked up for Mike Stanley at first base the next game. I get a hit there, a home run there, drive in a couple runs there, and all of a sudden, every day I was picking up for Mike Stanley at first base. Eventually, I would catch a game or DH.

Did I ever think I was gonna make the team? Absolutely not. I knew Varitek and Hatteberg were there, and barring one of those guys getting hurt, that would be my only potential opportunity.

I was the last guy to get sent down out of spring training. I knew I was getting sent down the last day. I'm like, "All right, we'll see what happens." There was no talk like, "Hey, man, if anybody gets hurt, we'll call you."

It was the last day of spring training, and I'm in a pair of shorts and a t-shirt. I drive over to where the Twins play in Fort Myers. Everyone else is dressed up because they're gonna jump on a plane and go to Colorado for the exhibition games against the Rockies. I drive my truck over there in a pair of shorts and a t-shirt, planning to leave after the game.

I get back to the clubhouse, and I'm the only one with a locker that still has stuff in it. I have to pack up my stuff and go down to minor league camp for three or four days before breaking to go to Pawtucket. I'm starting to pack up my stuff as they come back in. They're like, "Hey, are you Creighton?" I go, "Yeah." They go, "You need to go on the flight with the team. The team's waiting for you. You've gotta go to Colorado." I go, "What?! Let me run home. I'll go get my suit and my clothes." They're like, "No, we don't have time. We're gonna pack up all your stuff."

They had already told me I was sent down and they didn't need me for the exhibition games because they had Varitek and Hatteberg going. So I drove myself to the last game 'cause I knew the team was going on a bus to the airport. I didn't have any clothes. I didn't have any toiletries. I had absolutely nothing on me, and they had me leave my truck.

I jump on the team flight in a pair of shorts and a t-shirt. I had to sit next to Dan Duquette, the general manager. He's like, "Man, you're underdressed for this." I go, "I asked them. I said my apartment was only five minutes away and I could have been there and back, but they said to just go to the mall in Colorado, buy stuff for the next couple days, and that they'd reimburse me for everything."

I walk off the plane. It's snowing. There's like eight inches of snow, and here I am, wearing Donnie Sadler's leather jacket in a pair of shorts and a t-shirt.

So we get snowed out the first two days. We finally play, and I made the last out. My buddy, Chris Sexton, was playing shortstop. I hit a hard ground ball up the middle. He makes a diving play and throws me out at first base. I was so pissed off. I'm like, "Man, couldn't you have just let me get this?"

I flew back, packed up my apartment, and drove all the way to Pawtucket. Then we started on the road for a week and a half before we went back.

It was after our first or second game back in Pawtucket, and we're still in hotels. I got a phone call from Gary Jones, who was the manager at the time. We didn't have the best relationship. He called me at the hotel and was like, "Hey, Gubanich, what are you doing?" I go, "I'm at the hotel." He goes, "We need you back at the clubhouse." I'm like, "What?" He goes, "Dude, it's important. You need to get back here." When you hear that, you're like, "Oh my God! What the hell just happened? I'm getting released."

I drive all the way back. Gene Tenace was the hitting coach, and Rich Bombard was the pitching coach. They were all sitting in the office. Gary

Jones was like, "Gubes, sit down." I'm like, "What?" He goes, "Every time we talk, it doesn't have to be a bad thing." I'm like, "What are you talking about?" He goes, "I just wanted to see the look on your face when I told you that you're going to the big leagues." I was like, "What?" He's like, "Yeah, man. Congratulations. You've earned it. You had a great spring training. Hatteberg needs to go on the DL, and you need to report to Boston tomorrow by 3:00. Pack up your stuff. Good luck."

Not in my wildest dreams did I think that call was gonna come after nine years of being in the minor leagues and thinking, "Did I make the right decision? Should I have gone to college?"

Obviously, then you've gotta call the parents. I'm like, "Hey, Mom, what are you guys doing tomorrow?" She's like, "Well, your father has a couple meetings and I have to work. What's wrong?" I go, "I wanted to see if you wanted to come watch me play up in Boston." She's like, "What do you mean? I thought you were in Pawtucket." I go, "Mom, think about it." She drops the phone. My dad gets on the phone and goes, "What the hell's going on?" I go, "I got called up. I'm going to the big leagues." He's like, "You better not be fucking with your mother right now. She's gonna have a heart attack." I go, "Why would I screw with you guys on this?" It was a Friday night, and my parents couldn't get off of work or get out of those meetings.

I go through BP and everything, then go to the bullpen. They called down and say, "All right, Gubes. You're gonna catch if Varitek gets on 'cause they're gonna pinch-run for him." Well, Varitek gets pulled in the bottom of the eighth.

I'm like, "Oh my God! Here we go!" I'm running from the bullpen in Boston with all my gear on, across right field, to get down to the dugout. My mind is going, "Oh my God! Oh my God! Oh my God!"

Derek Lowe was pitching. I'm like, "Okay. I know Derek Lowe. Not a big deal." Grady Little was like, "Okay, Gubes, you're going in." I'm like, "All right, here we go." Literally, it lasted maybe three minutes. Somebody got on. Wade Boggs comes up, hits into a double play. And then the last guy strikes out.

Three minutes, and all of a sudden you run back in. Grady Little comes up and says, "Gubes, congratulations. You just played in the big leagues."

Ray King (Cubs)

Ray King made his major league debut on May 21, 1999, with the Chicago Cubs. He played in 10 big league seasons. A lefty specialist with a durable arm, King ranked amongst the top 10 National League relievers in appearances from 2001 through 2005.

I remember on May 20, 1999, we were in Oklahoma City. I get back to the hotel room, and the phone light is flashing to let me know I got a message.

A bunch of guys went out, so it's probably about 1:30, 2:00, in the morning when we get back in. The light's flashing, I picked it up and call the front desk. Guy's like, "You have a message to call Bob Grimes." He was our trainer.

I call Bob and he's like, "Pack your bags, kid. You're going to the big leagues tomorrow."

I remember at two o'clock in the morning, I'm calling all my family, friends, and high school coaches. I'm all giddy.

The next morning, the team is leaving as well. It's about a seven o'clock flight. I'm flying into Atlanta, and the team's going to Nashville. I get to the airport with the team and I'm like, "Okay, this bag's separate."

I land in Atlanta, and I've got no baseball equipment. It went to Nashville with the team. Felix Heredia, another lefty, let me borrow a glove. The clubhouse guys went out to a local sporting goods store and got me a pair of cleats.

I remember walking in the clubhouse in Atlanta, seeing Mark Grace, Sammy Sosa, Glenallen Hill, Steve Trachsel, and all them guys. You go out for batting practice and you're in awe. I'm looking across the field and there's Andruw Jones, Chipper Jones, Bobby Cox, Leo Mazzone, John Smoltz, and Tom Glavine.

The grass is greener. The stadium's bigger. You go in after batting practice, and there's a full spread. You're like, "Man, no peanut butter and jelly after batting practice. This is awesome."

I got dressed, went out for the anthem, and was just standing there looking around at Turner Field like, "Wow. I finally made it. It's a dream come true." You remember being 10 years old in the backyard, pretending to be on a major league mound.

I remember sitting in the bullpen about the fifth or sixth inning. The phone rang, and they're like, "Get King up." My heart skipped a beat. I start warming up and then, next thing you know, I see the manager coming out. He raises his left hand, and my bullpen coach says, "You're in, kid."

I remember jogging from the bullpen to the mound, and it seemed like it took me about 30 minutes to get there. It was like I was floating.

I get to the mound and start warming up. Benito Santiago's my catcher. I finish warming up, and Benito comes out. I was like, "One—

slider, two—curve, three—blah, blah, blah." He's like, "Just throw it, I'll catch it." I'm like, "What do you mean?" Gracie's laughing. He's like, "Just throw it. He'll catch it." I'm looking for a sign, and Benito just waves his glove, like, "Throw it!"

I get runners on first and second and then here it comes, "Now batting, number 10, Chipper Jones." The stadium goes crazy with the tomahawk chop chant. I come set, and my heart is just thumping through my chest. I step off and look at Gracie at first. He's slicking his arms like, "Throw a slider!" I get back on the mound and throw a slider. Chipper Jones hits a ground ball, and they flip a double play.

I come out and I'm like, "Wow! I just pitched my first big league game!" It happened so fast, but it was also like it was in slow motion.

Back in the clubhouse that night, guys are congratulating and welcoming me. Then I get back to the hotel, and I'm calling everybody. I think when I checked out of the hotel, my phone bill was about $150.

David Lee (Rockies)

David Lee made his major league debut on May 22, 1999, with the Colorado Rockies. He played in five big league seasons.

In '98, I was in spring training with the Double-A and Triple-A group. I'm doing well. I'm 25 and thinking I should be in Double-A or Triple-A.

The next thing you know, I'm in High-A in Salem. I stayed there the whole year. I made the all-star team, and I just couldn't believe I was there. I was doing really well, and other guys

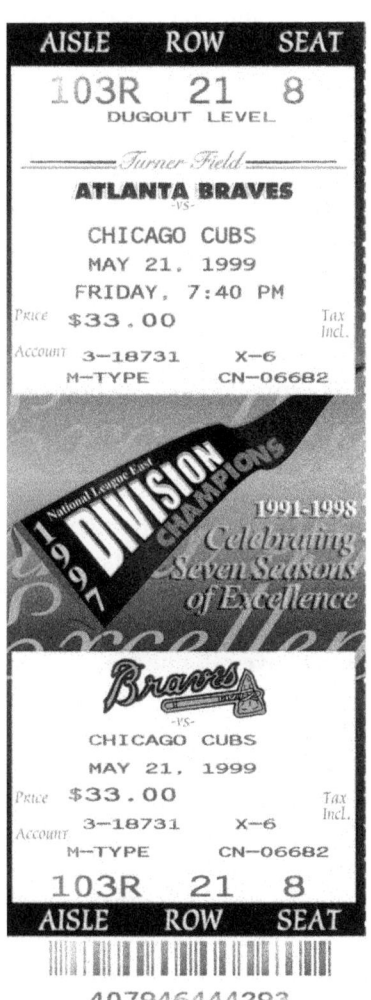

Ticket stub from Ray King's major league debut with the Chicago Cubs in Atlanta. He got Chipper Jones to hit into a double play in his debut (author's collection).

that weren't doing as well were getting called up. It was my protection year, meaning they either had to put me on the 40-man roster or someone could Rule 5 me.

Jim Leyland became the manager of the Rockies in '99, and I actually knew him through my grandmother's cousin, believe it or not. The big thing for me every year was going to lunch with Jim Leyland at the country club.

Leyland calls me. I go to the country club and he's like, "You earned the major league roster. I didn't put you on it. I just wanna let you know that. I'll see you in spring training." I'm in spring training with all the big names, and I was doing well. In fact, I was doing so well I thought I belonged there. I thought I had a good shot.

Leyland calls me to his office and says, "Listen, you haven't pitched above A-Ball. Right now, you're pitching just about as good as anybody here, but realistically, you're not going to make this team just on the basis you haven't pitched in Double-A. We're going to send you down. I gotta make some tough decisions. If you keep pitching the way you're pitching, when we need somebody, I'll call you up."

I go to Double-A in North Carolina and was doing real well closing games. There were a couple guys that got hurt in Triple-A, so I thought I might have a shot at going to Triple-A.

We were in Huntsville, Alabama, and it was May 20. My wife wasn't with me traveling, so we had this thing. If I told her I was calling her at 7:00 at night, I was calling her at 7:00 at night. That was the way it was. We didn't have cell phones.

Jay Loviglio, the manager, calls down to my room. He goes, "Hey, Dave, I want you to come up. We're gonna play a game of cards in my room." I told him, "Skip, normally I would, but I told my wife I'm calling her at 7:00. We have this thing. I don't miss it for anything. It's important." He's like, "I think you wanna play this game." That's exactly what he told me. So I'm thinking maybe I'm gonna get called up to Triple-A.

I go up to his room, and the other coaches are there. He says, "Okay, we're gonna cut the deck. Whoever gets the highest one gets to name the game." I get a two, and they all start laughing. Jay goes, "You're going to the big leagues." My whole body went numb. I couldn't believe it.

I go downstairs back to my room. I call my wife and tell her to quit her job. I told her, "You're not working anymore." She goes, "What do you mean?" I said, "I'm going to the big leagues."

I get to Coors Field, which is an awesome stadium. I went in the clubhouse, and everyone congratulated me. I walked out to the dugout, looked at the stands, and took it all in. I don't know how this happened, but I was very fortunate to have a locker between Larry Walker on my right and Darryl Kile on my left. Kile was the best. He took me under his wing and showed me what it was like to be a big leaguer.

We're playing the Diamondbacks. The first game, I get up in the bullpen but do not get in. The next day, Bobby Jones was pitching. He had a long sixth inning, and we were losing. I come in with guys on base, and the first guy I face is Jay Bell.

The first pitch I threw, the catcher didn't move the glove. The umpire called a ball. I couldn't believe it. I looked up at the board and it said 96. I'm like, "Okay, I've got my stuff." Next pitch was right there and a ball again. The next pitch, I threw a slider and Jay Bell hit a home run. I couldn't believe it. He hit it good.

There were two outs in the inning. I walked Luis Gonzalez, and the next batter was Matt Williams, a really good big leaguer. I struck him out, but we were losing by four runs now.

Leyland tells me I'm going to hit. I go up there and end up striking out. The next inning, I go out and don't give up a run.

After the game, there were reporters asking me questions, and I didn't want to talk. I was too mad. I walked away. Larry Walker pulled me aside and goes, "Listen, kid. I know you didn't play the way you wanted to play, especially with that first batter, but this is the big leagues. Part of your responsibility as a player is to talk to the media."

The next day, I'm in the weight room, and a couple Diamondbacks were in there. Jay Bell came over and said, "Man, you've got a really good arm. You'll be here a long time." That was reassuring and good to hear.

Juan Alvarez (Angels)

Juan Alvarez made his major league debut on September 1, 1999, with the Anaheim Angels. He played in four big league seasons.

I was playing with Edmonton, and we were on the road in Calgary. It was before a Sunday game, and I was throwing down the line.

Our manager was Carney Lansford, and Carney didn't say much to anybody. He always kept to himself. He was a good baseball guy, and he was a good manager, but I'd been there two months, and he hadn't said maybe three words to me the whole time. He's standing behind me while I'm warmin' up, and I'm thinking, "Man, this guy wants to tell me something." Sure enough, I finish warmin' up, and he pulls me over to the side.

He says, "I've gotta tell you something, but you can't tell anybody until tomorrow." I'm like, "What?" My heart stopped. I was like, "What do you mean I can't tell anybody?" He tells me, "Nobody on this team can find out what I'm gonna tell you. I just got off the phone with Bill Bavasi and Terry Collins. You're gonna get called up." I was like, "Oh!" That was the best feeling ever.

He's telling me, "Please, you've gotta keep it quiet." I'm like, "Can I at least call my family?" He goes, "Yes, you can call your family." I go to a pay phone, because I didn't have enough money to buy a cell phone then, but I couldn't get in touch with anybody.

So we had to play the game. I'm sitting there in the bullpen, keeping this to myself and nobody knows. I'm excited. It's the best news I've ever gotten in my life, and I can't tell anybody. The game ends, and I got to talk to my parents and some friends. I let them know what was happening. Otherwise, I kept it hush. We had a three-hour drive back to Edmonton after the game.

I get to the field the next day, early. Carney comes up and goes, "You need to do me a favor." I'm like, "Oh God, what now?" He goes, "When I call you in the office, Rick Wise wants to tell you. He doesn't know that you know." Rick was the pitching coach, and he had been my pitching coach in Double-A as well. Carney says, "Please, you've gotta act surprised." Sure enough, I went in, and Rick told me, "Hey, you're getting called up! You've done a great job the last couple years. Just go and do what you've always done and get those left-handers out."

The next day I was off to Cleveland. That night was very weird because the night before the Indians and the Angels had gotten in a bench-clearing brawl. I knew some of the guys 'cause I had played with them through the minors, but it was just a weird feeling. Everybody was to themselves. It was a very bizarre feeling in that clubhouse that day. The whole clubhouse atmosphere was very strange.

That night, we played against the Indians. Back at that time, the Indians were one of the best teams in baseball. The game's going on, and every time the phone rang in the bullpen, my heart started beating faster and faster. In the eighth inning, they told me, "Hey, if Roberto Alomar gets on, you're gonna go in there to face Jim Thome." Sure enough, I went in there to face Thome.

Terry Collins, our manager, gave me the ball, and goes, "Hey, just do your thing. Just do what you've done throughout your career in the minors. Throw strikes."

I come set right before the first pitch. I see 40,000. They used to sell out "The Jake" at that time. I look at first base, and I see Alomar taking his lead. Then I see Thome, who looks like he's 25 feet tall.

I had to step off for a second, handle my breath, gather my thoughts, and pitch. It was a cool feeling. I ended up striking him out, which was a good ending.

All call-ups are special, but that first one, with how bizarre it was with Carney, and not being able to tell anybody for a little bit, was special. It was funny, because Terry Collins was only my manager for one day. When we got back to Anaheim, he resigned. Joe Maddon took over the rest of the month of September as the interim manager. It was crazy.

Chad Hermansen (Pirates)

Chad Hermansen made his major league debut on September 7, 1999, with the Pittsburgh Pirates. He played in six big league seasons.

It was my second year in Triple-A. I was 21 years old. Back then guys were just starting to get cell phones and their own laptops, so they started to pay more attention to who teams might call up. You got sucked into that a little bit.

I was having a good year. I hit over 30 homers, so I thought it's gotta be time.

I played in Nashville, and our season had ended. Trent Jewett was our manager, and he called me and a couple other players into his office. It wasn't a one-on-one thing. He said, "You guys are going to the big leagues tomorrow."

I felt like it was going to happen, and I was certainly expecting it, but there's still all those emotions going through you. I called my wife right away and let her know, then my parents. That was a pretty cool and emotional thing, but there was more excitement than anything.

My wife and I were newly married. We had flown my mother-in-law out, and she helped pack up everything in Nashville. We figured either way, we were going to drive home or drive to Pittsburgh. She came out for the last few Nashville games, and then she drove the U-Haul up to Pittsburgh.

I remember flying in the next morning and playing that day. They had me hitting seventh and playing left field. They threw me right in the fire, which I was grateful for.

A funny backstory is I had caught walking pneumonia and got real sick for about three weeks in August. I lost 10 pounds, and I was barely 190 at that time. I lost a lot of strength. I was skinny and remember putting on that Pirates jersey. It felt like a big bag.

This was back at Three Rivers, the old stadium. It was the first time I played on turf. We were playing against the Padres and facing Sterling Hitchcock, a lefty.

I remember my first at-bat. I hit a line drive bullet to left field. Reggie

Sanders was playing left field and made an amazing catch. He stretched out and kind of snow-coned what would have been a standup, one-hop double off the wall. I'm like, "Holy crap! How did he get there? I smoked that ball!" I rounded first base and came back to the dugout.

I actually got a standing ovation from the fans. From the anticipation of me getting there, and then to have that happen right away, was pretty cool. I joke that's probably the only standing ovation I got in Pittsburgh. Things didn't go as well as planned, but to have that experience my first at-bat was cool. It took a couple games to get my first hit.

I participated in the 2019 MLB draft. Reggie Sanders was there representing the Royals. I was there as a scout representing the Angels. I saw him, and I went up to him. I told him that story. I go, "Reggie, you probably don't remember me, but you robbed me of my first hit in my first at-bat. You ruined my life because of that." He remembered me. We had a good laugh.

4

Since 2000

Since 2000, baseball has experienced record earnings and attendance and has grown internationally. A focus on statistical analysis has changed the style of play. Rule changes have been implemented to address the pace of play.

While steroids were suspected in the 1990s, for the most part, baseball turned a blind eye during the decade. Since 2000, baseball has adopted tough policies against performance enhancing drug use.

More than half of major league teams have opened new stadiums built primarily for only baseball. Many teams with older stadiums have struggled. While only the Montreal Expos moved to become the Washington Nationals, other teams have also threatened relocation without new ballparks. The Houston Astros moved from the National League to the American League. Playoffs have expanded considerably.

Minor leagues have been restructured. Rules relating to the injured list, previously known as the disabled list, have changed, and roster moves have become more frequent.

There are 35 stories that follow from players who have debuted since 2000.

Tarrik Brock (Cubs)

Tarrik Brock made his major league debut on March 29, 2000, with the Chicago Cubs. He played in one big league season. Following his playing days, Brock became a coach.

To make the team out of spring training in 2000, we have to backtrack to the year before, 1999. It was my first time in big league camp with the Cubs. I had a good spring by my thoughts but got sent down. I made a declaration to myself that the next time I would go to big league camp, I was going to leave everything out there.

I was bunting, playing defense, stealing bases, doing early work, late work, doing everything that I could do to improve my game. We start to get later in the camp. There are some send-downs, and I am still around, just keeping my head down, showing up early and working. There was a morning where they were doing cuts and sending guys down. I got a tap on my shoulder and was told that the manager at that time, Don Baylor, wanted to see me. I'm thinking, "Oh man. I'm going down. This is awful." At the same time, I'm like, "I've hung in there as long as I ever have." I go to the office, and the door's closed. I figured, "I'm going to go about my day. If they're going to send me down, they can come get me."

I walk up to Baylor a little bit before the game and said, "Did you want to see me?" He goes, "No." In the middle of the game, when they would normally tap me to let me know I'm going in, he takes me down in the hall. He sticks his right hand out and goes, "Congratulations, you're on the team." I couldn't process what he said after that, if I was going to left, center or right. I wasn't sure. All I kept thinking was, "I can't wait to tell my family." I didn't touch the ground for the rest of the day.

I went out and played. Afterwards, I remember being in the locker room and thinking, "Oh my gosh, I made it." That was the coolest thing ever. Then I made a bunch of phone calls. There are not enough calls that you can make at that time.

When I found out the news, I still had a week left of camp, and we were opening in Tokyo, Japan, as well. Everything was so new and foreign. I didn't know how to handle it. I remember running down a fly ball in spring training, hitting the wall, and Kerry Wood saying to me, "Hey man, watch that. We're gonna need you." That made it sink in, like, "I'm on this team."

It was weird because Opening Day wasn't in a stadium that you would imagine. You would think about it being somewhere stateside, but it was in Tokyo, which was completely different.

Flying over with the team was a different experience. We played two exhibition games, and I remember just wanting those exhibition games to be over as quickly as possible. I wanted to get to the regular season.

I made a base running mistake in the last exhibition game. I came in to pinch-run. A ball was hit, and I go. The third baseman tagged me out and I'm thinking, "I hope they don't send me down. That's gonna be a long flight all the way back." I was thinking the worst, but it wasn't that bad. They understood what I was doing and were like, "Okay."

I knew my role, but coming up in the minor leagues, I was always playing. I wasn't in the starting lineup Opening Day, but I knew what I needed to do in a completely different role. Watching the first half of the game, and taking in the experience, was so cool. I'd never been in a situation like that.

I got in the game late. I couldn't hear, was short of breath, and my heart was racing, jogging out to left field in the Tokyo Dome. I didn't know the history that I was making in that moment. I was just there playing the game that I had played since I was eight years old in Little League.

A fly ball was hit to end the inning by the late Darryl Hamilton. It was the first time I'd ever played in a dome. I remember the ball going up, and I realized in that moment, "I cannot see this ball. It is blending in with the ceiling." Utter panic came over me. Over the years of being in the minor leagues, and doing drills, I had to trust that that ball was gonna come out somewhere. The ball comes out, I make the catch, and I jog in. I'm telling everyone what I've experienced on the inside, and they're saying, "You didn't show that at all."

Later, I got an at-bat. Looking back at it, my first major league at-bat was the coolest thing ever. Rich Rodriguez was pitching, but also Mike Piazza was catching. Growing up in L.A., we all knew about Piazza.

I remember seeing the first pitch come in. It was a ball. I'm just trying to be composed. Then ball two comes in. I'm like, "This is okay." Then ball three. Mike Piazza is saying some choice words underneath his breath. Strike one comes in, 'cause I had the take sign. Then the next pitch comes in, and I swing.

I got a base hit in between the first baseman and the second baseman. I'm watching Sammy Sosa run around the bases, and it was like watching a movie, like, "I can't believe that this is actually happening." Sammy got thrown out at the plate to end the inning, but I had the biggest smile on my face. It brought me back to the very first hit I'd ever gotten playing the game. It was so cool.

The next day out, during BP, there were signs the local Japanese fans made that said, "Congratulations on your first hit out of the USA! You made history!" That was my only at-bat in Japan. I was grateful that I was able to make history in that moment.

The most important thing to remember is the many people that you carry with you in that first at-bat—every Little League coach, every Little League player, every teacher, and, of course, your family.

I remember being in the front yard as a kid, pretending I was Reggie Jackson or Rod Carew. We all dream of being professional ball players, and for some of us, the reality is just like how the dream was. The reality might have been a little bit shorter, but it's still just as impactful to be able to say, "I did make it."

Scott Forster (Expos)

Scott Forster made his major league debut on June 18, 2000, with the Montreal Expos. He played in one big league season.

I was playing for the Ottawa Lynx, the Triple-A affiliate for the Montreal Expos, at the time.

My pitching coach, Randy St. Claire, came out and said, "Hey, I want you to throw a bullpen session." I'm thinking, "That's weird, but okay." I threw a bullpen session of maybe 20 pitches. Then he's like, "All right, that's it. You're done."

We go through batting practice and all the normal pre-game rituals. The game started, and eventually somebody was getting loose in the bullpen. The bullpens were outside on the field, not behind any kind of enclosure or any kind of fence. I was told to protect the pitcher, watch the game, and make sure the pitcher warming up didn't get hit. That's normal.

My manager, Jeff Cox, walked down to the end of the dugout and he's like, "Scott, what's the date?" I go, "I don't know." He goes, "6-16-2000!" I go, "Okay." This guy was crazy fun. He kept saying it to me. I was looking at him like, "What are you talking about? Why do you keep saying this to me?" He goes, "6-16-2000." I'm like, "I don't get it one bit."

When the game's over, I go into the dugout. No one's in the dugout except my manager and my pitching coach, and they have me sitting down. Apparently, there were cameras on me that I did not know about, and the word spread that I was getting called up. I did not know at this point.

I was sitting between my manager and pitching coach. He goes, "6-16-2000." I'm like, "What are you talking about?!" Then my pitching coach says, "Dude, you're getting called up. You're going to Chicago."

I literally broke down. Then my entire team came out. Apparently, it's on video somewhere. I've never seen it, but my whole team came out and were high-fiving me, hugging me, and all that.

It was the moment you think about when you're seven years old. It was so amazing.

It was also sad for me because I called my dad, who was an athletic director for a high school. Every year he would chaperone a senior class trip to the South Pacific. I'm calling him from the parking lot in Ottawa, and I'm like, "Dad!" He's like, "What?" I go, "I just got called up." He broke into monster tears because he was leaving within about six hours for the South Pacific, and he couldn't come see my major league debut at Wrigley Field.

My then-girlfriend, my best friend, and my sister came. I didn't pitch the first night I was there, but they watched me pitch in my first game the second night, which was a nationally televised game that went extra innings.

The bullpens are outside at Wrigley Field. They got me up. I'm warming up in the bullpen, and I literally started about five feet away from the catcher, Charlie O'Brien. I'd get it close to him and move back a little bit. The game's going, and I started throwing him soft fastballs. He's like, "Throw the ball!" I started throwing harder, but if I did not throw a strike, he'd let it go. He was hazing me. He was trying to be like, "You're going into this game. You've got to throw a strike, so throw a strike. If you don't throw a strike, I'm not catching it." He did it four times. The game stopped and everybody in the dugout was popping their heads out and looking down like, "Who's down there?" I literally stopped the game.

The fans are right there next to the bullpen. They're in your face. Some dude yelled out, "You suck!" I was so frustrated with myself, I turned to the direction of where I heard it and yelled back, "I know!"

I faced one hitter. It was Henry Rodriguez, who was a former Expo. I got him to hit a ground ball, and I got a hold. Felipe Alou came out, patted me on the butt, and said, "Great job."

Later that night, I proposed to my wife. I went to my sister's hotel room and said, "I'm going to propose tonight." She had brought the ring, which was my mom's ring. My mom had passed away and never got to see me play, but she was my biggest fan. I called my wife's parents, got their blessing, and proposed the night I pitched.

I didn't have a long career or make millions of dollars, but I did something I had wanted to do since I was seven years old. I had so much fun and met so many great people. I have so many great relationships to this day from it. It's something I set out to do as a kid, and I did it as an adult.

Jose Ortiz (Athletics)

Jose Ortiz made his major league debut on September 15, 2000, with the Oakland Athletics. He played in three big league seasons. Ortiz also played nine seasons in Japan.

I had so much fun with Sacramento in 2000.

If you see my career, starting in rookie ball, I always had injuries that limited my play. My body would break down, and I would have some kind of injury. I always had trouble with my hamstring. In '99, I pulled my calf, I pulled my obliques, and I sprained my ankle. I had three injuries in '99 that prevented me from going to the big leagues that year. So 2000 was fun for me. I played 19 years professionally and that was the only year I didn't get hurt. It was a blessing.

We went to the playoffs and got eliminated right away. We were bummed and sad because we didn't get past the first playoff series in Salt Lake City.

My manager, Bob Geren, called me in after the game and said, "You're going to the major leagues tomorrow." I was really excited and happy. I was waiting for that moment. But at the same time, I was bummed because of the series loss.

My family were the first ones to know. It didn't matter what time it was in the Dominican Republic. It was, "Mom, they called me up to the major leagues!"

It felt like a dream when I went into the big league clubhouse. You see those guys in spring training, but there's different emotions when you're in the real big league clubhouse. So many emotions come to my mind. Everything felt like a dream.

I got into my first game, in Tampa, after about a week. I was 23 years old and nervous. I went in to bat in the sixth inning of a game.

Vinny Castilla played third base, and I'm a little guy, so he played in, expecting me to bunt. I didn't bunt much. I hit a sinking line drive down the third baseline. Vinny Castilla dove and robbed me of my first hit in my first at-bat. I saw him a couple years later in Mexico. I told him, "Man, you stole my first hit! I had a dream about getting my first hit in my first at-bat, and you took that away!"

Jose Ortiz was called up by the Oakland Athletics during his fifth professional season, following a Triple-A season which earned him the Pacific Coast League's Most Valuable Player Award (photography by Doug McWilliams).

My call-up time was a great experience. Where I come from, to go through the struggles, and to get that call, it's special. It's something I can barely describe.

Tom Wilson (Athletics)

Tom Wilson made his major league debut on May 19, 2001, with the Oakland Athletics. He played in four big league seasons. Wilson played in 11 minor league seasons before appearing in his first game.

I was stuck in the Yankees' system for a long time, and they never gave me a chance to get to the major leagues. I was kinda discouraged, but Shane Spencer's one of my best friends in the game, and he got there after a long time. That kept me going, trucking through the minor leagues.

I actually got called up with the Diamondbacks in '98, while playing for Tucson, but never played. Damien Miller and his wife were having a baby. We were in Vancouver, Canada, and we were getting ready to play a day game. Chris Speier was my manager. He comes out and he goes, "Hey, you've gotta motor and get to the big leagues. They need you in Arizona." We had just finished BP, so I showered up, packed my shit, and hauled ass to the airport.

I showed up at Bank One Ballpark in Phoenix, and it happened super-quick. I had known Buck Showalter already 'cause he came from the Yankees. Buck says, "Hey, I don't know if this is going to be a day, two days, or three days." It was dependent on whatever time Damien Miller took. He wasn't gone for very long, and when he came back, that obviously moved me out. I was there for two nights. So I went to the big leagues, never played, and went back down to Tucson.

That season, I stayed on the roster, and I figured I'd go up in September as a third catcher, at worst. I had a great year in Triple-A and was the everyday guy there, but the last week of the season, I got hit by a pitch in Las Vegas and broke the zygomatic arch in my cheek, so I didn't get called up.

I didn't go back until 2001, so I played 11 seasons before I had my first chance. I finally got a shot with the Oakland A's. Billy Beane gave me my first shot. Billy Beane actually called me personally at home. He called me that winter of 2000. He goes, "Tom Wilson, this is Billy Beane." I'm like, "Oh shit, why is he calling me?" I mean, GMs don't call career minor league guys. We talked numbers. I had made more money before, but I took less money to go play with Oakland.

I had a lot of friends that were in the same boat I was in, and they went out there. I made some calls and talked to Jeff Tam. He said, "Billy

Beane's straight up, man. He's honest and you'll get a shot. You can take him at his word. You can trust him."

So I rolled the dice, took a lot less money on the Triple-A side, and it worked out. I played well that spring training, and I wasn't happy when they sent me out. I was the last guy there. It was obviously Ramon Hernandez, Sal Fasano, and myself. They were comfortable with Sal, so they kept him. I understood that.

I didn't get called up until May. I started off kinda slow, and then I got hot for about a week, and they called me up. I was in Tucson, Arizona, playing Triple-A for Sacramento, and Bob Geren was my manager. I was laying in bed that morning at the hotel, and Bob called me. He said, "Hey, you've gotta pack your shit. You're going to the big leagues." I packed my shit, and as soon as I could get the first flight out of Tucson, I flew to Oakland.

I didn't play that first game, but Art Howe started me the next day with Mark Mulder pitching. Art told me the night before. He says, "Hey, you're gonna start tomorrow with Mark, just so you know." He didn't want me to walk in the clubhouse the next day and be shocked.

I was a little nervous taking the field, just because it was my first major league game. With that being said, I had played 11 years already. So it was a lot more excitement than nervousness.

We actually went six and two-thirds into a no-hit game. Mark was pretty special. Then Magglio Ordonez hit a home run inside the left field foul pole to break it up.

It's pretty weird. I had faced James Baldwin over the years in the minor leagues, and he had my number. I never got a hit off him in the minor leagues. I knew he was starting that day and I'm like, "Awesome." In my last at-bat, I got to an advantage count, and he made a mistake with his fastball in the middle of the plate, with a little elevation, and luckily it snuck out. I got the first hit, home run, RBI, all of that out of the way. That was pretty cool.

It took a while to happen, but it finally happened. Obviously, you've gotta wait and pay your dues. It was perseverance, really. I kept chugging away, and the Oakland A's and Billy Beane finally gave me a shot.

Nick Johnson (Yankees)

Nick Johnson made his major league debut on August 21, 2001, with the New York Yankees. He played in 10 big league seasons. Known for his patience at the plate, he was among the top 10 hitters in on-base percentage three times while playing in the National League.

We're in Columbus. After a game, me and my buddy were watching SportsCenter. We saw Tino Martinez had a tight hamstring, so they took him out of the game. I didn't think anything of it and went to bed that night. I get a call at 7:30 in the morning. Rob Thompson, the Yankees' director of player development, called me.

Back then the Yankees wanted you to lift. If you didn't lift the amount of time they wanted you [to] per week, they'd fine you $100. I see this phone call. I'm like, "Shit, I'm getting fined $100." I wasn't lifting, so I screened the call. He calls me right back and leaves a voice message. So I called him, and he told me I was going to the big leagues. I was on my way to Texas that afternoon.

I called my mom. In Columbus, it was probably about 8:00, so it was 5:00 out there. I said, "Mom, I'm going to the big leagues." She said, "Nick, it's too early in the morning to be fucking around." I said, "No, I'm serious." She didn't really believe me. I called my dad, and then my girlfriend, that's now my wife, and she flew out to the game. I think she missed the first inning.

There's a lot of emotions and questions. What do you do here? What do you do there? I'm just trying to fit in. Once the game starts, you're trying to relax. You're so amped up.

My first hit was off Doug Davis in my first at-bat.... Hanging curve ball.... Off the top of Rafael Palmeiro's glove. Later in the game, I got a base hit past Alex Rodriguez at short. It was just crazy being on that field.

In Texas they have these little vans that take you back to the hotel. After the game, there were a couple players on it, so my girlfriend and I hop on it. I was like, "I don't know how I'm getting back. My girlfriend's here. Let's hop on it." The next day, they let me know it's just for players. You learn quick.

Cory Aldridge (Braves)

Cory Aldridge made his major league debut on September 5, 2001, with the Atlanta Braves. He played in two big league seasons. Aldridge's 2010 call-up with the Los Angeles Angels of Anaheim is also included, as he had spent nine years out of the majors at that time.

I went to my first major league camp in 2001 and had a great spring. I hit almost .400 and had a chance to make the team out of spring training, but I started having my first shoulder injuries. That kept me out of the lineup a lot, and I got sent down to Double-A.

I remember the last part of the season I went to the lineup card. I wasn't playing. I didn't know what was going on. I had never seen anybody get called up. I didn't know that a lot of times when you got called up, you're out of the lineup.

The manager, Paul Runge, calls me into his office and goes, "Hey, man, you know, I'm taking you out of the lineup today." He talked through some things and just slipped in "Well, they want to see you up top." I said, "What do you mean?" He goes, "You're going to Montreal." I said, "Oh my God. Really?" I didn't think about it because, again, I had a lot of injuries, so me getting called up caught me off-guard. I was like, "Wow. This is awesome."

I remember calling my mom. She knew it was the end of the season. I said, "Hey, Mom, I've got to go." She goes, "What do you mean?" I go, "Yeah, they're letting me go. They're making me leave Double-A." I was trying to make it seem like I was getting sent home. She's getting amped up. Now mind you, she's a school nurse at a high school. She's getting pissed. The other nurse is like, "Jean, what's going on? Why are you so mad?" She goes, "I can't believe they're going to send you home." I said, "Mom, they're sending me to Montreal." She's like, "Why the hell are they sending you to Montreal?" I said, "That's where the Expos play." She's like, "So?" I said, "Mom, I'm getting called to the big leagues." She goes, "Oh my God." It was funny she was cussing in the nursing office. She's pretty soft-spoken, so she never says any bad words. It was funny because I went along with her for a little bit.

They made us get passports before the season. I'd never had a passport before. Growing up where I grew up, passports were one of those things that were far-fetched. You never saw yourself going outside of where you lived. The only time you ever saw anything outside Texas, or the United States, was on TV. I just never thought about getting a passport. I never thought I was going to use it.

I remember everybody started telling me how Canadians always say "Eh." It was a running joke for some reason. We had a couple Canadians that we played with, so we were making jokes about Canadians always saying, "Eh, eh, eh, eh."

I get to Canada. The cab picks me up and takes me to the stadium. The whole way to the stadium he's like, "Eh…. Where you going, eh?" I'm dying laughing in his cab, and he's like, "Why you laughing?" I go, "I didn't realize that y'all did say eh after everything." Me and the cab driver had a laugh.

I arrived, and it's a huge stadium. I remember walking in, like, "Where am I supposed to go?" They don't really give you instructions. I just walked around this huge complex, looking for a locker room, asking people. Everything was new. Nothing about the situation was familiar to me because I'd never done it and never seen it done.

4. Since 2000

I'm walking through the stadium looking for a locker room. I didn't know to go in and see the manager. I was not hip to any game of how to act in that setting.

Watching my first batting practice and seeing Vladimir Guerrero crush balls was cool. It was also cool because it's now a super historic stadium that most people will never see. Probably the best part about that was just being in Montreal. That was a team I was interested in when I was a younger player.

The first day, I came in for Brian Jordan to play right field. I was honestly a nervous wreck. I had never been prepared for that stage. I got a ground ball and threw it in. Once I got that first ball, I was okay. I hadn't gotten acclimated to the league. You try to put a kid in the position where he can succeed, so putting him on defense is easy to do.

It was like, "Don't mess up! The fans are looking." The good thing about Montreal is there were no fans. It wasn't like in New York, where there's 50,000 people.

The second call-up was a better story.

I go to the Angels for spring training in 2010 and tear it up, but they sent me to Triple-A. Well, I had a bad attitude 'cause they told us whoever had the best numbers was going to make the team. I led the team in almost every category.

I got frustrated. My Triple-A manager comes up to me and says, "You know what, Cory? You deserve to be in the big leagues but doing what you're doing right now is not going to make it." He goes, "I need you to tighten it back up and have some fun again." So I did. I started hitting.

About a week after that, one of my friends gets called up. He had a better attitude than I did, and I was like, "Dang! That could've been me."

I told the Angels at the first part of the year that my brother was getting married in July. They were like, "Okay, just keep reminding us." So I did. We're in Colorado Springs, and I hadn't played a game in three or four days. I was just kind of sitting the bench and getting frustrated.

My coach comes up to me and says, "Hey, Cory. Don't worry, man. You're back in the lineup tomorrow." I was like, "No, I'm not." He goes, "What do you mean?" I go, "I'm going out of town tomorrow." He's like, "What are you talking about?" I go, "I told you, my brother has his wedding. I've been telling you this all year." He goes, "Okay, my bad. Don't worry about it. I'll go ahead and talk to the front office. We'll make it work."

I get to my brother's wedding, and we're having a good party. I notice my phone hasn't rung in a while, and I'm used to getting text messages. I don't have any service. I say, "This is kind of weird."

I go outside and my phone starts beeping. I check the messages, and it's Tony Reagins, the Angels' GM, saying, "Hey, Cory, I need you to call me right now." So I call. He goes, "How fast can you get to Anaheim?" I said, "How fast can you get me there?" He goes, "You'll be on a plane tomorrow." I was like, "For what?" He goes, "You're getting called up."

I got the call-up at my brother's wedding!

Immediately, I'm thinking about all the surgeries and stuff—problems, divorce, kids. The funny thing is I had all my family there, which is kind of neat. My kids were there. I think even my ex-wife was there. It was nice having that situation happen where everybody that I knew was around me. To get called up to the major leagues again, after all I had been through, I cried like a baby.

It was one of those things I'm very emotional about. I'm very emotional about things that happened to me in my career in sports. I think that was probably the most emotional I've ever been in my life because of getting called back up and knowing the path I took to get there.

All my stuff was in Salt Lake City. I didn't have any equipment. I did have some old suits I got when I was called up with Atlanta in 2001. Because I was in my hometown, I went through some of my old clothes at my mom's house. I had to take a bunch of random stuff.

Somehow, I got a glove, but I didn't have any bats. For my first at-bat, I was using Kendrys Morales's bat. I didn't even have my own bat. The hit that I got wasn't even with my own bat.

The second call-up was a lot more special to me. The first was awesome, but the story is better on the second one.

Jalal Leach (Giants)

Jalal Leach made his major league debut on September 5, 2001, with the San Francisco Giants. He played in one big league season. Leach played in 12 minor league seasons before reaching the majors.

I can't remember where I ranked as the minor leaguer with the most minor league games played without a major league call-up, but it was up there.

It was our last game of the season, and they had already made the initial September call-ups, so if you didn't go in that first wave, you kind of thought, "It's probably not going to happen this year." I didn't think too much of it.

We used the Fresno State facilities and had to share with the college. We had a weird set-up. We had a game on Saturday, we didn't have a game on Sunday, and then we had to come back and play a meaningless last game of the season on Monday.

Living in Sacramento, I took almost all my stuff home that Saturday. My dad and I were just going to drive down, play the game on Monday, and then turn around and go right back. I don't even think we took batting practice or anything. It was pretty much just a show and go. It seemed like the game went by rather fast.

I remember at one point, I was sitting next to our trainer, Rick Lembo, and saying, "Ah, another year by, no call-up, blah, blah." I was venting a little bit, just to see if anyone was listening. He just got up, walked away from me, and I was like, "All right, he's not even listening."

The game ended, and usually I'm slow to undress and get all my stuff, but we had to drive all the way back to Sac, so I hurried in. I knew once the game was over, guys were going to scatter because the season was over. We started all the pleasantries of saying goodbye to different guys.

I was in the locker room. My manager, Shane Turner, comes in and he just starts screaming at me. He goes, "Get in my office, right now. You're in trouble for the signs you missed." I was like, "Shane, really? It's the fricking last game of the season! You're going to fine me the last day? All right, whatever."

I go in, and he's yelling at me. He slammed the door and he's just going on and on and on. Our hitting coach at the time, Mike Hart, was in there as well and he goes, "And by the way, not only are you being fined, but they want you to get to San Francisco to play for the Giants tomorrow." He just mixed it into all that. I was like, "What?" He goes, "You heard me!" He's yelling in a real authoritative voice.

I was like, "Are you saying what I think you're saying?" I looked at Mike Hart, because I'd known him for a long time, and he's like, "Yeah, you're going to play for the Giants tomorrow, if you want to go." I was like, "Oh, wow."

All the guys in the locker room knew I had been around forever, so they were ear hustling. The guys were yelling and cheering and screaming. It was exciting to share with everyone.

My dad was in the stands, working his way toward the locker room. I told one of our clubhouse guys, "Can you get my dad real quick?" He runs out there in a fit of rage. He's like, "Mr. Leach! Mr. Leach! Jalal wants to see you! He needs to see you now!" My dad didn't know if I was hurt, so he comes in the locker room, and I said, "Dad, I'm going to the big leagues tomorrow." He goes, "Oh, I thought something was wrong with you." So we shared a moment.

We're excited, and we start calling people. Then on the way home, my dad goes, "I think I should drive because you're way too excited." While he drove back to Sac, I started calling old teammates that were in the big leagues, told them what happened, and got advice.

We got back home to Sac, and I couldn't sleep at all. My dad, who was a cop in San Francisco at that time, commuted from Sacramento to San Francisco. He left early, and the traffic was bad that day, so he let us know. Then my wife and I left, overanalyzing it. We gathered our stuff and started trekking toward San Francisco because I didn't want to be late my first day. We left really early.

We checked into the hotel, and we're just sitting there with a baby and one on the way. All I kept thinking was, "I just wish she would give me the green light to go to the field." That's all I was thinking about. She was like, "I know you want to go to the field. You've been waiting a long time for this. Go for it."

I got all my stuff and hailed a cab out front. The guy's like, "Where you going?" I said, "I'm going to Pac Bell." He goes, "Are you a player?" I said, "Yup. I just got called up." He goes, "Right on!" He took me through the gate, where you park out back, and security makes sure you're on the list and whatnot.

Once they cleared me, the equipment guys from the clubhouse came out. When you're playing in the big leagues, you don't carry your own equipment. They grabbed my stuff, and I walked in, underneath the stadium, into the clubhouse.

I think it was about noon. It was early for a 7:00 game, so there was no one there but the clubhouse attendant, Mike Murphy. He said, "I put your locker down there, a few stalls from the bathroom." He goes, "I think you deserved a good number, so I didn't give you a high number." I thought that was cool. I put my uniform on, went in the bathroom, and looked in the mirror just like I did when I was in Little League.

Then Dusty Baker, who was the manager at the time, came in. He looked in the locker room to see if anyone was there. He looked to the left, and he looked to the right. He saw me sitting at my locker and started laughing. He goes, "I should've known you'd be ready to go your first day on the job."

I went over, we shook hands, and he's all "Come in my office." I went in the office, and he congratulated me. Then he gave me the rundown on what my role was going to be. The team was still in contention, so I knew the opportunities to play were going to be few and far between. It was pretty much pinch-hit early if the starter was getting knocked out. Pretty much garbage time or mop-up time, whatever you want to call it.

The guys started coming in and congratulating me. Then the game started. He was going to pinch-hit me. I went out on deck and then they did something to counteract me pinch-hitting, so he called me back. My first time, I got all the way up there, ready to go, and then he's "Ah, nope. Come back. I'm going to use so-and-so." We called that a dry hump. So my first day I didn't get to play.

The next day, our pitcher was having a tough go, so Bake told me, "This is it for him. You're going to lead off the next inning." I had a whole half-inning to get ready. It felt like an hour.

Shawon Dunston and Eric Davis were taking bets on if I was going to get sick or not before my at-bat. They were like, "He's going to get sick. He's going to throw up." I just had to keep going to the bathroom.

Finally, the inning ended and Bake's like, "Hey, you've been waiting a long time for this. Go get 'em." I got a standing ovation my first at-bat. Everyone's like, "You should step out." I'm like, "Man, this is my first time up. I haven't earned that, to wave to the crowd or tip my hat or anything."

Curt Schilling was pitching, and he was on. I kept saying, "I've gotta swing quick." His split finger was filthy that day. I was thinking, "If he comes with a first pitch fastball, I'm going to be ready to swing."

He grooved one for me. I didn't think he would groove it because [of] the way he was pitching. He was going in and out, up and down, and then the split finger was "See ya!" I was looking on the edge, and he threw it right down the middle. I hit it off the end of my bat and ended up popping up to right field. That was my first AB.

As soon as I got in the box, I was ready to hit. I wasn't thinking about the standing ovation. I guess that's just from all the time labored in the minor leagues.

Andy Shibilo (Padres)

Andy Shibilo was called up to the major leagues and warmed up for a debut on May 8, 2002, with the San Diego Padres. However, due to a unique double play, he did not appear in the game. He was sent down the following day and never returned to the majors.

It was definitely unexpected. I wasn't even pitching that well.

We were in Mobile, and we were playing at home. After a game, the manager, Craig Colbert, called me into the office. Like I said, I wasn't pitching that well, so I started thinking negative things.

He says, "I've got some good news and I've got some bad news." At the time, I was pitching late relief, typically in the seventh and eighth innings, and one to two innings at a time. He says, "The bad news is we're gonna move you to long relief, but the good news is it will be long relief in the big leagues." It was definitely a shock and caught me by surprise.

I had a flight early the next morning. The Padres were in Florida, playing [the] Marlins. I hardly got any sleep. I was just running on adrenaline and floating around like it was a dream.

I go through the whole warmups. The newest guy in the bullpen has to carry a backpack of seeds, chew, gum, candy, and snacks. Of course, it was a hot pink Barbie backpack I had to wear in front of the whole crowd on the way to the bullpen.

I remember Brett Tomko started for us that game. I was sitting in the bullpen, watching him warm up. He was throwing gas, and I was like, "I dunno if I really belong here." The game starts, and I'm taking everything in.

We're losing by a few runs in the bottom of the eighth. The bullpen phone rings, and they tell me to warm up. I get up, and the ball's all over the place. I can hardly feel my body. I finally settled down a little bit. It was the bottom of the eighth with one out and runners on second and third. They called down to make sure I was ready if the batter got a hit.

Sure enough, the guy gets a base hit. However, the runner that was on second got thrown out at the plate for the second out. Then the guy who got the base hit tries to advance on the throw home and gets thrown out at second. That's the third out and the end of the bottom of the eighth. We hit in the top of the ninth, don't score, and that's the ballgame.

I didn't think anything of it at the time. I figured there would be another opportunity, but that was it. I was there for one more game. I didn't get action warming up or anything like that. We flew to Atlanta after that game. Bruce Bochy called me up to the front of the plane and told me they needed a starter. They brought up a starter and sent me back down.

I got about as close as you can come without getting in. I definitely feel blessed to have been put in that situation, even though I didn't get in.

Jason Jimenez (Devil Rays)

Jason Jimenez made his major league debut on June 3, 2002, with the Tampa Bay Devil Rays. He played in one big league season.

I was in Triple-A, and we had just gotten off a six-hour bus ride going from Scranton to Ottawa. It was early. I wanna say maybe 3:30, 4:00 in the morning. We had just gotten into the hotel. Our manager at the time for the Durham Bulls was Bill Evers.

4. Since 2000

We were in the lobby, waiting to get our rooms. Bill called me over and asked if I thought I could get Eric Chavez of the Oakland Athletics out. I said, "Yeah, I think I can get him out." He said, "Great, 'cause you'll probably be facing him tonight." That's how he broke the news to me that I was going to the big leagues. At first, I was in shock and thought maybe he was messing with me. Once he confirmed he wasn't messing with me, I obviously had to give him a huge hug, to his surprise.

The conversation continued with "Your flight's already been made, and you're gonna leave from here in Ottawa." It was only a few hours later that the trainer was gonna take me to the airport to jump on the plane to meet the team in Tampa. Unfortunately, the trainer and I miscommunicated, so I ended up missing the flight.

Instead of getting to Tampa prior to the game, I ended up not getting there until about the sixth inning. I literally walked off the plane and went straight to Tropicana Field. I walked into the locker room, and no one was in there with the game going on. I got dressed and headed out to the bullpen.

It was a surreal moment, walking out there and realizing that I had made it.

That night they got me loose, but I ended up not going in. I sat for a couple days. We fly to Toronto, and I'm starting to get anxious. I wanna get my first outing out of the way. It was June 3, and they make a call down to the bullpen. We're losing, but I'm gonna go in and pitch. That's when the nerves kicked in. I get loose. Having to start that inning, I run in from the bullpen, which is out in right-center field. It was kind of an out-of-body experience. It's hard to believe, but you've got to quickly get over that. In my mind I'm thinking, "Just throw strikes. Just throw strikes." I didn't want to be that guy that goes out there and walks the park in his first outing.

My first pitch, I could barely feel the baseball in my hand. I let it go, and it was a strike. I remember that relief coming over me, like, "All right, you know you can do this."

Thankfully, I faced three Blue Jays I had faced coming up through the minor leagues, so they weren't people I was unfamiliar with. I only threw one inning. I threw nine pitches, and eight were strikes. I got three up, three down.

I remember sitting there in the dugout after the game. It was what you might see in a movie, where they start shutting down some of the lights. I'm still in the dugout. The pitching coach, Jackie Brown, came out and said, "I was looking for you." I said, "Oh, I just don't want to leave." He said, "I don't blame ya. Take it all in because you'll never forget this."

Jim Rushford (Brewers)

Jim Rushford made his major league debut on September 3, 2002, with the Milwaukee Brewers. He played in one big league season.

I had a less than spectacular college career. I played four years at San Diego State, but no one showed any interest, and I didn't really do anything that would get anyone particularly interested in me. I was undrafted, and I gave it up for a year. Then I played independent ball a couple years. I was released from independent ball and gave it up for a couple more years. Then I decided to give it one last try in independent ball, and a lot of things came together for me at that point.

I reassessed everything, from where I was, to where I needed to go, what my goals were, and what things I needed to change to get myself there. I plugged away and worked at it. All the pieces started comin' together, and I started performing well.

I got picked up by the Brewers out of independent ball, and once I got on with the Brewers, I absolutely tore it up and shot through their system. But gettin' my call-up was pretty lucky. It took a lot of other circumstances outside of my control for me to have that opportunity.

With a few games left in the 2002 Triple-A season, my manager gave me a heads-up I'd probably be going up and that I better buy some nicer clothes. I was wearin' a bunch of hand-me-downs from a friend of mine. Fashion wasn't my thing.

I was supposed to go up on September 1 to Cincinnati, but a few days before that, I was rounding third, going home, and I felt my groin pull a little bit. It was slight. It wasn't bad, but it was bad enough, I felt I might need a day or two off for it to heal.

When I told the manager, it put my whole call-up in jeopardy. I was in tears 'cause I thought I'd overcome insurmountable odds to get this call-up, and now it wasn't gonna happen. Fortunately, they worked with me. I worked with the trainers and took a couple days off. Then I played a game on September 2 without incident.

When I played the game September 2, the manager took me out about the sixth inning. The team called to the dugout, and he said, "Yeah, he played. He's good." Then he told me, "Get your stuff and go to Chicago."

We were on the road in Louisville. My wife had our daughter, who was just months old. Our minivan was packed with all our stuff 'cause we'd already moved out of the apartment. I grabbed my stuff, ran out of the clubhouse and into the minivan. I said, "Hurry up! Go before they change their mind!" We got right in the car and drove straight to whatever five-star hotel it was in Chicago. I wanna say it was six hours. It was a day game, so it gave me time to get there by that night and stop at a shopping mall to get some nicer clothes.

I was really nervous 'cause I never even went to big league spring training. Everything that goes on in the major leagues was completely unknown to me. I didn't know the players. I didn't know the etiquette. I didn't know how I was supposed to get into Wrigley Field. I don't even remember how I ended up getting in. I was just walkin' around, lookin' for a way in.

I grew up in Chicago and I grew up a Cubs fan. My first game was a night game against the Cubs, and I was on the Brewers, which are pretty much the archenemy of the Cubs. It was sort of a fairy tale. It kinda makes you feel like everything was meant to turn out that way. It coulda been any team, but it was the Cubs.

When I got in, I had my uniform hangin' in a locker, and all that stuff. I thought, "Okay, I'm good." Then after BP, one of the coaches took me out to the field, and he's like, "I'm just gonna fungo you some balls on the left." He's fungoing me balls all over, making me run for balls, and I realize they're testing me to see if my groin was okay. To be honest, I was afraid the whole time that I might tweak it again. But I made it through without hurtin' it and without lookin' like it was bothering me. They were okay with it, and that's when I went in and signed my contract. I realized I wasn't even official 'til I jumped through that hoop. They didn't want to put an injured player on a major league roster, 'cause then they'd risk a guy being stuck on the major league disabled list. It was a very touchy situation.

I was in the starting lineup that first night, and the fans heckled me for nine straight innings out there. I was pretty nervous. I had always played right field and they put me in left field. I wasn't gonna say anything, but I was very uncomfortable playing left field.

The very first ball hit to me was in the first inning. Fred McGriff popped one up down the third baseline into foul territory. It's twilight, so it's hard to see the ball, and at Wrigley, they've got the bullpen on the field. I literally had to run up the bullpen mound, catch it, and then step off the mound and gun it home. I made a perfect throw home. It was a bang-bang play, as close as it could possibly be, but they called the runner safe.

To go along with it, two innings later, I had a ball over my shoulder, and I took a good route back on it, but it went off the pinkie of my glove. I didn't put my glove quite in the right place, and I made an error. I was pretty mortified, you know. The fans were all over me. I just wanted to dig a hole and crawl in it in the outfield. Then a couple innings later, I got a soft liner to shallow left. I came in and made a full-extension diving catch on it and made up for my error.

But by the third inning, I was just exhausted. Because of my nerves,

Jim Rushford on-deck during his major league debut with the Milwaukee Brewers in Chicago (courtesy Jim Rushford).

Jim Rushford taking a swing during his major league debut with the Milwaukee Brewers in Chicago (courtesy Jim Rushford).

I felt like maybe 12 hours had gone by, and we were only an hour into the game. I didn't get a hit in my first game. I was 0-for-4 off Matt Clement. I was always a patient hitter. My first at-bat, I thought, "Well, I'll just do what got me here. I'll take a pitch, size it up, and measure it out." That first pitch was a cock-shot, right down the middle. He just served it up. I just watched it go by for strike one. To this day I regret not takin' a huge hack at that first one, 'cause you only get one first pitch. I say had I gotten a hit in that first at-bat, it would have taken so much pressure off me and set the momentum in a different direction for me. It ended up taking me to my 13th at-bat.

I went home that night, and all that night and the next day, there was my error and my diving catch on *SportsCenter*. I was like, "Oh, man. This is a big deal here." Everything you do goes national. It's not like the minors, where maybe the stadium heckles you for a minute and then it's forgotten about. I realized the magnitude of everything I was doing right then and there.

For me, it was like winning the lottery. I got a one in a million lottery ticket. I had to do so much and overcome so many odds to get there. The odds were so far against me, I'm just grateful that somehow it worked out. I accomplished the thing I wanted to do in life. I wouldn't trade it for anything and it's kinda made everything else in life easier for me. When you know you did what you always wanted to do, you're more at peace with yourself.

Josh Stewart (White Sox)

Josh Stewart made his major league debut on April 6, 2003, with the Chicago White Sox. He played in two big league seasons. Stewart also played one season in Japan.

I wasn't really on the radar to get called up going into 2002. I went to Birmingham to pitch in Double-A. Everything clicked. I had a great year, and our team won the Southern League championship. They sent me to the Arizona Fall League, and I continued the roll I was on. I was playing with, and pitching against, a lot of future All-Stars. That's what propelled me into the next year.

I go to spring training in 2003, which was my first big league spring training, and I stayed in that groove. I was one of the guys they were considering as a fifth starter. Danny Wright, who was pretty much penciled in on the team, hurt his elbow that spring, and that opened a spot. I was just pitching well at the right time and stayed with the team all through spring. Well, we're down to the last few days. Danny throws and he does well.

The next day, I was supposed to pitch against the Colorado Rockies, which I thought was fantastic. They had guys like Todd Helton and Larry Walker, and I wanted to pitch against them. However, I was given the impression Danny was healthy enough to go with the team. I thought I would throw against the Rockies and then get sent to Charlotte in Triple-A.

I pitched to the Rockies. I'd thrown five or six innings and was having a pretty good game. All the while, I was expecting to be sent to Charlotte. I come out and go to sit down. Jerry Manuel, who was the manager at the time, comes over. I was thinking he was going to tell me, "Hey, good job. You're out of the game." However, he asks, "Hey, do you have a suit?" I said, "No." He said, "Well, you need to go buy one tonight 'cause you're going with us."

It hit me, and I got the chills. I was like, "Oh my goodness!" Apparently, Danny's elbow had not healed enough to where he could pitch in a healthy way.

My wife at the time was driving across the country while I was pitching that game. We had become really good friends with Dave Sanders and his wife. He was a reliever, and we had drove to Tucson together. Well, our wives had already taken off and were heading to Charlotte because that's where we thought we were all going. After the game, I called my wife and was like, "Hey, don't go to Charlotte. You need to take the other interstate and go up to Chicago because I'm heading that way."

Dave and I had an apartment in Tucson, and we had become friends with the neighbors. Neither Dave nor I had a car because our wives had already left in our cars. We were just sitting there in the apartment. This was the day before he went to Charlotte, and I was going up. There was no jealousy or animosity. He was thrilled for me, and I would have been thrilled for him. We were that close. We were sitting there on the couch, and I was like, "Man, I wanna celebrate, but we don't have a car." I knocked on the neighbor's door. She threw her keys at me and insisted I take her car so Dave and I could go out and celebrate. I always thought that was sweet of her.

My wife's mom and stepdad lived in a suburb of Chicago called Naperville. They had a gathering at their house the evening before I pitched. My family came up from western Kentucky, which was about a six-hour drive to Chicago. My mother-in-law made us dinner, and we all hung out. It was a nice celebration and good to get everybody together. I really appreciated it.

That night, I stayed at a hotel closer to the field. Naperville is about an hour away, and with Chicago traffic, I didn't want to be stuck in traffic on a day I was supposed to pitch. I get up and go to the field. I'm sick to my stomach. I can hardly eat. I was trying my best to stay calm. When I go out on the field to warm up, I look up, and there's my family and friends. That calmed me a little, knowing they were there to support me, but I was still so nervous the entire time.

We were playing the Detroit Tigers. We were the home team, so that was a good thing. I could go out and throw the first pitch. My catcher was Miguel Olivo. He was a guy I'd pitched to the year before in Birmingham, so I was familiar with him. That was kind of calming. I had to pause after my warmup pitches for a TV break, and I had never heard of that. I was standing there on the mound like, "Okay, here we go."

Bobby Higginson was the first batter. I wound up and threw the first pitch right down the middle. Higginson took it for a strike. At that point I was like, "Okay, I'm here. Time to get to work." Higginson eventually got to a 3–2 count, and I got him to ground out to second base. In the first inning, I got a couple ground outs and a flyout to right field. Once I got the one-two-three and walked off the field, it was a relief. At the same time, I was like, "Okay, I gotta keep this up."

My strengths as a pitcher were mixing speeds and trying to get ground balls. I had my two-seamer and sinker working well that day, and they were hitting a lot of ground balls without incredibly solid contact.

I gave up a run in the fifth and then threw a scoreless sixth. In the seventh, I gave up a walk and hit. Damaso Marte came in and gave up a little dribbler that found a hole. At that time, we were behind by one. We came back and scored nine runs in the eighth to win the game.

Billy Koch was the closer at the time. He had gone out and bought a bottle of champagne. They were planning on doing the shower and everything, but since I didn't get a win, he just gave me the bottle as a celebration.

About three weeks later, my friend Dave Sanders got called up. One of the proudest things I've done is show him around. I felt since I had been there a few weeks, I could help him out.

Lance Niekro (Giants)

Lance Niekro made his major league debut on September 5, 2003, with the San Francisco Giants. He played in four big league seasons. Lance's dad, Joe, and uncle, Phil, also played in the majors.

We were in Tucson, playing the Diamondbacks' Triple-A team. I was with Fresno, and it was before our last game of the season.

We were getting ready to go on the field, and one of our pitchers, Luis

Estrella, walked out on the field with me. He said, "I'll bet you a steak dinner you get called up after the game." I was anticipating it and hopeful, but I didn't want to jinx anything. I was like, "Yeah, I'll take the bet. I'll say I don't."

After the game, our manager, Fred Stanley, called me and a few other guys in, one at a time, and said, "Hey, congratulations. You're going to the big leagues tomorrow." It was plain and simple, straight to the point. I was excited.

Walking out of his office to go get my phone to make a couple calls, I noticed Luis standing there. I said, "Well, I guess I owe you a dinner." He goes, "Yeah, I saw the names on the list before the game. That's why I knew you were going up." I think Fred maybe wrote names down and had it on his desk, and Luis kind of put it all together.

The best part was that my dad played 22 years in the big leagues, so he had a lot of connections through baseball and with the Giants. He was the first call I made. It's 11:00 Arizona time, so it's 1:00 or 2:00 in the morning in Florida. I called him, expecting to wake him up. I said, "Hey, Dad. I just want to let you know I got called up to the big leagues." He said, "Yeah, I know. I'm packing up. I'm on a flight out there tomorrow." I said, "How'd you know?" He goes, "I know things way before you do."

We had a coach named Carlos Alfonso. My dad and Carlos had played together, and they were friends. Carlos knew about it and let my dad know so he could get his ticket and everything. We fly from Tucson to Phoenix, and Phoenix to San Francisco. My dad was on our connector in Phoenix, coming from Tampa. We were getting called up, so we sat first class, and he was sitting coach. He had a couple choice words for me about why he was sitting coach and how I got first class.

We were in a playoff race. We had J.T. Snow and Andres Galarraga at first, so I wasn't expecting much playing time. It was just more about getting up there, soaking it in, and hopefully learning as much as I could for any future experiences.

It was about a week before I made my debut late in a game. I had just faced the pitcher a week or so before in Triple-A, and then I get my first at-bat off him in the big leagues. I wasn't going to go up there and get cheated. If I was going to go down, I was going to go down swinging, and swinging hard. I flied out.

I remember Robb Nen coming up afterwards and saying, "Hey, man. You're a big leaguer now." It's such a surreal moment that you work so hard for. Hundreds of thousands of kids work so hard at it, and not many ever get a chance to go back to their hotel, sit there, and be like, "Oh, man. It happened."

Vinnie Chulk (Blue Jays)

Vinnie Chulk made his major league debut on September 8, 2003, with the Toronto Blue Jays. He played in eight big league seasons. Chulk also played one season in Japan.

We were at home in Syracuse with the SkyChiefs. Omar Malave, my manager, called me in the office. It was him and Tom Filer, my pitching coach. We started talking. They said, "We don't know if you are going to be excited about this news, but they have sold your contract to Japan for the remainder of the playoffs." Obviously, I knew something was up because I definitely wasn't going to Japan.

Omar came up, shook my hand, hugged me, and then told me I was going to Toronto as a September call-up, and I was going a little bit early.

Tom Filer was a good pitching coach, and we had become good friends throughout the season. We had gone golfing one day, and he goes, "Man, that is a really nice driver you've got." I said, "Well, if you get me good enough to get called up, maybe I'll give it to you." So as I get called up, he goes, "Hey, I didn't forget about when we were golfing." I went out to my car, grabbed the driver, and gave it to him.

It was amazing, obviously. I didn't feel anything at the time. I took about 30 minutes to myself at my locker, and then I called my dad.

The Blue Jays were at home. I had a little Pontiac Grand Prix that somebody had almost given me, and I drove it up to Toronto. It was a little nerve-wracking. You get there in the locker room, go see the traveling secretary, go see the manager, and then start seeing Carlos Delgado and everybody else that you grew up watching. I saw Roy Halladay in spring training, but I never thought I'd be on the same team as him.

Quite honestly, I was a little bit overwhelmed. I was trying not to show too much emotion. I wanted to cry out of joy, but I also was scared because I didn't know what to do.

We were there for a couple days, and then we took off. I think it was about 10 days before I got into a game. Carlos Tosca, the Blue Jays' manager, couldn't get me in. We were trying to win games, and everything was close.

Then all of a sudden, 10 days later we're in Yankee Stadium. Of course, he calls my name. I'm like, "No, not here! That's Derek Jeter coming up to bat!" I was happy, but I was scared and nervous. It was nervous energy. They called and said, "Hey, Vinnie! You're going in the next inning!" I kind of wanted to tell them my arm hurt or something because I was so scared. I started warming up, and sure enough, the inning ends.

I start running out, 'cause I wanted to get some of the jitters out, and

"God Bless America" starts. I'm in left-center field by myself, looking at this crowd, which wasn't that big 'cause it was a make-up game, but my legs are shaking. I'm thinking about my warmup pitches when I get to the mound, that I don't throw them over everybody, and stuff like that. They were the weirdest thoughts I had never really thought of before.

The whole time I was thinking, "I'm pretty much gonna give up the house right now. I just don't want to walk anybody." I wanted to throw as good of pitches as I could without hitting somebody in the face, throwing it into the back net, or spiking one 15 feet in front of me.

I just didn't feel right. I didn't have a good grip on the ball. Everything felt a little out of whack. I knew who I was coming in to face, and when you know you got those guys, you're just trying to get out of there without making a fool of yourself. I thank God I did a little better than I thought I was gonna do. It started off kind of shaky.

I battled Jeter a little bit, and then he put a swing on a slider. He hit a swinging bunt down the third base line a little bit. I ran over there and thought I had some time. I picked up the ball, and I was gonna fire it to first. That's when I realized how fast the game is up there. He was already crossing first base.

Once that happened, I'm like, "Okay, now I've just gotta try to get a ground ball." Honestly, I was just trying to think of things to not understand who I was facing. Then Jason Giambi dinked one off the end of the bat into shallow center field, and it felt like all the wheels were gonna fall off at that point. I had made two good pitches, and I figured it just doesn't matter when you're in the big leagues. I got Hideki Matsui to swing at a slider, and when I got him to swing at the slider, I kind of realized, "That's the pitch that got me here. He's a really good hitter and he just struck out. Maybe I can compete with these guys."

We lost, and I went into the locker room. I'm sitting there, and I want to call my dad 'cause he and my mom weren't able to be there. I'm just waiting. We get on the bus, and that's when I realized it, driving back from the stadium to the hotel. I'm like, "Oh my goodness. I'm in New York. I just pitched against the Yankees. I'm now going back to the Plaza Hotel."

Coming from where I came from as a kid in South Miami Heights, I was probably the last guy that was expected to make it out of Southridge and Palmetto. Then I'm in New York, and it all started coming to me, like, "This is real. I'm gonna enjoy this."

Later, calling my dad was just awesome. He's like, "You made it." I was on cloud nine, but when I finally got to speak to him, he pulled me back down to being his son.

Travis Hughes (Rangers)

Travis Hughes made his major league debut on September 26, 2004, with the Texas Rangers. He played in three big league seasons. Hughes also played one season in Japan.

I was at home with my brothers. We were at Randy's Bar and Grill here in Lincoln, Nebraska.

I got a call from John Lombardo, the Rangers' minor league director, and he was like, "Hey, Travis, how's everything going?" I thought it was a joke, honestly. It was the middle of September. I was like, "This is not John." He's like, "No, it is. It's John. What would you think about driving down here to Arlington and throwing a bullpen?" I was like, "What? Come down and throw a bullpen?" He goes, "Yeah, we're short a couple arms and just wondering if you would mind coming down." I was like, "Yeah, I'll be down there tomorrow. I'll leave now if you want me to."

We finished our beers. I waited 'til the next morning, took off, drove down there, and threw a bullpen. I had a big ole beard, and Orel Hershiser came up to me. He was like, "Well, I've got good news and bad news. If you wanna be a big leaguer, you can be one today, but you've gotta shave that beard." I was like, "It's done. Give me a razor. I will shave right now." Orel's got a pretty good sense of humor.

Two games later, I pitched against Seattle at home.

I got the call in the bullpen, got up, and was like, "Oh my gosh!" My first two throws to Gerald Laird went about 35 feet. I was like, "What in the hell was that?" He looked at me and threw the ball back. Then I threw another one and it went about 25 feet. I was like, "Holy shit! This is not happening!" Then I just lobbed one, started getting into it, and was fine. But I'd never done that before in my life. I didn't even get it halfway.

They swung the gate open, and I jogged out there, soaking it in, looking up and around. I'd never played in front of 35,000 people. I was like, "Holy cow."

I got in the game, and I walked the first guy. I'm like, "You've gotta be kidding me." Then I had two strikes on the next guy, but I walked him too. I struck out the next two, and then Jose Lopez, who I struck out 100 times in the minor leagues, gets a double down the line. I was like, "You little shit." I don't think he ever got a hit off me except for then.

After settling down, I started thinking, "Man, I just pitched in the big leagues." It was surreal. Ending the season in Triple-A, then going home for a week or so, and not expecting anything, was totally mind-blowing. I never expected anything like that. It was pretty amazing.

Kameron Loe (Rangers)

Kameron Loe made his major league debut on September 26, 2004, with the Texas Rangers. He played in nine big league seasons. Loe also played one season in Japan.

I was a mid-round guy, but I was going up through the system because the Rangers needed pitching help at that point. I kept putting up good numbers and had a good season.

I was back home and hanging out with my mom, running errands, when I got the phone call.

I had seen two days before that Frankie Francisco and Doug Brocail got into an altercation in Oakland with one of the fans. Frankie ended up throwing a chair into the stands, and it was a big deal. A lady got hit in the face with the chair and her husband was coming on the field to attack the guys. In Oakland, the bullpen is so close to the fans that they can basically reach over and punch you if they want.

I saw that, and two days later I got the call. I can't remember exactly who called me, but they were in Anaheim, and they needed another pitcher 'cause Frankie was being suspended.

My parents live in L.A., so I basically just took a drive down the 405 freeway and met the team in Anaheim. I sat around in the clubhouse, worked out with them, and shagged BP. I think they were kind of filling me out for the first two days. I wasn't on the roster. Then, I believe it was a Sunday, I was put on the roster.

I wanna say I was on the roster around six or seven days before I got into a game. I was available every day. The anticipation was the worst part of it. They got me up, I think two days before my first game, like I was going to go in the game. Then the pitcher got out of it. That kinda helped me get over [it] a little bit, getting to warm up and getting the adrenaline flowing.

When that phone rings, your heart jumps. Everybody looks at the bullpen coach like, "Does that mean me?" Once you get into the game and the hitter steps in the box, then it's game time, you know. For my very first outing, I remember coming out of the bullpen. As I was running across the field, I had insane adrenaline flowing. My back leg was shaking.

I was pitching against the Seattle Mariners and went two and two-thirds with one hit. The one hit that I gave up was to Ichiro Suzuki. They stopped the game and got the ball. I'm like, "All right, I guess everybody gives up a hit, and the first one might as well be to the guy that gets the most in one season."

I don't remember who my first strikeout was, but my second strikeout was Edgar Martinez. I threw him a sinker first pitch, threw a slider second pitch for a swing and miss, and then came with a curveball that kind of buckled him. It was a little good morning, good afternoon, good night. My buddy said a lot of our friends were gathered at somebody's house watching the game, and one of my buddies just dumped a full beer on his head after I struck out Edgar Martinez. He was a guy I used to watch growing up, and it was his last year.

It was surreal, and I definitely remember the adrenaline pumping hard. They told me afterwards, "You've gotta control your breathing. Your shoulders were going pretty hard out there." I was doing a lot of upper chest breathing, almost hyperventilating.

Adam Greenberg (Cubs)

Adam Greenberg made his major league debut on July 9, 2005, with the Chicago Cubs. He played in two big league seasons. Due to the uniqueness of his story, his second call-up with the Miami Marlins in 2012 is included.

I was in Double-A with the Cubs in Tennessee. It was the last game before we were traveling down to Jacksonville, Florida, which was like a 13-hour bus ride.

I walked into the clubhouse, and my name and Matt Murton's were not on the lineup card. The manager, Bobby Dickerson, called us in and he's like, "You guys just take it easy today." At the end of the game, he calls us back in and says, "Guys, you're not coming on the bus to Jacksonville. You're either going to fly and meet us there or you're going to be going to Triple-A and meeting the team wherever they are." We went back to the hotel, said goodbye to our teammates, and watched them get on a long bus ride.

Matt and I stayed in the hotel room for the next few hours, and we were watching the Cubs play a doubleheader. We both shared the same agent at the time, and we were told by our agent to root against the Cubs more than we'd ever rooted against a team in our life. We didn't know why but were like, "Okay, sure."

The Braves swept the doubleheader, putting the Cubs at an eight-game losing streak.

Almost immediately the phone rang, and it was the Double-A manager. He called my phone and asked me to put the phone on speaker so Matt could hear. He started saying, "Hey, I just want to let you guys know you're going to be meeting the team in Miami." Matt and I both looked at each other like, "Aren't they going to Jacksonville?" He then said, "Congratulations, you guys are going to meet the major league team in Miami to play the Marlins."

Oftentimes in that situation, one guy's getting called up and the other is not. You're happy for your teammate, but anyone who says they're genuinely happy when they weren't the one to get called up is lying through their teeth. When I got that call with Matt, there could have been no cooler experience because we both got to be excited for each other genuinely.

That night I looked over, and Matt was sleeping like a baby. I don't think I slept more than five seconds. I was so amped up.

We got into Miami, went straight to the hotel, dropped off our bags, and then we went to the field. It might've been 12 o'clock, maybe even earlier. I always got to the park early anyway, but this was extra early.

The traveling secretary was there, and he had me sign my contract. That's when it was like, "This is real." I don't even know what it said. I didn't read a word of it. He just said, "Sign." I said, "Okay." Then he handed me an envelope filled with cash. I asked him, "What is this for?" He said, "Well, if you don't want it, give it back. This is your meal money." It was probably more money than I made the whole month in Double-A, and it was just meal money.

I went onto the field and to home plate. There wasn't a soul around. I dug into the batter's box, looked around, and I was like, "Man, this is it. I get to unpack my bags for the first time ever in my life, being satisfied where I am." It was pretty magical.

Dontrelle Willis was pitching and I'm a left-handed hitter. Dontrelle was on top of the world that year, so I did not play that first game there. July 9 was my first game, but it was the same thing. There was a left-hand starter, and I was going to be starting the following night, but I ended up pinch-hitting in the ninth inning.

I was ready. I knew the opportunity would come. Mentally, I was watching the game, paying attention to everything that was going on, knew the circumstances and who I would probably be facing. When my opportunity came, I was prepared to be aggressive. Valerio De Los Santos, a lefty, came in, but it didn't matter. My mentality was to just be aggressive.

When a ball is released, you've got three-tenths of a second.

My thought process when the ball was released, coming out of his hand and towards my head, was to stay in there and not look stupid bailing on my first major league pitch. That was all in the first two-tenths of a second. Then the third tenth of a second was realizing it wasn't a breaking ball and to get the hell out of the way.

I never lost consciousness. I remember everything vividly. I said, "Stay alive! Stay alive! Stay alive!" I said it three times. It wasn't, "Stay with it!" or "Stay awake!" It was, "Stay alive!" I thought my skull split open. I thought I was dying.

My eyes rolled to the back of my head. I grabbed my head and thought I was holding it together, bleeding out, and legitimately dying. I was scared for my life.

My eyes rolled back, and that's when I noticed Paul Lo Duca, who was catching, standing over me. He said, "Stay down, kid. You're going to be okay." That was my only comfort, the fact that he didn't say, "Go get towels!" He wasn't freaking out like that.

It's a good assumption that I went right to the hospital, but I did not go to the hospital then, and I did not go to the hospital that night. I finally went to the hospital the next morning when I walked outside, and the sunlight was killing me. My head was throbbing. I wanted to vomit. My eyes were shifting out of control, from side to side. At that point, I went to the hospital.

I was there just a couple hours that morning. They did a CT scan. It's been reported there was a skull fracture, but there was no skull fracture. Obviously, I wasn't going to be playing, but I got sent to the stadium. I was laying in the clubhouse most of the game.

It was tough. Here I was, the kid that just got called up to bring energy to the team, and I'm in the clubhouse and can't even stay awake. It was embarrassing. That was my only way to describe it. I wasn't nervous at that time for my future. I didn't think I was that badly hurt. Embarrassing is the best way that I could describe it.

My first bit of nervousness was in the airport. I basically fell over. Fortunately, I caught myself against the wall.

Then it was the All-Star break. I was home in Connecticut with my family. I remember laying down in bed, and my eyes just uncontrollably going side to side. The pain was just excruciating. That was really when I was concerned. I didn't know what was going on.

After the All-Star break, I went back to Chicago and was trying to do anything that I could. I remember taking batting practice, and I told the trainer that my eyes felt like they were floating and disconnected from my skull. Four games go by with the Pirates at home, and then the Cubs are going on the road. Obviously, I didn't play in any of those games. That's when they're like, "We're going to send you down to Arizona and do whatever rehab you need to do."

I was in Arizona during that rehab, and that was when I was concerned for the quality of my life, less baseball, for the first time ever.

I was really just tricking them and myself that I was okay. I knew I was a mess. I knew I wasn't right, but they said, "As long as you don't have symptoms for 72 hours, you can come back and play." As a 24-year-old kid, I figured I had to get out on the field.

Fast-forward to the winter of 2011. I got a phone call from Matt Liston, who was a baseball fanatic. He told me he got my number from Willie Weinbaum, an ESPN producer, and just a wonderful guy. With the credibility of Matt having the relationship with Willie, I figured, "All right, I'll listen to what this guy has to say." He was a filmmaker, passionate about being a baseball fan, he knew my story, and was a Cubs fanatic. He was like, "It's unfair what happened to you." He's like, "I was watching *Field of Dreams* with my wife, and she felt bad for Moonlight Graham. I told her Moonlight Graham has nothing on Adam Greenberg." It got his mind swirling. He called me to check in and see what I was doing.

He essentially wanted to be my agent. Our arrangement was not necessarily wanting to get me back to the big leagues. He was going to just bring attention to my story.

I told him, "Matt, I'm not a charity case. I got called up to the major leagues and I want to go back, but I don't want to go to independent ball again." I told him I wanted an opportunity to go to spring training with a team and get called up that way. I said, "I'll allow you to do this, but I don't want any favors. I wanna earn this. You've got my blessing if that's your approach." That's how the whole thing started.

I got contacted by Brad Ausmus from Team Israel, and he said he wanted me to be a part of the team or at least try out. At that point, I became a little kid again. I had a batting tee, and I would hit every day. I started throwing the ball off the brick building I worked out at. I'd take my cleats and go run bases at the park. My brother would throw me flips. I was doing whatever the case was, just to stay baseball ready. Then I went down to Florida to hit with the hitting coach that I had trained with for years, back when I was doing well.

Team Israel was in September, and I played with them for a few weeks. That's where the Marlins sent scouts to watch me play and work out.

Our team lost the championship game, and I thought that I had taken off my cleats for the last time. Matt Liston was calling me obsessively, and it was pissing me off. He was at the game and wanted to know when I was going to be out for an exit interview. At that point, Matt and I were good buddies, but I was like, "Bro, leave me alone. I'll be out when I'm out." Obviously, he knew something I didn't.

I got out, he hooked me up to a mic to do that exit interview, and that's when David Samson, the president of the Marlins, called his phone. It was like 11:30 on a Sunday night. I was like, "What the hell is Samson calling his phone for?"

Samson told me they were there seven years prior when I got hit.

He said they didn't follow my story much and thought I was okay. More recently, my story had come to their attention, which is what Matt did, acting as my agent. He brought my story to the team, and they sent their scouts. Samson said, "You were a big leaguer seven years ago and from what we've seen you're still a big leaguer. We'd like you to be part of the Marlins and get your at-bat."

It was crazy 'cause I flew up to New York and I went on the *Today Show* to announce it nationally. Until then I couldn't tell anyone for at least two or three days. It was this top-secret thing.

I knew I was going to get in that game on October 2. I knew I was pinch-hitting. I didn't know exactly what inning or who I was going to be facing.

I waited seven years, and R.A. Dickey, the Cy Young Award–winning knuckleballer, was pitching. My approach was the same as before—to be aggressive. I wanted to get the best swing, or swings, I possibly could early in the count.

The crowd was going insane. It was so loud. I dug into the batter's box and then stepped out. I was hearing it, and I said to myself, "I waited seven years for this. I don't know if it'll ever happen again. I'm just going to enjoy it."

It might only have been about two seconds that I stepped out, but it felt like five minutes. Those two seconds are moments that I cherished then and still do to this day. I enjoyed my time being up there.

Seven seasons after his debut with the Chicago Cubs, fans held these signs when Adam Greenberg had his at-bat with the Miami Marlins (author's collection).

I was ready for it. I thought the first pitch crossed the plate high. It was a knuckleball that started up in my eyeballs and then plummeted down. When the umpire called strike one, it became much more challenging because I knew I then had to be overly aggressive.

The next pitch that he threw me was a knuckleball that started on the outer third of the plate. I tried to put the bat on the ball, trying to hit it to left field. It darted off the plate and I swung through it for strike two.

Then once I got two strikes, with everything that was at stake, I couldn't go down looking. I joke that if he threw the ball anywhere in the stratosphere of the universe, which means that ball left his hand, I was swinging. It's not an awesome way to approach any at-bat. He threw the last one, and it was a very similar trajectory as the first one. It darted in towards me instead of down, and I swung through it.

I got a standing ovation for striking out from the home team fans. I don't know how many times that's ever happened.

Jason Bergmann (Nationals)

Jason Bergmann made his major league debut on August 28, 2005, for the Washington Nationals. He played in six big league seasons.

Hurricanes became a common theme in my progression. In 2004, in the Florida State League, a hurricane was hitting, so they cancelled the rest of the season and sent a few of us to Double-A because of it. I think Double-A was the first time I had a former major leaguer on the team, and it started to set in that making the major leagues could actually happen.

The next year I started in Double-A, and I was doing extremely well. I ended up getting called up to Triple-A about halfway through, and my eyes started widening. I was pitching well against the Pacific Coast League, which was a hitter-friendly league.

As I said before, hurricanes became a commonality in my progression. I was a New Orleans Zephyr, and Hurricane Katrina was bearing down on us. We had a home stand against the Iowa Cubs that was cancelled, and we weren't sure what our schedule was going to entail after that.

We went to bed, and Hurricane Katrina was in the gulf as a Category 1. The next morning, we woke up with a Category 5. We were supposed to report to the field around 10 or 11 a.m., but it got cancelled.

My manager, Tim Foli, gave me a call and said, "Hey, you've gotta get to the airport." I said, "Where are we going? Are we going to Oklahoma City?" That was our next opponent. He goes, "No, dude. You're going to the big leagues." I said, "What?" He goes, "You're getting called up. You need to get your ass to the airport." The kicker was it was about 1:45 when he called. And I said, "Okay. What time is my flight?" He said, "Your flight's at 2:30."

My girlfriend, now wife, and I had been preparing for the hurricane because we were going on the road and the hurricane was coming down. We were on a ground floor apartment and were thinking about practical things. I didn't have any inkling I was going to the major leagues. When I got the call from my manager, I expected him to give us instructions for our next destination for Triple-A. He shocked the hell outta me, saying I was going to the major leagues.

My apartment was probably five to 10 minutes from the field, and from there about 10 to 15 minutes from the airport. We got in the car and zoomed over to the field to get my gear. I got back in the car and realized something—everyone else was trying to get the hell out of there because there was a hurricane.

We were in the car for about 10 minutes and moved about five car lengths because everyone was on the road now, trying to get out of the New Orleans area. I called the guy with the Nationals who was our coordinator for flights. I said, "There's no possible way I can make it to the airport in the next 20 minutes, even if it was optimal conditions." I said, "The hurricane's bearing down on us. Everybody's getting out. Traffic is awful." He said he'd do what he could, and I hung up the phone.

I'm sitting there in the car looking at my girlfriend, and I'm like, "What if this hurricane screws up my chance of going to the major leagues?" I'm in New Orleans. I can't get to the airport, and they need a guy for tomorrow. They could just call a guy from Harrisburg, and he'd drive down in no time. That was running through my head. Obviously, the hurricane was also a major issue because our stuff was there, her family was there, and everything else.

I get a call back and he says, "Get to Baton Rouge. We've got a flight for you at 5:30." We have three hours to get to Baton Rouge and it takes about two and a half hours to get there. I barely made that flight.

Then we had a decision to make. My girlfriend was driving me to the airport, but she couldn't get back to be with her family because they had closed off all access due to the hurricane. I'm sitting there at the gate and I'm like, "Well, how much does it cost for her to fly with me?" They named their price, and I decided at that point with not only my baseball life, but my [future] marriage, "Come with me. Let's do it." We both flew to Atlanta. I had a connection to D.C., and she stayed. The team was only gonna be in D.C. for one day and then head to Atlanta. I said, "I'll meet you in 24 hours."

It was the most amazing and worst day ever. We lost all our stuff because of the flooding, but I got to realize my dream of going to the big leagues.

I get there Saturday night around midnight. I'm not sure what to do 'cause I'd never been in the majors before. I'm at the team hotel, and I woke up about 8:00. I had no idea what time to get there, so I just figured I'd go early. I got to the field around 8:30, and no one was there except for the equipment manager.

I got my locker squared away with all my gear and just sat there for I think two more hours with no one at all. I just watched TV on the couch, and of course the only thing on was Katrina coverage.

Frank Robinson was one of the first people I saw. He just kinda looked at me like, "Who are you?" Frank was a cool but different manager. He liked to joke with you a little bit and mess with you, but the way the structure was, everything I did went through the pitching coach.

It just happened so fast. I honestly couldn't tell how I felt. I was just so enamored with the feeling of being there. It was everything I wanted it to be. I grew up in New Jersey a big Yankees fan and always wished to be a Yankee, but it didn't matter at that point. It was like, "This is the greatest thing ever." Mike Stanton was on the team as a relief pitcher. I watched Stanton win world championships for the Yankees. Just getting to pick his brain, and talk to him before the game, was cool.

A couple of relievers joked with me, like, "Dude, you're getting in today, 'cause all our arms are barking. We're all tired." They had been worn out the last couple days. Through the whole experience, it was very difficult to concentrate until the game started. There were so many things going on for me personally. It was a dream playing catch with a major league baseball, putting my uniform on, seeing the sights, and hearing the sounds of everything you dreamed of as a kid. At the same time, I've got all this other stuff going on.

When the game started, I was able to focus in. Once they called me to warm up, I got in that zone where I didn't hear anything else. I was just very focused on what I was supposed to be doing.

I ended up getting in, but not [until] after Stanton loaded the bases. Again, he was a guy I had looked up to. They called me in the top of the eighth inning with two outs and [the] bases loaded. It was crazy.

Imagine warming up and being so nervous that you're running on the field with jelly legs. I gave up a hit with bases loaded and a run scored. The next batter hit a swinging bunt, and I ended up short-hopping first base 'cause my legs gave out.

I go in the dugout, and they say to grab a bat. We had some guys that were banged up pretty good. When I got into the game, I guess they never double-switched. I don't even have batting gloves or a bat. I used someone's bat. Alberto Reyes was pitching, and I didn't even see the pitch. I swung and was like, "Holy crap, I hit the ball."

I grounded out hard to first base. I was the third out. I ended up running down to first base and turning around to grab my glove and go back out for the top of the ninth. I couldn't feel my legs. However, I ended up striking the next three guys out.

Craig Hansen (Red Sox)

Craig Hansen made his major league debut on September 19, 2005, with the Boston Red Sox. He played in four big league seasons. Hansen had a quick journey to the majors.

Before the draft, it was widely known amongst front offices that the first initial talk my agent and I had with teams was, "When is he gonna be in the big leagues?"

Our thing was, "If you're ready now, you get up there now." There was no need to go into a system, sit in the system, and have them try to change how you pitch. If they think you're ready and can play at that level, then they shouldn't be allowing you to sit in the minor league system. Teams knew that going in, so interested teams knew they were likely calling me up that year.

We were just finishing up our season in Double-A in Portland, which is Double-A for the Red Sox. We'd lost in the playoffs.

It was me and Hanley Ramirez that got called up. Everyone knew he was being called up. We didn't get called up September 1, though. They wanted to make sure our season was complete, we made a playoff run, and tried to win the championship.

I was packing up and getting ready to go back home. I thought, "All right, I guess I'm not getting called up." I was pretty much prepared to go home, and all of a sudden, I get the call. Todd Claus, the manager, was the one that told me.

I go see Hanley and say, "All right, bud, we've gotta go to the airport tomorrow." We flew into Tampa Bay, and the team was already there. When Claus told me that I was getting called up, he told me, "When you get there, go straight to the manager's office." That's what I did, and Terry Francona was in there.

I introduced myself. He's talking to me and tells me, "We're not going to put you in any pressure situation. We're going to look for a comfortable lead. I want to see what you have, but it probably won't be during a close game because we wanna break you in." I said, "Okay. I'm here whenever you need me."

Hanley had been with the Red Sox system since he was 16. He'd been in camps, and he knew some of those guys that were in the clubhouse. I go in there, look around, and go, "I was just watching these guys a couple months ago on TV."

I grew up a Yankee fan. I was watching them beat the Yankees the prior year in the playoffs. I watched Curt Schilling and his bloody sock, and he's right there. I'm like, "This is pretty fucking cool."

When I was in college, I was being recruited by different agencies so they could represent me for the draft. A couple of them had big leaguers reach out to me, and Kevin Millar was one that reached out. He was on the team when I got there. I went over to him and introduced myself. I'm like, "Hey, we spoke over the phone." He was like, "Holy shit! That was fucking quick!"

It's a one-run game, and Francona told me he wasn't going to put me in a close game, but I know from playing that you've always gotta stay ready. The phone rings, and I hear, "Hansen, get up!" I'm like, "What?!"

Tampa Bay had their bullpens on the field. You warmed up on the field, not behind a fence or anything. If you threw one in the dirt and it got by the catcher, everyone saw it. You try not to think about that type of stuff, and luckily, I didn't let one go. However, it added that extra bit of nervousness.

I went in for the fifth and it went one-two-three, with two strike-outs and an infield popup. I get back to the dugout and everyone's super excited because you've now broken in and are part of a fraternity that is very limited.

It was a surreal experience to get that acknowledgment from the guys. Everyone in that dugout had one thing in common—the dream to play major league baseball, and everyone was living that one dream. You can't go into many workplaces and sit next to someone who has the same exact dream as you.

It was crazy being called up to Boston with such a diehard fan base. I couldn't have asked to be called up in a better place. They put me on a pedestal. They were following every footstep throughout my outings in the minor leagues and counting down to when my debut would happen.

James Loney (Dodgers)

James Loney made his major league debut on April 4, 2006, with the Los Angeles Dodgers. He played in 11 big league seasons. In 2006, Loney was named the Dodgers' Minor League Player of the Year.

We had just landed in Las Vegas for the start of our Triple-A season, and I had just come off a Double-A year. I think our first game was going to be in two days.

Nomar Garciaparra got hurt before the first game of the season for Los Angeles. I was in my hotel room, getting ready for the Triple-A season, and Jerry Royster, the manager, called me. He said, "You're getting called up." It was pretty cool to go from Double-A to the big leagues. I'd just come off two years of Double-A, so I knew that Triple-A was the next step.

I left the next morning and was in the game that night. With Nomar being hurt, I had a pretty good feeling I would be starting. I just tried to think, "You belong here. They're giving you this uniform for a reason."

It was a blur, because you're trying to get your pants and jersey on, and you've got to do some of the media stuff too. My manager was Grady Little, so I met with him and did all that. The first day was definitely a little hectic.

Growing up, I watched a lot of Braves games because they were on TBS a lot. That was special too, because I have a lot of family on the East Coast from South Carolina that watch Braves games. I'm pretty sure the first game I played in was on TBS. A lot of people got to see it.

I remember facing John Smoltz, and he walked me the very first time. I always tell people that he was really scared of me. My second time up, I ended up going to a 2–2 count, and he threw me a slider down and in. It was a pretty good pitch, but I got it up in the air for a line drive single to right field. It was nice to get on base the first two times. It took some of the pressure off me.

It's funny, because when I got called up, I was thinking, "I'm going to stay here forever." Then I got sent down about two weeks later. I was back and forth a lot that year, but it was a great experience. I got to see how great it can be in the big leagues and how hard you've got to keep working in Triple-A to get back there.

Zach McClellan (Rockies)

Zach McClellan made his major league debut on April 16, 2007, with the Colorado Rockies. He played in one big league season.

I was coming off a winter league situation in Mexico where I pitched pretty well. I had an outstanding major league camp but didn't make the team. I believe I even pitched in the last spring training game, even though I was sent down. I came back and pitched against the Cubs before going to Triple-A.

We were in a tight game in Tucson, Arizona, and I was frustrated that I didn't get a chance to pitch. Those key situations were when I'd throw. I had no idea they were going to call me up. I go into the locker room in Tucson, and Bill Geivett, who was the minor league director at that time, called me into the office and told me. Tom Runnells was the manager, Chuck Kniffin was my pitching coach, and Heath Townsend was the trainer. Those guys were the ones in the room. What made it special to me was it felt like they were just as excited as I was.

It was pretty cool. I had a lot of teammates I'd played with for years. They knew the work I'd put in and how long it took for me to get called up. When I came out, there was a lot of people congratulating me and celebrating.

When you're in Triple-A, everybody wants to get called up, so you know some of the teammates were disappointed it wasn't them. At least for that time, they acted excited, and I appreciated that very much. I felt like it was respecting the time I had put in the minors and sticking through some hard times. I hit every path you could possibly hit before I got called up. There wasn't a level that I missed, and some of them I liked so much, I repeated.

My wife was the first one I called. I give her a lot of credit 'cause we got married after my first year of pro ball. She saw me through all the ups and downs, all the mental and physical anguish, and what I was willing to put myself through to get there. I could hear the joy in her voice. That was the first call. Then I called my parents.

Josh Newman was my roommate. I went back to the hotel after getting the news, and I couldn't sleep. I didn't wanna stay up all night and interrupt Josh's sleep, but I couldn't sleep at all. I'd close my eyes, and I swear I could see the insides of my eyelids.

I flew in the next morning. It felt awkward. I'd known most of those guys, but I'd never been in that setting before. I was like, "Man, I don't know if I belong here." You kinda go through that mental challenge of "Do I really deserve this type of stuff?"

I show up in the clubhouse, and I run into Todd Helton. To me, Helton was like a saint. It was almost like there was a halo around him when he walked around me. I don't know how to describe it. I wasn't like a fan, I just respected him so much. When I showed up and he's like, "Hey, Zach.

Congratulations. How's it going?" and shook my hand. That made it all feel normal.

Then LaTroy Hawkins. He was one of the greatest teammates you'll ever find. He said, "I want Zach's locker next to mine." We sat down and he said, "Man, you did it. You can do this. You belong here." He kept telling me, "You belong here." So when I got to the mound that night, at that point, I kinda felt like, "Who's put more work in than me to get here?"

They put me in the very first game. It was against the Giants. I give Clint Hurdle a lot of props for doing that, because it made it all normal for me if that makes sense. But it was a surprise.

Running out from the bullpen to the mound, I couldn't feel my feet. It felt like I was running on a cloud to the field. Everything was super bright. The lights were brighter, the lines were white, the balls were brand new. It was sensory overload. You get out there, and the mound is perfect. There's no holes. It's just perfectly set up. Coors Field might as well be a nature channel site. It's immaculate.

So I get out there. Once I hit that pitching rubber and started to throw, it really did feel normal. Mark Sweeney was the first batter I faced. The first pitch I threw was a backdoor curve ball for a strike. I threw a second backdoor curve ball, and Mark Sweeney hit it in the gap for a double. He ended up scoring.

Imagine you get called up, and the first batter you face hits a leadoff double on a backdoor curve ball that you executed. You're like, "Okay, maybe my stuff's not good enough." But mentally it's all about executing pitches. I have no control over what Sweeney does with his bat. The only thing I can control is where I throw the ball, how to execute the pitches they're calling, and to make sure it's the right pitch. I didn't really panic. I just started executing other pitches.

The other hit I gave up was a ground ball through the hole. I never really took those as, "The hitter beat me." It's more like they found a hole, and that's just the game. That's how I mentally absorbed those hits as I got older.

I could literally count on one hand the people that supported me continuing to play. Those people knew what was in my heart. They knew what my ability was. A lot of other people were saying things, especially behind my back, like, "This guy's never gonna make it. He doesn't throw anything above average."

The journey for me was getting my inner circle small and listening to those people and then using the other stuff as fire to fuel me when times were down. It was a tough journey, but I would not change my journey for anything. Not one bit. I didn't take any days for granted. I knew it wasn't gonna last forever.

Ryan Rowland-Smith (Mariners)

Ryan Rowland-Smith made his major league debut on June 22, 2007, with the Seattle Mariners. He played in five big league seasons. Rowland-Smith struck out the first batter he faced, former Mariners star Ken Griffey, Jr. He played for Australia in the 2004 Summer Olympic games and helped the team win a silver medal.

In 2006 I was in Double-A, and my pitching coach was Brad Holman. He was awesome and would say things like, "You are really good. You have a chance to play in the major leagues."

He was fightin' for me to go to the Arizona Fall League that off-season. The farm director's like, "No, he's not a prospect. He's not gonna go to the Fall League. Sorry." I was pretty bummed out. Then a couple guys went to the big leagues and their spots opened. Brad was the pitching coach on the Fall League team, and he pushed and pushed. I went to the Arizona Fall League, and I was laser-focused. I knew that was my protection year. I had to get on that 40-man roster. I started pitching really well in the Arizona Fall League and I'm like, "Man, I'm gonna pitch in the big leagues. I know I am at this point."

I got put on the major league roster, and then I figured, "I'm gonna go to Triple-A with guns blazing and try to get to the big leagues as fast as I can."

In May of 2007, we're in Round Rock, Texas. Darren Brown, my manager, calls me in the office and says, "Can you pitch tomorrow?" I said, "Aw, my arm's kinda hangin', but yeah, of course I can pitch." He said, "It won't be here. You're gonna be pitchin' for Seattle. You're goin' to the big leagues."

I got outside and Googled who we were playin'. We were playin' the Yankees. They had a bunch of lefties in their lineup, like Jason Giambi, Hideki Matsui, Johnny Damon, and those guys. I'm like, "No friggin' way. Not the Yankees. I can't just face the Tampa Bay Rays on a Tuesday? Man, I can't handle this."

I call everyone. It's 3 o'clock in the morning my time, but it's primetime back in Australia. Everyone says, "Oh, we wanna fly over." I said, "Well, don't fly over just yet. I don't know how long I'm gonna be there for."

I get there, and my name's spelled wrong on my jersey. I'm like, "Do I tell the clubby?" I didn't wanna make anyone do anything extra. I thought maybe they were tryin' to mess with me or somethin'. I go to the clubhouse manager and let him know my name's not spelled right. He goes, "I'm so sorry. We're gonna fix it and have it done about the third inning." I had to go out to the bullpen with no jersey, but they fixed the jersey and rushed it out to me.

We're facin' the Yankees for the weekend. The first game Friday, we're gettin' crushed and I'm like, "I'm gonna pitch to them." I'm freakin' out, scared in the bullpen. I don't pitch. Saturday was the same thing. I don't pitch. Sunday, I don't pitch. At this point I'm like, "Ah, man. I just wanna get this outta the way." Monday rolls around, and I get sent back down.

I get three days in the big leagues, and I don't pitch. There were a good couple weeks where I thought that was gonna be my story. I actually got called up, never pitched, and no kid's gonna believe me. I was freakin' out. I'm in Triple-A and I'm like, "Don't get hurt. Just be patient." I was scared I was never gonna have any stat line to prove I was a major league baseball player.

Then three weeks later, I get called back up.

We're in Sacramento. We knew something had happened because I was supposed to pitch, and I didn't. I was gettin' loose and they said, "Hey, stop throwin'. You're not gonna pitch this inning." I sat back down. We had a guy, Julio Mateo, who was sent down to us after he had a domestic violence case. Everyone's like, "Ah, he's gettin' traded. I bet you'll get traded with him."

I get in the locker room that night and nothing happens. I go back to the hotel. It's about midnight, and I get a call from my manager sayin', "Hey, I know it's late, but early tomorrow morning you're gonna fly off to Seattle." Here I go again.

I went back up, and that first night we're playin' the Reds. Ken Griffey, Jr., was back in town for the first time. Again, no soft landing. I'm like, "Man, can't we just be playin' someone who's not very good and make it easy for me?" They had a ceremony, and the place was packed.

We were down, 16–1. I'm like, "Okay, tonight's my night. This is gonna happen." I start getting loose and they said, "You're gonna face a lefty." The three lefties in the lineup were Josh Hamilton, Adam Dunn, and Ken Griffey, Jr. They're All-Stars. I just didn't want to face Griffey my first time. I was so nervous.

Lo and behold, the first hitter I ever faced was Ken Griffey, Jr. Everyone's on their feet. They all wanna see him hit a home run. I come in, and they're all on their feet, but not for me. I felt like I hadn't thrown a baseball in two months. My hand was numb and all I was thinkin' was, "Just throw strikes. Don't walk him."

You gotta remember somethin'. I grew up in Australia in the 90s before the internet. We didn't have access to players, but we had access to guys like Ken Griffey, Jr., 'cause he was on *The Simpsons*. Here I am, thinkin', "Man, this dude was on the friggin' *Simpsons*. People back home know who this guy is."

I remember I threw my last warmup pitch and walked a little around the mound, tryin' to look cool. I'm like, "What am I doing here? I don't belong here." Willie Bloomquist was playin' shortstop. He walked over to me and said, "Hey, man. Just enjoy it. It's just another hitter. Have some fun." That calmed me down.

I said to myself, "Just throw strikes." All of a sudden, I had two strikes against him. I'm looking at that iconic stance, and I'm like, "I am gonna try and snap off the biggest curveball of my life here." I did, and he swung right over it. I swear the place booed me.

My mom and stepdad had flown over, but their flight got delayed and they missed the game. When I picked them up, my mom asked, "Did you pitch?" I said, "Yeah, I did." She was bummed. Then I told her I faced Ken Griffey, Jr. She's like, "Oh my God!"

Josh Newman (Rockies)

Josh Newman made his major league debut on September 12, 2007, with the Colorado Rockies. He played in two big league seasons.

I was in Colorado Springs, and if you know anything about the Pacific Coast League and Triple-A baseball, those are hitters' parks. I would have some good and some not so good games. It was up and down throughout the year, inconsistent for my standards, anyways.

The season ended, and we had our meeting. They said the player development guys will follow up with you. I got my flight information back to Ohio. Columbus, Ohio, is where my wife and I were living.

As I'm flying home, I got a message from my agent that I needed to call the Rockies' front office as soon as possible.

My wife and I had a condo, and we didn't have anything in it. It was just an air mattress, a little TV, and odds and ends that we had piled up through our first two years of marriage. I get in there, and I called Bill Geivett of the Rockies. I believe Dan O'Dowd, the GM, was on the call as well. We're talking about the year, and Bill said, "Well, we're going to be calling you back later today. The travel secretary is going to be giving you flight information. We're calling you up."

People ask, "What was that like?" I couldn't even talk. I just broke down on my knees and sobbed for a solid hour probably. You think about the many sacrifices people were willing to make from an early age to where you're at. I get emotional just talking about it now. You can't explain that moment.

My wife was a schoolteacher, so she was just getting back into school and the routine. We didn't have much at the time. I knew I was going to have to work in the off-season. I had my degree and was a substitute teacher. I called her once I was able to get ahold of myself and told her.

It was one of those moments in your life that you never forget. We were able to be together throughout the minor leagues, and I was a senior sign, so I signed for $1,000. You don't make much coming up through the minor leagues, but we were able to manage, and she was supportive from the beginning.

The Rockies told me I was going to be getting on a flight the next morning. I'd be flying into Denver, and they would have a person there to pick me up and take me into the stadium. It was a quick turnaround. They said I had to make sure to have some clothes because we were going on a road trip in a few days. I had a suit and just threw what I could in my suitcase. I didn't sleep the night before.

It was a Sunday day game, and we were playing at home. My flight left early in the morning, but when I got to the stadium, the game had already started. LaTroy Hawkins is one of the guys I owe a lot to because he took me under his wing. My locker was supposed to be beside his, and they didn't have the locker for me yet. I'll never forget, LaTroy getting after our clubhouse staff because they didn't have a locker ready. Veteran relievers sometimes will have their own routines. I didn't expect anybody to be in the locker room. LaTroy was in there, just kind of doing his own thing. He came up, introduced himself, and said, "I've heard a lot about you. We're going to get your locker." I didn't care. I was in the big leagues and was like, "Just give me a uniform."

LaTroy rode with me on the golf cart to the bullpen. It was a very emotional moment when I got there. Rick Mathews was our bullpen coach and gave me a big hug. He's from Iowa, so he's a Big Ten guy. He kind of

Josh Newman was called up by the Colorado Rockies during his fourth professional season. He threw a one-two-three inning in his debut (courtesy Josh Newman).

ragged on me a little bit about being a Buckeye. I made a connection with him right away.

I'll never forget my first road trip either. As rookies, they always want to dress us up and do something fun. It was a fun flight for the rookies. I was an adult baby. I had an adult diaper and a pacifier.

Philadelphia was my major league debut. The Philadelphia fans are very passionate. The visitors' bullpen is in center field, and the fans let you know where you're at very quickly. When you're warming up, they are right on top of you. At that time, Philadelphia had a really talented lineup.

We were winning, and Rick said, "This could be your time. You need to start locking it in." The ninth inning comes, I open the gate, and I don't remember my feet touching the ground.

I was so jacked up, my first two warm up pitches went to the net and backstop. Chris Iannetta came up to me. I'll never forget, because he was my guy all the way up through the minor leagues, and he was catching me that day. He comes out to the mound and he's like, "Just relax, dude. This is the same thing." Then we went through how we're going to get the guys out. He locked me in. It was just slowing things down and doing what got you there.

I was able to strike out my first batter, and I had a one-two-three inning. So it was very, very memorable.

After our first road trip, LaTroy took me out, bought me a suit, showed me how to dress, and how to represent yourself at the major league level. I'm forever grateful for that.

Steve Holm (Giants)

Steve Holm made his major league debut on April 4, 2008, with the San Francisco Giants. He played in three big league seasons. Holm played in seven minor league seasons before reaching the majors.

I went to spring training, hoping to make the Triple-A team. I'd never been in Triple-A. I made the all-star team in Double-A, so I thought it was a realistic chance. There was Bengie Molina as the starting catcher and two other catchers who were both on the 40-man roster. One of the stories that spring training was which of those guys was gonna end up being the backup catcher.

Well, luckily for me, Bengie Molina pulls his quad on like the second game of the spring. So those two guys now start going head-to-head and are starting. They're sharing the bulk of the time because Bengie's obviously sitting out. Bengie, like a true veteran, said, "Hey, I'm gonna make sure I get this thing right, it's not gonna linger through the season." He sits out maybe an extra five days than he really had to. That's what you do if you're a veteran in spring training, make sure you get it right.

Well, because of Bengie's innings not being used by him, those guys are getting to play, and I'm getting their innings. I'm playing well, but I'm playing with house money because those two guys feel the heat. They've got a lot on the line. I've got everything to win and nothing to lose.

Pretty soon, I'm starting a game. Then I start another game. Then one of them gets sent down, and it's just me and the other guy. Now the story starts to change a little bit.

Now we have this guy that's never played in the big leagues. At that point, I'd put seven years in the minors, and six of them were in A-Ball. People are going, "Is this guy really gonna make the team?" People start to come up to me like, "Hey man, you're having a pretty good spring."

It gets down to the end, and we're at the exhibition games in San Francisco. You know, those games where we play against the A's. We go there, we play the A's, and it's just me and the other guy left.

After the second of the three games, they send the other guy down. I'm looking around the room like, "Well, there's just Benji and me." I wasn't a math major, but I can figure this part out. I'm thinking I'm in a pretty good spot. I'm staying in the team hotel. I wake up and there's a newspaper underneath my door. I open it up. It says, "Giants searching for a catcher on waiver wire." I'm like, "Oh, you've gotta be kidding me. I've come this far, it's been such a good spring, and now they're gonna pick somebody else off the waiver wire."

I pulled up to the field in my truck and they go, "Hey, can we get your suitcase? They're supposed to put your suitcase on the van. It's gotta get put on the plane." I hadn't been told anything yet. I said, "No, you can't have my suitcase."

I pull past him, park my truck. I get out. I have my suitcase and wheel it in. Now Murph, who's the head clubby for the Giants, goes, "Hey, give me your suitcase." I go, "Murph, you can't have my suitcase."

He goes, "I changed your number. You made the team." I said, "I'm not giving you my suitcase until they tell me I made the team." So I wheel my suitcase to my locker and stuff it in. It's way too big. I'm standing around and I'm like, "Gosh, I look like an idiot. I'm the only guy with a suitcase here."

Finally, they come and get me. Ron Wotus says, "Hey, Bochy wants to talk to ya."

At that point, I walked in. I sit down and they had a couple other people walk in. Brian Sabean walked in. Dick Tidrow, who was in charge of the minor leagues, and the one that wanted to convert me to a catcher all those years ago, was there. Bochy, obviously, was in there. He said, "Hey, I just wanted to congratulate you and let you know you made the team."

You're 28 years old and he says, "You made the team." I don't know what he said after that. You're sitting there spinning like crazy. I couldn't tell you if it was 10 minutes or one minute. All I knew was I made the team.

My parents were on their way down to the exhibition game. They live in Sacramento. I shot a text to my brother, who was with them. I said, "Hey, tell Mom and Dad that I made the team." At that point, I turned around and had like 10 reporters at my locker.

I shot that text and that was it. I started going through all the reporter stuff. By the time I go through that, all the sudden I look up and my phone has gone crazy. They'd put it out on KNBR or something at that point, and everyone back home was listening.

For my debut, I came in against the Brewers, late in the game, and I had to catch Erick Threets. He was a 97 to 100 left-handed guy that didn't have a lot of command. The one thing a catcher has to do is catch the frickin' baseball. You don't want to go out there and have passed balls, and I'm catching the easiest guy to have a passed ball against. Anyway, I caught clean. It was fine.

I got one at-bat. It was against Salomon Torres. First pitch, fastball. My whole career I swung at it every time I saw it. I hit a line drive to the left and was out.

I was never one of those people that was sitting there in the big leagues going, "Oh man, this is great!" I always appreciated it because I knew how close I was to never getting that opportunity.

Jonathan Van Every (Red Sox)

Jonathan Van Every made his major league debut on May 14, 2008, with the Boston Red Sox. He played in three big league seasons. Van Every played in eight minor league seasons before reaching the majors.

We were in Buffalo, New York, and it's funny because I had played for Buffalo the previous two years as the Triple-A affiliate of Cleveland. So now, I'm with Pawtucket, on a visiting team. I knew they had some issues at the big league level.

Ron Johnson was my manager at the time. He gives me call at 8:00 a.m. I had an idea, if the manager's calling at 8:00 a.m., he probably wants something important. He gave me the news. He's like, "Hey, pack your bags. You've got to be at the airport in an hour and a half." I was ecstatic and immediately called my family, my parents, and my brother, and gave them the news.

Typically, when you get called up to the big leagues, they fly you first class 'cause everything in the big leagues is first class. I had a middle seat on Southwest. I wasn't going to complain. I was on cloud nine. I was just beside myself.

We were in Baltimore, and it was a Wednesday day game of all things. It was kind of trial by fire. I land, and I've got all my gear with me. I'm sitting in the airport like, "Okay, do I get a cab? Is somebody coming for me?" Typically, you'd have a liaison from the club assigned to shuttle guys to and from the airport, to the field, or to the hotel. I was assuming that was going to be the situation. Well, it was not. After about 30 minutes, I realized that I've got to get a cab and get to the stadium. The game's going to start without me. I can't let that happen. Ultimately, I get in a cab and I'm on the way.

Finally, the traveling secretary called to make sure I got in okay. I was on the way to the field. I hear a little rumbling in the background. It was a couple of the coaches in the background, "Well, do you want me to tell him?" They told me, "By the way, you're starting in center field today." I'm like, "Holy shit!"

It's great and was a dream come true. Usually, when you're an older guy getting called up, you're just kind of warming the bench until somebody gets hurt or somebody goes down. In this case, they threw me right into the fire, which couldn't be any better.

The cab driver literally just dumped me off in the parking lot outside the stadium. I had to call the traveling secretary like, "Hey, man, how do I get to the locker room?" A guy came out, got me on a golf cart, and took me all the way down the tunnels to the visitors' locker room. If I had to walk that, it would have been a nice 15- to 20-minute walk from the parking lot down to the dungeons of Camden Yards.

A lot of guys weren't in the locker room because I arrived late. They were already on the field, stretching and getting ready for batting practice. I had to hustle to get out there. The last thing you want to do when you get called up, on that kind of stage, is be late.

The main thing that stands out was just taking batting practice on a big league field for the first time. Catching fly balls on a big league field for the first time. Seeing how the ball travels with the big backdrop of the stadium. The stadium seats way off in the distance. It's definitely a different experience as far as depth perception versus a normal minor league field. That was intriguing. Just taking it all in, looking at the light poles, the scoreboard, and seeing my name up on the starting lineup, was a surreal environment.

Making my way up to the plate for the first time, over the loudspeaker in the stadium, I hear the announcer, "Now making his major league debut, number 30, Jonathan Van Every." The catcher patted me on the back and said, "Congratulations. Welcome." The umpire told me the same.

I was facing a guy I faced before, coming up through the minor league system, Daniel Cabrera. I won't forget that. He threw mid-90s, had some tail on his balls, and was a sinker ball pitcher. Traditionally, I did well against sinker ball pitchers. Unfortunately, I struck out, but the second at-bat, I got a knock up the middle.

As soon as the ball hit the bat, I knew it was a hit. Kevin Millar was playing first. He hit me on the butt and said, "Congratulations." He was happy for me.

I look in the dugout and see Sean Casey, "The Mayor," jumping up and down. The third out's made. I run over to go get my glove in the dugout, and Casey's on the first step trying to give me a big hug. He picked me off the ground. I'm like, "Okay, dude, you're going way too overboard with this. Do I have a sign on my back? What's going on here?" But he's just genuinely a super nice guy.

He signed one of his bats for me, saying, "Glad I was there to see your first big league knock, Sean Casey." I've still got it framed in a shadow box with the lineup card, the jersey, a picture of me getting my first hit, and the ball from the first hit.

Tim Dillard (Brewers)

Tim Dillard made his major league debut on May 23, 2008, with the Milwaukee Brewers. He played in four big league seasons. Tim's father, Steve, also played in the majors.

I was playing in Nashville for the Nashville Sounds, and this is before my wife and I had smart phones.

I've got this flip phone, and during that time, you didn't just text or call people all the time. It was still in that era of something better be important. You would leave your phone on loud at night because nobody would ever call unless it was an emergency. I left my phone on and woke up to one of those old ringtones that you had to buy. I had Led Zeppelin's "Kashmir."

We were busing to Memphis for a road trip at around 7:30 a.m., and I get this call around 5:30 a.m. It's our manager, Frank Kremblas, and he's like, "Hey, what are you doing?" I was like, "Uh, sleeping." He was like, "Oh, okay." He was a very high energy guy. So it wasn't surprising to me that he was probably up and hanging out and lifting weights or whatever. He says, "Hey, you've got called up. You need to go to the field, get your stuff, and then go to the airport. You've got a flight at like 10:00." I was like, "Oh, okay." He goes, "Oh yeah, by the way, you're going to D.C." I was like, "Oh, okay." He goes, "Okay, all right, bye." That was it. I was just like, "Oh, wow."

So I was like, "Honey, wake up. I've got called up to the big leagues." She's like, "Oh, that's nice." We like sleep in our house. Anyway, once we came to our senses, we had to go to the field, get my stuff, and drive straight to the airport.

My wife and I went together, and this was Memorial Day weekend. To get an emergency ticket at that time, to Washington, D.C., on Memorial Day weekend, was like $1,000. That was about all the money we had to our name. We had one credit card for emergencies, and we didn't use it. We didn't want to use it, so we're like, "Goodness gracious, we're going to have to spend $1,000." We were contemplating at the airport if I should just leave her behind, and I was like, "Well, even if I get sent down tomorrow, I'll make $1,000 in the big leagues. We can pay for it with one day."

So we bit the bullet and went. One of the things I learned early on is that it's not just me, my life, and my career. We're in this together, and she's a huge part of that, so there was no way I was going to not take her.

By the time we flew in, the place was a zoo. By the time we got to a taxi, I realized I had to go straight to the field. I shoved my wife and suitcases into a taxi going to the team hotel, and then I went separately.

I was wearing a suit. I thought that was the dress code, and I was looking cool in a suit, but it was really hot. I've [got] this giant baseball bag, this suit on, and I'm in this taxi, and the guy's like, "Where do I drop you off at the stadium?" I was like, "At the player's entrance." The guy's like, "Oh, I know exactly where that is." But he dropped me off on literally the other side of the stadium of where I needed to be. I still got in somehow, even though I didn't have any form of identification saying I was a player, which is probably a security risk. I guess I've got a trusting face.

I walk down the tunnel underneath the stadium, and I just kept walking. It's endless and I'm asking, "Where's this clubhouse?" They're like, "Just keep going. It's way down there." By the time I got there, I had sweat all through my suit. I walk in there and guys are like, "Hey, it's about time you're here. Get changed. Go out and play catch."

I changed fast and went outside literally when they're getting the field ready for the game. I played catch and came back in. They're like, "Hey, what are you doing? Get your game stuff on. We've got to get out there for the game." I'm scrambling. I'm like, "Well, at least they spelled my name right on the jersey."

I got ready, and they were like, "Hey, you've got to do the candy bag since you're in the bullpen. You're the low man on the totem pole. You better get this candy bag right." I've got no time, but I'm like, "All right, I'll just figure it out." I'm throwing Red Bulls, waters, candy, gum, and whatever I could find in. Then they're like, "Get out there. The anthem's about to start."

By the time I got out there, I realized there was like 40,000 people in this stadium, and it was loud. The first thing I remember is the jumbotron—the biggest jumbotron I'd ever seen. It almost looked like a widescreen television sitting right in front of your face everywhere you walked.

The anthem happened, and it was probably the first time where I felt like, "Okay, everything seems to have calmed down a little bit. I can finally relax and take a breath." I walked down to the bullpen, sat down, and I'm like, "Okay, now it's time to watch some baseball."

The game flew by. In the fifth or sixth inning, they called down, and they're like, "Get Dillard hot." Everything sped up again. I threw, like, five pitches, and they ask, "Hey, you ready?" I said, "Of course I'm ready."

Finally, they say, "Dillard, you're in." I went jogging in. I didn't want to trip in front of all those people. Running out to the mound, I'm literally going, "Left, right, left, right, left, right."

I came out of left-center, where their bullpens were. I made it to the mound and was trying to take a deep breath but look calm. I didn't want anybody to be like, "Wow, he looks like he's freaking out."

My catcher was Jason Kendall. So, luckily, the Brewers had a catcher that had many years in the show. He was like, "Hey. You all right? You good to go?" I was like, "Yeah." He goes, "Okay, what are your signs?" I was like, "One, fastball, uh, three, slider." He was like, "Great, let's do this. Here we go." I said, "All right! Let's do this, man!" I was kind of too aggressive for the point in the game. He looked back at me like, "Wow, that was pretty aggressive." You know if it was Game Seven of the World Series, yeah, but it was May.

He's talking to the umpire while I'm warming up. The umpire's laughing and he's pointing at me, and Kendall's back there nodding his head, like, "Yeah, he said that." I'm self-conscious already. I've been a big leaguer for two hours, and this is my intro.

We got through the inning. I struck a guy out and got a couple ground balls. I got back to the dugout and didn't think anything of it other than, like, "Thank God it's over." People were coming up like, "Great job." They're hugging me.

I didn't know it, but after I struck out the batter, they kept the baseball. I thought they were just throwing it out. Bill Hall was at third base, and when he got the ball back after they threw it around, he acted like it was scuffed and threw it into the dugout. At the moment, that's not really what I was caring about. I found out later I'd struck out Aaron Boone, who now is the manager for the New York Yankees. So I have the ball. It's got a little hologram sticker and [is] in a little plastic case on my shelf.

I remember thinking, before I went out there, that my whole goal was to look like I had done it before.

After the game was over, my wife and I took a taxi back to the team hotel, and we were walking through the lobby. Jason Kendall was with a couple of coaches in the lounge area. He sees me through this window, waves me in, and I sit down. He says, "Hey, man, can I buy you a beer?" I was like, "Oh, sure, man."

We sat down and he says, "I just wanted to give you a cheers, man. You went out there to have your debut in the big leagues in front of a sellout crowd. Dude, you looked like you knew what you were doing. You looked like you had done it before."

I thought that was the ultimate compliment. He said exactly what I wanted to have happen.

Ticket stub from Tim Dillard's major league debut with the Milwaukee Brewers in Washington. His debut took place during the busy Memorial Day weekend in the nation's capital (author's collection).

Jared Wells (Padres)

Jared Wells made his major league debut on May 24, 2008, with the San Diego Padres. He played in one big league season. In 2005 Wells was named the Padres' Minor League Pitcher of the Year.

I started off my first year on the 40-man at Double-A in 2006 and was pitching really well. Then I pulled my hamstring. I was running down the first baseline and ended up pulling my hamstring in the second inning of a game.

The manager was Gary Jones at the time. He came over, and obviously I couldn't pitch after that. He was like, "Man, I want to apologize to you." I was like, "For what?" He said, "Because you were only supposed to throw at the beginning and get called up." I was like, "Ah." That would have been my first time. Hearing that news, I tried to come back a little too soon. I didn't really get back to form, where I was at that point, until I got called up in '08.

The funny thing is, I literally didn't have any idea I was gonna be called up at the time I did. I was throwing the ball okay. I didn't think about it.

I was asleep in my apartment in Portland. My wife wakes me up, "Jared, you need to call your manager. He's trying to get in touch with you." This was like at midnight. I'm like, "What?" I look at my phone, and I had four missed calls from him.

The reason she found out is because Mike Adams, a teammate of mine, knew and got called up with me at the same time. His wife had called my wife and was like, "Hey, where's Jared at? Randy Ready is trying to get in touch with him!" She was like, "For what?" And she gets, "I don't want to tell you. It's gonna ruin it." So she wakes me up and I call my manager. He's like, "Hey, man. You're going up to the big leagues. You almost missed it."

I called my parents right away. Unfortunately, at midnight on the West Coast, it was a lot later down in Texas. They answered right away and were excited. They were on a flight the next day and met us out there. I was fortunate my brother lives in San Diego as well. He served in the Marine Corps, stayed out there, and made a life for himself. So it was a pretty good deal. Most of my family got to attend.

Before leaving Portland, we went to the locker room, gathered our stuff, and were on a flight at 6 o'clock that morning to go to San Diego. It was me, Mike Adams, and Josh Banks who got called up together.

We check into the hotel, and mind you, it's still early in the morning at that point. It's hard for me to go to sleep, 'cause I'm excited waiting to go to the field. We got settled into the hotel they put us up in and went to the stadium for a normal night game.

I left for the field, and it was within walking distance. I walked through downtown, to the stadium, and it was just a perfect day of California weather. I was pumped to be there.

We go through the players' entrance. We met the guards at the entrance, and we were pretty pumped. They were all very friendly. Of course, the first people there are the clubhouse manager and traveling agent. We talked to all of them, all the training staff, and I go in to talk to Bud Black, who's the manager. He just said, "Hey, man, glad you're here. Be ready to pitch. You're here to help the ball club win the games."

We kinda knew everybody already, just from spring training and being on the 40-man. I was amped up, and the adrenaline was going the whole time, just excited about being there.

I wanna say it was the second day I was there that I threw one inning. It went pretty good. I ended up walking Bronson Arroyo, which was not good, 'cause he was the pitcher, but I didn't give up any runs. I was probably more nervous in the bullpen than when I was going out on the field. The process in the minor leagues kinda prepares you for these situations, 'cause once I was on the field, I was ready to pitch.

The crazy thing about that whole situation is that they put us in the hotel for seven days. We were playing the Reds at the time, and then the Nationals came. Well, right after we got done playing the Nationals, we were about to go on the road. They called me in the office and let me know I was traded to Seattle.

Justin Thomas (Mariners)

Justin Thomas made his major league debut on September 1, 2008, with the Seattle Mariners. He played in three big league seasons. Thomas also played one season in Japan.

We were in Tacoma. We had a home game, and it was the last week of the season. We weren't going to make the playoffs that year, so people were starting to make travel arrangements to get home. I had a feeling I had a chance to get called up, and I didn't want to jinx it, so I didn't book a flight back to Phoenix.

After that night's game, my manager, Daren Brown, called me into the office and started talking to me. They were having exit interviews with everybody at the time. I went in, and he asked me what my winter plans were. He asked, "Are you still planning on going down and pitching in Venezuela?"

I said, "Yeah, I'm going to go down and pitch in Lara for the Cardenales, just to get more accustomed to pitching out of the pen." He said,

"Well, what if there's a better league you could pitch in through the end of the season here?" I was like, "That would be great." He asked, "You know what the next level is?"

I said, "Yeah, pitching in the big leagues would be the only level above here." He was like, "Well, you're going to get a chance to pitch in the big leagues through the end of the year. You're getting called up. You're going to be leaving in the morning, flying down to Texas to meet the team, playing the Texas Rangers."

I was on the West Coast, and being from Ohio, it was late at night. But I called and woke up both my parents and told them the news. Then I called my wife, who was my fiancée then, Theresa. She was a schoolteacher, so she was back in Peoria, Arizona. The school year had started, so she was back at work. I called her and gave her the news.

It was myself and another guy who I spent a ton of time with in the minor leagues, Luis Valbuena. He and I played at the same levels at the same time. We started together in Everett and kind of worked our way up through the system. He and I got called up together.

Valbuena and I got picked up in a black car at the hotel at about 6:00 in the morning and taken from Tacoma down to Seattle. We flew to Texas and got there later in the morning. We went to the hotel, got situated, and then met the team at the stadium in Arlington for the game on September 1.

I had a normal pregame routine and was sitting in the bullpen watching the game. It was anxious nerves sitting out in the bullpen, trying to get acclimated to the situation. We were winning by quite a bit. We had a six-run lead after the eighth inning.

They called down, and I was told to start warming up. I was going to throw the ninth inning. I was pretty jittered up and anxiously nervous getting warmed up in the bullpen, making sure I was ready.

I went in and threw the bottom of the ninth. I had a one-two-three inning. I struck out Marlon Byrd to end the game, so it was pretty fantastic. Texas had some pretty big names in their lineup back at the time, so being able to pitch in that game was pretty amazing.

Freddy Sandoval (Angels)

Freddy Sandoval made his major league debut on September 8, 2008, with the Los Angeles Angels of Anaheim. He played in two big league seasons. In 2008, Sandoval was named the Angels' Minor League Player of the Year.

In 2007, I had the opportunity to go to the Futures Game. That was the first time I realized I had a shot. Pretty much everyone who goes has a shot to get to the big leagues. Rich Thompson went with me to the Futures Game, and he got called up that year. I had a pretty good year in Double-A, but I didn't get close to being a call-up.

I go to winter ball, come back for spring training, look at the roster, and I'm like, "Man, it's gonna be difficult even to make the Triple-A team." The Angels were pretty stacked. I ended up making the Triple-A team. I was hitting ninth the first eight games of the season, without a position. I was playing DH, hitting ninth. We had seven guys in our starting lineup with big league experience. *Baseball America* did a story and said the 2008 Salt Lake Bees had the best start in the history of baseball. We started 21–1. It was insane showin' up to the ballpark and knowing you're gonna win.

I did pretty well my first eight games, and then I ended up hitting third the rest of the year. I was putting up pretty good numbers. However, I had experienced the year before what it was like to not get called up after you've put up good numbers. I knew I had to continue to be diligent about my work and continue to improve because of the type of team the Angels had in 2008.

September came, and a bunch of guys that already had big league service got called up. I didn't get called up. I wasn't upset. It was just like, "We have a phenomenal team in the big leagues." We went through the playoffs, and we lost to Sacramento at home.

I'm divorced now, but at that time my wife and I had planned that on our way back from Salt Lake City, we'd drive through L.A., watch a game, and then head back home to Arizona. We had a close friendship with Sean Rodriguez and his wife, Giselle. He was with the Angels.

When the season ended, in our minds, we thought, "Okay, we didn't get called up September 1. There's no way we're getting called up after." We had everything packed and figured we'd leave the next day, see an Angels game, visit with Sean, and then head back home. That was the original plan.

Bobby Mitchell, the manager, comes up and he grabs me. He's like, "Hey, Freddy, they need to talk to you in the office." The clubhouse is full of people, but everyone's dead silent at that moment. Everyone's like, "Hey, you're getting called up." I'm like, "Nah, it didn't happen before, it's not gonna happen right now."

I get called in, and Bobby started talking about how I had a great season. He's like, "I just called you into the office to let you know ahead of time that the voting was done, and you were named the organization's Minor League Player of the Year." I was like, "Oh, that's awesome." Bobby's like, "Well, have a great offseason. I know you're gonna continue to work and get better." I was like, "Yeah, thank you so much."

I open the door to leave, and as I'm pulling the door back, Bobby's like, "Hey, by the way, make sure you continue to do the same thing in Anaheim." I turned around, almost like I didn't hear him. I'm like, "What?" He's like, "Yeah, make sure you continue to have the same success in Anaheim when you head over there tomorrow."

I came out of the clubhouse and went to my wife. I said, "It was a great season. I just wanted to let you know I got named Minor League Player of the Year." She was excited.

I was like, "Are you ready to go because we're leaving tomorrow?" She's like, "Oh yeah, I'm so excited to see Sean and Giselle. I can't wait." Then I was like, "Oh yeah, but I won't be able to watch the game with you." She was completely thrown off and was like, "What do you mean?" I was like, "Well, we can't be watching the game together when I have to be in the dugout, you know?"

It took her a minute and then she was like, "Oh my gosh!" I don't even know if the feeling can be put into words. It was a dream come true.

We ended up driving to Anaheim the next day. I got there on September 7 and had to report to the stadium the next day, on September 8. I couldn't sleep the whole night. It was one of those times when you're trying to go to bed, and you can't. I slept very little.

At that time, I had really long hair. The next morning, I went to the mall and got a haircut. I wanted to be presentable. I also bought a suit. I was always that guy that would go to the stadium early, but I headed to the stadium around noon, super early. I drive in the parking lot and people are like, "Who are you?" I'm like, "I'm a player. I just got called up."

The walk from the players lot in Anaheim is super far. You park behind the rocks in center field. I'd never been there, so there was a security guard that escorted me from center field all the way through the tunnels to the clubhouse behind third base. It was a phenomenal feeling seeing my locker and my jersey with number 59. I sat on my chair and looked around the clubhouse at all the names like, "Wow. I'm here. I did it."

I knew that Mike Scioscia always did a phenomenal job trying to get guys in the game their first day. But the first thought that crossed my mind when I looked at the nine players on the lineup was, "Golly, I'm never gonna play. We have a ridiculous lineup. These guys are insanely good."

The game starts and gets blown open. Ron Roenicke, the bench coach, comes up to me and says, "Hey, grab a bat. You're gonna hit." I grab my helmet and go to the on-deck circle. I didn't feel any nerves. It was something I had wished for and lived so many times in my mind that when it happened, it was normal.

I got announced, went in, and took the first pitch. Then I took a hack on the second pitch. I hit a ball that I thought was gone. Bobby Abreu was in right field for the Yankees, and he caught the ball against the wall for the third out of the inning.

When I was walking near the third base line back to the dugout, that's when it hit me. The nerves came uncontrollably. I couldn't control my body from shaking. It was just such an amazing feeling. It didn't happen at all when I was on-deck or during the game. It happened afterwards. It was almost like since it happened already, I could get all the feelings and emotions out.

I go to drink some water. I grab a cup, and my hand is shaking. The water is hitting the sides of the cup and I'm getting wet. Maicer Izturis comes up to me and I'm like, "Man, I don't know what's goin' on." He's like, "Congratulations, man. You're here now."

After that, I talked to Maicer and everything kinda went back to normal, but it was funny how things happened afterwards.

Casper Wells (Tigers)

Casper Wells made his major league debut on May 15, 2010, with the Detroit Tigers. He played in four big league seasons.

I had a really good spring training, to the point where I thought I had a chance of making the team. I was a little disappointed when I didn't make the team, but some of those things are somewhat established, especially for the outliers on the bubble, barring injury. It would've been tough for me to go from Double-A to the big leagues, but I did hit well that spring training.

I ended up going to Toledo, and I didn't start out real hot. I know some of it was the disappointment from wanting to be in the big leagues. I let some of those emotions get the best of me and didn't allow myself to be present and make the most of the opportunities I had in front of me in Triple-A. Plus, I was facing tough guys. A lot of them were big league guys, just riding the cusp like me. It was a big jump from Double-A to Triple-A.

I saw one of my buddies, Brennan Boesch, get called up to the big leagues when Magglio Ordonez got hurt. I thought I might've been the one to go up, but I was very happy for my buddy, Brennan, and was with him, in my apartment in Toledo, when he got called up.

I remember we were in Durham, and I had started to get back into it. I had changed my approach a little bit, but unfortunately, I had struck out one of my last at-bats.

I get called into the office, and I'm thinking the worst. I'm thinking, "Great, I'm gonna get sent down to Double-A." Larry Parrish was our manager at the time. He called me in and said, "Well, we're gonna be flying back to Detroit tomorrow. We'll head back to Toledo, but you're just gonna stay there." I was like, "What?" He's like, "Yeah, you're gonna stay in Detroit." I say, "I don't know what that means." Then he's like, "You're going to the show, man." I was like, "Oh, wow! Great! I thought I was gonna get sent down to Double-A." He was laughing.

At the time, I know it wasn't 'cause of my performance. I was the outfielder on the 40-man that they needed to fill a spot.

I'm walking back to the hotel in Durham, and I call my dad. As soon as my dad answered the phone, he's reaming me out about a curveball in the dirt that I had swung at my last at-bat. He's like, "I don't know how you're swinging at that." He had been watching the video stream of the game on his computer.

I told him I was getting called up to the big leagues, and it was a good moment. We both got teary-eyed and cried, 'cause we knew this was something I had wanted my whole life. I kinda needed validation though. He's like, "Yeah, it's on the internet now." I still was kinda in shock. Once it was out on the internet, it seemed real.

I met the team in Detroit, and we were facing the red-hot Red Sox at Comerica Park. It was surreal. It was a nervous excitement, or nervous energy. You've got all these big-name guys there, and you're just trying to fit in as a rookie.

I wouldn't say it was tense, but Jim Leyland ran a tight ship. It wasn't a very loose clubhouse. It was kinda business. I get in there, and I'm just trying not to mess up because they're already in the rhythm of what they're doing. I knew Tom Brookens, the first base coach, really well. He was the outfield guy too, so he told me what to do, where to go, and what meetings I was supposed to be in. It was exciting.

Then we had a game that day against the Red Sox. I didn't get in. After the game's over, we're walking up the stairs to get back into the clubhouse. Jim Leyland's like, "You're starting tomorrow, so let your family know you're gonna be in there." I told my parents, but they didn't get a chance to make it out on such short notice.

I was facing Jon Lester, who at the time was probably having his best statistical start to a season, and the Red Sox were on fire. Needless to say, I didn't sleep at all that night. I remember I called my mom at four or five in the morning. I'm like, "Mom, I didn't sleep at all." She's like, "You've been doing this your whole life, so you're prepared for it. Just have fun and know you're meant to be there." My mom's always had that gentle side. My dad would just be like, "Toughen it up." But my mom would always bring me back down and make everything relative.

I got a piece of advice before I got called up. Jeff Larish was a player in Toledo with big league experience. When we were down in Durham, he said, "I'll give you a piece of advice. Make sure to take it all in your first game and really take hold of being there."

Well, when I went out to left field, I remember looking around and taking it all in. I'll tell you what, that made me about a hundred times more nervous. In the big leagues, you've got stands, then you've got stands on top of those stands, and then you've got more stands on top of those stands. And you've got stands in the outfield, where stands wouldn't be in the minor leagues. Looking around, I was like, "Oh man! I shouldn't have done that!"

It's funny, 'cause I used that same piece of advice at my wedding, when I was with my wife, and we were doing our vows. I said to look around and soak it all in. I still visually remember those images. You're often so hyper-focused in those moments that you forget to do those things.

I remember being on deck before my first at-bat and feeling a nervousness, but it was a good nervousness. It's not like, "I'm scared to do this." It's just a certain excitement, like an out-of-body experience. It's like you're anticipating things being different, but it's just another game of baseball, just at a different level.

You can see the ball so much better in the big leagues than you can in the minors because of the lights and the batter's eye. Everything was crystal clear. I remember seeing Jon Lester. I could see the seams better, and the cutter he was throwing. However, he struck me out looking twice in that game, and I was pinch-hit for at one point. But I did throw out Dustin Pedroia at the plate in that game.

I just wanted to get a hit so bad. I feel like a lot of minor leaguers that get called to the big leagues have that same thought, "I just wanna get a hit! I just wanna get a hit!" That's why it takes a lot of them so long to get a hit, 'cause that's their only thought as opposed to just getting a good pitch to hit and letting your ability take over.

There were so many emotions, and that hyper-awareness of trying to soak it all in. It was definitely an interesting experience.

Mike Belfiore (Orioles)

Mike Belfiore made his major league debut on September 27, 2013, with the Baltimore Orioles. He played in one big league season. Belfiore was called up multiple times before appearing in a single major league game.

The first time, I was in Syracuse, New York. It was late at night, I would say, like, 11:00 p.m., and my manager in Triple-A called me.

It was one of those surreal moments. I had a roommate at the time, on the road, and I was in complete shock. You don't believe it. You don't understand how this is even possible. How are you gonna sleep that night? I don't even know how I did go to sleep, after making all those phone calls to all the people that were so important to me. It was definitely emotional telling my parents. I feel like I went to bed at 2:00 a.m., and I had to be up at 3:00 a.m. for a flight to Minnesota.

I'll never forget, I had a college roommate who worked in Syracuse. He picked me up at 4:00 a.m. to drive me to the airport, so I got to share the moment with a buddy. That was quite the day, to say the least. It was Mother's Day. I rushed to the game at Target Field, which was awesome. It happened fast.

In spring training, being in big league camp, I was around the guys there all the time. It wasn't as if, "Oh, here's a new team and a new group of guys." It's great when you walk in, and everyone's congratulating you, like buddies I would talk [to] on a normal day basis. It was a welcoming feeling.

It was just a one-day thing. We had a guy coming off the DL the next day, so it was more of a safety thing, just in case the game got outta hand. They didn't wanna waste relievers. It was that type of situation. I got sent back down, without getting in, unfortunately.

I remember my velocity was the best it's ever been the next game I threw in Triple-A. I was obviously a little mad, but it's the process, and that's kinda how it works. People could look at it and go, "Oh, that sucks. That's the worst thing that can happen." The reality is I knew I was next in line, that my name was gonna be called. That gave me a little assurance that it could happen any day, and I'd get that opportunity yet again.

The next call-up was to join the team in Tampa Bay. I had people fly down, thinking, "All right, I'm not gonna get sent down the next day again." It was the same situation. Pedro Strop came off the DL the next day. The worst part was having friends and family come in and out. I got about 30 tickets, but it didn't happen. At least I got to fly back on the plane with the team, so I got to experience being a big leaguer. That was nice.

My third call-up was when I got into a game.

September call-ups happened and, in this case, our minor league season had ended. Zack Britton and I were sent down to Florida to continue throwing in case we were needed. We were doing our stuff and staying loose. Within a day or so, they gave us the call. They were actually in Tampa again.

The third call-up, I was like, "Okay. Enough of this jitters stuff. I'm ready to play in a game."

It took about two weeks for me to get into a game. They were still in playoff contention, so I was there for the same reason as in the past—just in case they didn't wanna waste a key bullpen guy. We were home at Camden for the rest of the season, and the Red Sox were in town. We were outta the playoffs by then, and the Red Sox, who went on to win the World Series, were getting geared up.

I feel like every game, for a series or two before that, I was getting ready and jacked up. I was ready to go. Then at the end of the year, I'm like, "All right. They're gonna put me in one time. I've gotta get ready for that."

It was funny, 'cause it all came full circle. I was a big Yankees fan growing up, and then I went to Boston College. I'm playing the Red Sox. Being a Northeast guy, it was surreal.

The moment was crazy. I saw it all evolving. I remember Dustin Pedroia being up. They said, "Get ready." I start throwing bullets as fast as I can. I didn't even realize who was on deck, but it was obviously David Ortiz. I just figured left on left is when I'm coming in.

I get the call to run outta the gate, and from there your adrenaline just completely takes over. Your heart's pumping. Running to the mound, you're saying, "Find a way to get out of it! Find a way to get out of this jam!"

I got deep in the count against Ortiz and gave up a homer in the first row, left center. Obviously, I gave up a homer, but I felt like I made a good pitch there too. He put a good swing on it. I give credit to him. In the moment, I was obviously mad. I thought, "This is the worst thing that could happen." Now, telling buddies and new friends, it's quite the story to tell.

I remember going into the locker room, and obviously I was mad at the time, but a lotta guys were reminding me, "You're officially in the record books as a big leaguer. Don't worry. Congratulations." It was weird. I didn't have a great outing, but everyone's coming up and shaking my hand. It was a surreal moment.

I remember going out with my family after. My parents were at every game I got called up for. It was kinda the same thing, like, "I can't believe it! You're a big league ballplayer!" That kinda talk.

It definitely took me a day or so to step back and realize what I accomplished. It's a dream that you dream about forever, and not many people get that opportunity.

A.J. Achter (Twins)

A.J. Achter made his major league debut on September 3, 2014, with the Minnesota Twins. He played in three big league seasons. Selected in the 46th round of the 2010 draft, he is one of the latest Twins picks to reach the majors.

I was playing for Rochester in Triple-A, and there were two series left—one at home and one on the road. Terry Ryan, the Twins' GM, was in town to see who was going to be a September call-up. I pitched well and kind of pitched my way into a potential call-up.

We're loading the bus to go to Pawtucket for the final three games, and I'm on the bus already. I get called back into the office from the bus by Gene Glynn, the manager. He tells me, "You're going to the big leagues." I about lose it. I break down. Then he says, "But you're not going until we're out of playoff contention. You can't tell anyone you're going."

I leave Gene's office, and obviously I'm very excited. I called my wife, who was my girlfriend at the time, and tell her, "I'm going to the big leagues, but don't know when." I couldn't tell anyone else because I come from a small community outside of Toledo that was very supportive of me as a player. I knew the second I told someone back home, it would spread like wildfire. I had to lay on pins and needles for a couple days.

I believe we lost the second-to-last day, so we were out of contention, and it was official I was going up. However, the other caveat was I had to pitch the final game of the regular season, knowing I was going to the big leagues, because I hadn't thrown in a while. I had to throw two innings. It was probably the most scared I've ever been to throw in my entire life, to not get hurt. Thankfully I had two clean innings, stayed healthy, and went to the big leagues the next day.

I have a seven-month-old daughter now, and her birth's by far the coolest thing I've been able to enjoy. Probably the second-coolest thing was being able to call my parents to tell them I was going to the big leagues. To think of all the time and effort they put in driving me around as a kid and following my professional career, it was pretty special.

There were six or seven of us that were going up. I was the only one that hadn't been up before. I wasn't even on the 40-man and had to be put on the roster. Not only didn't I have major league experience, but I also hadn't been to a big league spring training.

The team left us behind in Pawtucket that night. It was pretty cool to have that night to hang out with the guys and take a little deep breath before getting to experience the joy of a lifetime. A lot of that night was spent asking questions. Who should I talk to? Who shouldn't I talk to? A lot of the groundwork was laid for me to have success just because of those guys, which was nice.

We got to Minnesota on September 2, but I didn't pitch in that first game. The game on September 3 got out of hand. We were winning, 11–4, and I got called on to pitch the ninth inning. It was a cool experience. I got to face guys I had played that year in Triple-A, so I was kind of familiar with the guys I was facing, and I was throwing to my catcher, Josmil Pinto, who was in Triple-A with me that year.

It was a great first experience. It went one, two, three, which obviously was a great way to get your feet wet in the big leagues. Also being able to make my debut with my wife and parents in the stands was something pretty special.

People often ask who I faced first, and as I said, I faced three guys from Triple-A on the White Sox. However, in my second outing, the first batter I faced was Albert Pujols. The first outing was a great way to get my feet wet, and the second was, "Holy shit! Let's get ready!"

Chris Heston (Giants)

Chris Heston made his major league debut on September 13, 2014, with the San Francisco Giants. He played in four big league seasons. In 2015, he pitched a no-hitter with the Giants.

It was a cool situation. When I got called up in 2014, it was with four or five buddies, who were also getting called up for the first time, and I had come up through the minor leagues with. We all got to make our debuts at the same time.

The way it unfolded was we had the last game of the season and were playing Tacoma in Fresno. I had to start that day. I showed up, and they hadn't told us anything. As far as I knew, I'm waiting for my flight to Florida, to go home after the start.

I got to the field that day, I knew I had the start, and they called me in the office. Andy Skeels, Bobby Mariano, and Dwight Bernard sat me down. They told me the news that I was going to the big leagues after the game, with the kicker that I had to pitch in the game first.

It was a pretty good feeling going out there knowing if you just get through this one, you get to live out your dream of getting called up.

If I could just get through that game without an injury, I was going to the big leagues. As luck would have it, the second batter of the game hit a line drive off my arm. That was a little nail-biter, but I was fine and threw four or five innings. After the game, we had a flight for that day. We were meeting the team in Denver, Colorado.

So a bunch of buddies got to live out the dream of getting called up together. We all piled on a flight and got there. It's kinda funny 'cause when you get called up to the big leagues, they fly you first class, but we had so many people that were getting called up that day, not all of us could fly in first class.

Because I had just pitched, as soon as I got there, they said, "You're gonna be down for the next four days at least and then we'll start working you into the bullpen." So I knew there were four days I could just kinda soak it in, get acclimated the best I could, and then get ready to go. That was a blessing, just being able to get a feel for everything before I had to worry about facing hitters at that level.

We got lucky with the Giants. They were a bunch of good dudes. They all welcomed us with open arms like we had been there all year. It was an easy transition, knowing those guys were gonna be there to help you along the way, and they were truly excited for you to join them.

It was 10 days or so before I got in a game. We did that whole road trip, played against Arizona at home, and then I finally got in against the Dodgers. We were getting blown out, 17–0. I got to pitch the top of the ninth, which I think was another blessing. You're not getting thrown into the fire of a 2–1 ballgame and a serious situation. Being able to go out there and get your feet wet in a game that was already decided meant you really had nothing to lose.

But it was the most nervous I've ever been, hands down. You finally get that opportunity, and there's so many emotions going through your mind. Then you're pitching in front of a sold-out crowd. It was a dream come true, but you're just trying to breathe, trying not to pass out.

For me, I was just going out there, throwing every pitch as hard as I could, and hoping for the best. That's the way I attacked it. I just trusted that Guillermo Quiroz was gonna put down the right sign. I was able to get my first strikeout in that inning against Scott Van Slyke. But to be honest, I didn't have a feeling for where the ball was going. I was that nervous. I was just trusting what I'd done in the past would take over.

Deck McGuire (Reds)

Deck McGuire made his major league debut on September 12, 2017, with the Cincinnati Reds. He played in two big league seasons.

I would say my call-up experience was a microcosm of my entire career—kind of chaos.

We were in the Southern League playoffs, and they told us right before game one that there was gonna be co-champs that year, because the hurricane was about to hit Florida. We weren't gonna play a second round, so whoever won the north and south were gonna share the title. We had just beat Jacksonville, the Double-A team for the Marlins, in three games.

I had pitched the first game, and our pitching coach, Danny Darwin, had encouraged me, that just in case, I should keep working out and playing catch. He told me after the fact, "I had absolutely no idea it was gonna happen. I just didn't want you to shut it down and then all of a sudden, 'Hey, by the way, you're getting called up.'" I threw a bullpen on that Friday, just in case.

I had packed up my car, and I was driving home to Colorado. I got maybe 40 minutes outside of Pensacola when our manager, Pat Kelly, called me and told me I needed to turn around 'cause I was getting called up. I turned around, went back, met with our trainer, and got the whole situation figured out.

The Reds helped me out a ton. The team had an off-day on Monday, so they let me drive my car to Cincinnati so it would be out of the hurricane. Then I flew and met the team in St. Louis.

I got to St. Louis Sunday and just kind of hung out in the hotel. My wife and son flew in on that off-day, Monday. I went to the airport, picked them up, and got to hang out with them for the rest of the day. Then I showed up to the ballpark on Tuesday.

I got there roughly three hours before anybody else. Once I ate breakfast, I was like, "Okay, I'm ready to go." I Ubered to the park, unpacked my bags, and got everything squared away. Luckily, I had been with the Cardinals' organization the year before in big league camp. I had met the road clubbie of the Cardinals, so he took great care of me, made sure I knew where my locker was, and got me situated.

I pretty much sat at my locker for two hours, just kind of staring into the back of it and soaking in every moment that I could.

My first outing was that night. I'm warming up

One of Deck McGuire's uniforms from his call-up with the Cincinnati Reds (author's collection).

for the eighth. Well, baseball happens, and the game gets a little squirrelly. So I end up coming in with bases loaded and one out in the seventh.

It was kind of like a double-edged sword. Luckily, I had played with almost every guy that I pitched against the year before. That kind of relaxes you in a sense, seeing familiar faces. We were getting beat up a little bit, and it was raining. The crowd that started out the game at Busch Stadium had dwindled down to about 10,000. So it was kind of like pitching in a Triple-A game.

I just wanted to go out and throw strikes. I ended up getting the first guy I faced to ground into an inning-ending double play, which was probably the first ground ball double play I'd gotten in about three months. It's not really a thing I'm known for, ground balls, but I got an inning-ending double play.

I went back out for the eighth and had a little bit of an adventure. I got out of it and could take a breath from there.

Nick Kingham (Pirates)

Nick Kingham made his major league debut on April 29, 2018, with the Pittsburgh Pirates. During his debut, Kingham took a perfect game through six and two-thirds innings before allowing a hit. Entering the 2023 season, he is still playing professional baseball and has spent two years in the big leagues.

It took me a while. I was drafted in 2010, and I made my debut in 2018. It took me nine professional seasons.

I was a higher draft pick in the fourth round. I got to Triple-A young, when I was 22 years old. I was a top prospect within my organization. I knew I had a good shot to go up the ranks to the big leagues.

One Sunday afternoon, I threw a pitch and my elbow just popped. It didn't hurt at all. It just felt like when you pop your knuckles or your neck. Immediately after it happened, I thought it was the "Tommy John" ligament, but nothing ever hurt. I threw four or five more pitches. My velocity was down. I called the trainer out and said I felt a pop. He said, "Okay, you're getting out of here and we're getting you an MRI." I got one first thing in the morning, and it was completely torn.

Luckily, it didn't hurt at all, which was very surprising. For most people, it kind of like frays along. Mine went on one pitch.

I got hurt in May and got the surgery the last week of May. That was 2015, and I missed the rest of that year and basically all of 2016 as well. By the time I got back to full strength, and I was pitching games, the season ended.

It was poor timing, but I learned a lot. I learned a lot about my body. I learned a lot about the mental side and how to handle pressure and adversity, so it was not for nothing. It prepared me in ways that I couldn't have imagined if it hadn't happened.

Then in 2017, I missed about a month at the beginning of the season. I don't know what happened. I kicked off and my ankle popped. I didn't roll it or anything. It was just a little ligament or something that popped in my ankle, and I couldn't walk for about five days. I missed five or six weeks. So I got off to the slow start and didn't get called up that year. That made me determined, going into that off-season, to put in extra work, heal up, and get as strong as I could. It worked out for the best when I got the call near the end of April in 2018.

I was at the field when I got the news. The manager called me into the office, and he said something like, "You're the leader of this team and you're not doing a good job with manning the clubhouse and everything." I was kind of confused. He said, "You know what? I think we're gonna suspend you a game. You're not gonna pitch on Saturday." This is on a Wednesday, and I'm so confused. I don't understand, and I'm kind of pissed off. Then he goes, "You're not gonna be pitching because you're gonna be pitching against St. Louis on Sunday. You're going to the big leagues." That's when it hit me. Finally, all this hard work had paid off. He got me pretty good on the practical joke. I didn't see it coming.

It was Wednesday and I was pitching on Sunday, so I had plenty of time to get family and friends there. I called my parents immediately, and my dad was the first one I talk to. He's been my biggest inspiration. He taught me how to play the game, and he's the reason I play. Then I called my mom, then my brother, then my fiancé. Luckily, everybody made it to the game. I had some friends that made it too.

I fly to meet up with the team on Friday night. I go to the field and play catch, but I can't be in the dugout because I'm not active yet. I go back to the hotel and watch the game on TV. Then on Saturday, I go to the field and go through a normal pre-game routine, but once again I go back to the hotel because I can't be at the field yet for the game.

I didn't get much sleep, but at the same time, I knew I was more prepared than I ever could have been, physically and mentally. I was just anxious and ready to get going. Then it's Sunday, the day of the game. My family and I go out for breakfast, we walk across the bridge, take pictures, and everything.

I show up around 11 o'clock for a one o'clock game. Apparently, that was a little late. Some guys were saying they thought I got scared and wasn't gonna show up. I figured two hours was plenty early.

I get to the field. I get going and it's freezing. Also not many people were in the stands because the Pittsburgh Penguins were in the playoffs and playing at home. I'm warming up and playing catch in a beanie and a heavy jacket because it's so cold. I wanted to stay warm as long as I could. Everybody's looking at me like I'm crazy.

I go out for the first inning. I threw the first pitch for a strike and felt relieved a little bit. As soon as I got the first batter out, Matt Carpenter flew out to center field, it eased the rest of my tension. I ended up going one-two-three that inning. I go back to the dugout everybody said, "Good job!"

I go back out for the second, one-two-three. I go back out for the third, again, one-two-three. Then after one-two-three in the fourth inning, I come back and sit down in the dugout. That's when it hit me like, "I don't think I've let a base runner on yet. I'm perfect through four. That's kind of neat."

In the back of [my] mind, I know when people have really good debuts, perfect games, or no-hitters going, people get updates on their phones from MLB. I'm wondering if anybody's getting updates about my debut. That's what I'm thinking in the dugout. I go out for the fifth, and I come back in. I'm like, "Oh, man, they should probably get an update now about it."

Nobody's talking to me at this time. Nobody's coming up to me because I have a perfect game for five innings.

I go out for the sixth, come back in, and I'm still perfect. I wasn't thinking too much about it, but I'd never heard of anybody in their debut going perfect that long. I know people are getting updates now.

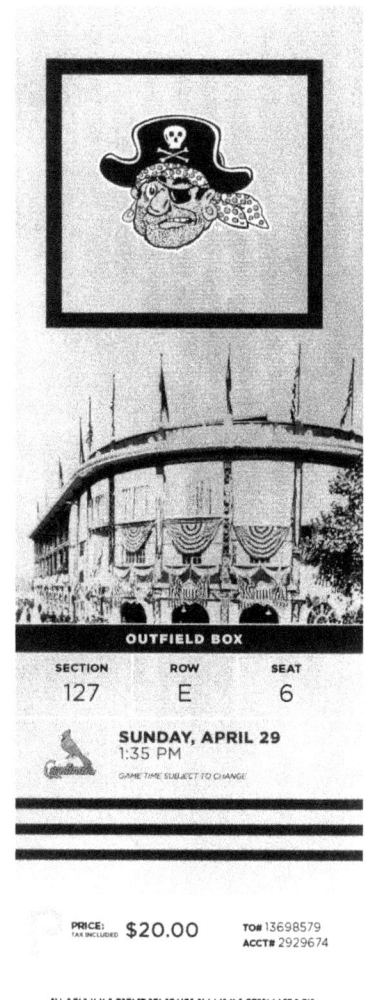

Ticket stub from Nick Kingham's major league debut with the Pittsburgh Pirates. He took a perfect game through 6⅔ innings before allowing a single (author's collection).

Then I go out for the seventh inning. I get the first two guys out and have a 2–2 count against Paul DeJong. I throw a slider, which I had nine strikeouts with that day. It hung a little bit, and he hit it down the line, past the third baseman, for a single. That was the end of the perfect bid, but I ended up getting Marcell Ozuna out, who was the next batter.

I got a standing ovation by the 43 people in the stands. Everybody was cheering me on and waiting for me at the top step of the dugout. It was awesome and everything I could imagine.

I'm done pitching and watch the next half-inning when the team hits. Then I end up going inside to do my arm care, ice, and strengthening stuff. I check my phone, and I have 200 text messages. I have MLB updates. I've got people on social media contacting me, tweeting at me, and stuff. That's when it hit me that it was a bigger deal than I thought.

The next day, I'm getting calls from MLB network, doing radio shows, and everything.

It was a really cool, special experience.

Patrick Wisdom (Cardinals)

Patrick Wisdom made his major league debut August 12, 2018, with the St. Louis Cardinals. In 2021, Wisdom broke the Chicago Cubs' rookie home run record and finished fourth in National League Rookie of the Year voting. Entering the 2023 season, he is still playing professional baseball and has spent five years in the big leagues.

I was in Triple-A, playing for Memphis, and we were in Oklahoma City. Our game went to extra innings, and I got hit by a pitch on my shin. After the game, I threw a little ice pack on it.

Our skipper at the time was Stubby Clapp, and we had a great relationship. He's like, "Hey, Wiz, come to my office real quick. I just wanna run some things by you." I was like, "Okay." I wasn't thinking anything of it. I didn't look at how the big league team had done, or if anyone was hurt, so I had no inclination of what was going on. I walked in there, and he closed the door. That was the telltale sign to the whole clubhouse that something's going to happen, but being oblivious, I didn't think anything of it.

I'm sitting there and he's like, "How's your leg?" I'm like, "It's fine." He asks, "Well, why do you have ice on it?" I say, "Just precaution. I'm fine. I'm good to go." He's like, "You don't need a day off or anything?" I'm like, "No, I'm good." He says, "You sure? I could give you the day off." I'm like, "No, no, no. I'm good."

He was kinda beating around the bush and he's like, "Well, how about I give you the day off tomorrow?" I'm like, "Nah, I'm good. Seriously, I'm good to play." He says, "Well, you're gonna need a day off 'cause you're gonna be flying to Kansas City." I'm like, "What?" He says, "You're going to the big leagues." I didn't know what to say. I was speechless 'cause it caught me off-guard. The pitching coach was in there too, and he had filmed the entire thing. I was so oblivious to him having his phone out, I didn't even notice. It caught me by surprise, and I kept asking him, "You sure?" He said, "Congrats." I said my thank you's, and I was just bewildered.

I open the door, which opened to the clubhouse, and the whole team is standing there. They're dumping water on me, cheering loud, and there were hugs all around.

I didn't know what to do. Thankfully, I had other guys on the team that had been up and down and they're like, "All right, this is what you need to do. You need to call your wife and your family." All that stuff. My wife didn't answer my first calls, and then my parents didn't answer either. I was like, "This has got to be some kind of joke. No one's answering their phones." They finally got back to me before I left the clubhouse. They called me back, and they're like, "Is everything okay? What's going on?" I told them the whole spiel, and they were super-excited with tears of joy.

I didn't get any sleep that night since our game went long. I didn't find out 'til probably 11:30 at night, and then my flight was at 5 in the morning. I just packed my stuff. The word got out, and my phone was blowing up, so I was trying to get back to as many people as I could. Then I flew out to Kansas City.

My family flew out too. My wife, who's a rock star, drove from Memphis to Kansas City. She packed the car with as much as she could and hauled up to Kansas City to meet me.

Everything was topnotch. I was in constant contact with the clubhouse guys, and they coordinated everything. When I got there, they helped me with where to go and leading me to the clubhouse. I knew everyone in the clubhouse from playing with the organization the last six years, so I was familiar with everyone in there.

Probably the coolest part was opening those double doors and seeing everyone. When they saw me, everyone's like, "What?!" That was really special. They came over and gave me hugs and congrats. Everyone was super excited, but everyone was working and getting ready for the game. I didn't want to distract them, so I said hi and everything and went to the skipper's office. I know Mike Shildt really well, so he was pumped to see me. Then I just jumped into my routine and figured things out on the fly.

I didn't play that night game but played the day game the next day. I crossed a lot off the list. I got a couple base hits, an RBI, a run scored, and I had my first error.

For my first at-bat, I faced Jakob Junis, who I faced in [the] minors before. I'd always said, "I'm swinging on the first pitch. No matter where it is, I'm swinging when I get to big leagues." I fouled it back, and I was like, "All right, here we go." Then he threw me a slider, and I hit it right off the end of the bat. It got past him, and I got a nice little base hit. A swinging bunt.

Probably the funniest thing was that error. I'm playing first and I'm comfortable over there, but it's my debut. Tons of guys are saying congrats from the other team and you just feel like the spotlight's on you. The first ball hit to me, "Boom!" I clank it right off my chest and it's an error. I'm like, "Oh great! What a way to start your big league career, a freakin' ball right off the chest." Then of course, the way it works out, he comes around and scores. I'm like, "Oh great! My error led to a run. That's just what I needed on my first day." But it's a long game, and I shook it off.

I was able to come up clutch and tie the game with a bases-loaded hit, so I kind of redeemed myself. I was more nervous and excited after that bases-loaded hit than I was my first hit. I was over there at first base, shaking in my boots with excitement.

It was cool seeing the excitement from everybody when I got my first hit and coming up clutch for the team later. It was a very special day. To have my family, my wife, and everyone around me, was really cool.

Index

Abreu, Bobby 201
Achter, A.J. 205–7
Acker, Jim 46
Acre, Mark 100–3, 114
Adams, Mike 196
Aldridge, Cory 151–4
Alfonso, Carlos 166
Allen, Dick 8, 25, 28
Alomar, Roberto 140
Alou, Felipe 147
Alvarez, Jose 43–7
Alvarez, Juan 139–41
Alvis, Max 6
Amalfitano, Joey 17
American Association 25–6, 82
American Family Field 129–31
Anaheim Angels/California Angels/ Los Angeles Angels of Anaheim 14–16, 27–8, 42, 60, 142; Aldridge, Cory 151–4, Alvarez, Juan 139–41; Grahe, Joe 71–3; Machemer, Dave 34–7; Sandoval, Freddy 198–201
Anaheim Stadium 72
Andersen, Larry 98
Anderson, Garret 104
Anderson, Sparky 8, 20
Arizona Fall League 163, 184
Arroyo, Bronson 197
Ashby, Andy 99
Aspromonte, Ken 20, 26, 27
Astrodome 56
Atlanta Braves 88; Aldridge, Cory 151–4; Alvarez, Jose 43–7
Atlanta-Fulton County Stadium 44, 47
Ausmus, Brad 99, 174
Avery, Steve 88, 117

Baerga, Carlos 84
Baker, Dusty 109, 130, 156, 157
Baldwin, James 150

Baltimore Orioles 26, 43; Belfiore, Mike 203–5; Grich, Bobby 14–16
Bando, Chris 100
Bando, Sal 11
Bank One Ballpark 149
Banks, Ernie 17
Banks, Josh 196
Barberie, Bret 96
Barrios, Francisco 32
Bavasi, Bill 140
Baylor, Don 14, 144
Beane, Billy 149–50
Beauchamp, Jim 45–7
Bedrosian, Steve 44
Belanger, Mark 27
Belfiore, Mike 203–5
Bell, Jay 66, 110, 139
Belle, Albert 83, 84
Bench, Johnny 8–9
Bergmann, Jason 176–9
Bernard, Dwight 207
Bevacqua, Kurt 19–21
Bevington, Terry 61
Blackaby, Ethan 23
Blauser, Jeff 71
Bloomquist, Willie 186
Blue, Vida 57
Blum, Geoff 120
Blyleven, Bert 72, 73
Bochy, Bruce 97, 158, 189–90
Bodie, Keith 76, 84
Boesch, Brennan 201
Boggs, Wade 135
Bohanon, Brian 83
Bolton, Tom 78
Bombard, Marc 91
Bombard, Rich 134–5
Bonds, Barry 66, 108, 130
Bonifay, Cam 105
Bonilla, Bobby 49, 66
Boone, Bret 84–6

217

Booty, Josh 116–18
Bordick, Mike 115
Borland, Toby 98
Boston Braves 3
Boston Red Sox 3; Gubanich, Creighton 133–5; Hansen, Craig 179–80; Van Every, Jonathan 190–2
Bourjos, Chris 41–2
Bowling, Steve 32
Bradshaw, Kevin 79
Brett, George 42, 51, 102
Brett, Ken 32
Brickhouse, Jack 37
Bridges, Rocky 41
Briggs, John 7–8
Briscoe, John 74–5
Bristol Red Sox 29
Britton, Zack 204
Brocail, Doug 170
Brock, Lou 19
Brock, Tarrik 143–5
Brogna, Rico 119, 122
Brookens, Tom 202
Brosius, Scott 115
Brower, Bobby 82
Brown, Darren 184, 197
Brown, Jackie 159
Brown, Kevin 111, 112
Brumfield, Jacob 110
Brunansky, Tom 69
Bulls, Durham 158–9
Burke, Joe 33
Busch Stadium 69, 210
Bush, Randy 78
Bush Stadium 91
Butler, Brett 63
Byrd, Marlon 198

Cabrera, Daniel 192
Caldwell, Mike 125
Calgary Cannons 58, 86
California Angels/Anaheim Angels/Los Angeles Angels of Anaheim 14–16, 27–8, 42, 60, 142; Aldridge, Cory 151–4, Alvarez, Juan 139–41; Grahe, Joe 71–3; Machemer, Dave 34–7; Sandoval, Freddy 198–201
California League 8
Camden Yards 191, 205
Campanis, Jim, Jr. 76, 86
Campbell, Mike 58–60
Candlestick Park 3, 24, 63, 110, 130
Canseco, Jose 73, 81–2
Cardenal, Jose 31
Carew, Rod 22, 145

Carlton, Steve 30–1
Carolina League 9
Carpenter, Matt 212
Carr, Chuck 96
Carter, Andy 97–9
Carter, Joe 126
Carty, Rico 26
Casey, Sean 192
Castilla, Vinny 148
Castro, Billy 123
Chaney, Darrel 20
Charlton, Norm 70
Chavez, Eric 159
Chicago Cubs 63, 137, 175; Brock, Tarrik 143–5; Greenberg, Adam 171–6; King, Ray 135–7; Plummer, Bill 8–9; Skidmore, Roe 16–19; Trachsel, Steve 94–6; Walbeck, Matt 87–8
Chicago White Sox 7, 32, 76; Howry, Bob 131–2; Kittle, Ron 48–9; Kucek, Jack 24–5; Nyman, Nyls 27–8; Schaefer, Jeff 60–2; Stewart, Josh 163–5
Chulk, Vinnie 167–8
Cincinnati Reds 7, 20, 90–2; Gross, Kip 69–71; McGuire, Deck 208–10; Spradlin, Jerry 90–2
Cirillo, Jeff 99–100
Clapp, Stubby 213
Clark, Will 3, 57, 64, 117
Claus, Todd 179
Clayton, Royce 108
Clear, Bob 36
Clemens, Roger 100, 115, 124–7
Clement, Matt 163
Cleveland Indians: Bevacqua, Kurt 19–21; Kern, Jim 25–6; McDowell, Sam 5–7
Cline, Ty 20
Coggins, Rich 27
Colbert, Craig 157
Coleman, Vince 69, 103
Collins, Terry 140, 141
Colorado Rockies 92, 164; Lee, David 137–9; McClellan, Zach 181–3; Newman, Josh 186–8
Columbus Clippers 112
Combs, Pat 65–7
Comerica Park 202
Comiskey Park 27, 48
Concepción, Dave 20
Conine, Jeff 96
Connie Mack Stadium 8
Connors, Billy 42
Coomer, Ron 132

Coors Field 138-9, 183
Cordova, Francisco 129
Cordova, Marty 103-4
Cox, Bobby 43, 45, 47, 136
Cox, Casey 15
Cox, Jeff 146
Craig, Roger 63, 65
Culver, George 65
Cumberland, John 90

D'Acquisto, John 22-4
Dalrymple, Clay 14
Damon, Johnny 184
Dark, Alvin 20
Darling, Ron 101-2
Darwin, Danny 208-9
Davis, Chili 57
Davis, Doug 151
Davis, Eric 157
Davis, Red 26
Decatur Commodores 17
DeHart, Rick 119-22
DeJong, Paul 213
Delgado, Carlos 126, 167
De Los Santos, Valerio 172
Denehy, Bill 7-8
Dent, Bucky 25
Deshaies, Jim 56
Destrade, Orestes 96
Detroit Tigers 58, 82, 165; Knudsen, Kurt 78-80; Wells, Casper 201-3
Dewey, Mark 110
Dickerson, Bobby 171
Dickey, R.A. 175
Dillard, Tim 192-5
Dorfman, Harvey 74
Dravecky, Dave 45
Dressendorfer, Kirk 75
Duncan, Dave 128
Duncan, Mariano 98, 99
Dunegan, Jim 17
Dunn, Adam 185
Dunne, Mike 55
Dunston, Shawon 64, 157
Duquette, Dan 134
Durocher, Leo 8, 18

Earley, Bill 94
Eckersley, Dennis 102, 127
Edmonton Trappers 114
Eisenreich, Jim 105
Eldred, Cal 123
Epstein, Mike 14
Erickson, Scott 104
Ermer, Cal 31

Essegian, Chuck 6
Estes, Shawn 106-10
Estrella, Luis 165-6
Evans, Bobby 108
Evers, Bill 158-9

Falcone, Pete 39
Fasano, Sal 150
Ferraro, Mike 14
Fielder, Cecil 51
Filer, Tom 167
Fisher, Jack 7
Fisk, Carlton 62
Fitzsimmons, Freddie 6
Flannery, Tim 50
Florida Marlins/Miami Marlins 95, 111; Booty, Josh 116-18; Greenberg, Adam 171-6; Millar, Kevin 128-9
Florida State League 176
Foley, Marv 94
Foli, Tim 38, 176
Forbes Field 41
Forster, Scott 146-7
Forster, Terry 25
Fox, Charlie 23
Fox, Eric 80-2, 101
Francisco, Frankie 170
Francona, Terry 179
Franklin, Micah 118-19
Freed, Roger 14
Fregosi, Jim 55, 99
Frey, Jim 42
Frost, Dave 35
Frye, Jeff 82-4
Fryman, Travis 124

Galarraga, Andres 166
Gallagher, Dave 61
Garcia, Carlos 111
Garciaparra, Nomar 181
Garr, Ralph 24
Gayle 108
Geivett, Bill 182, 186
Geren, Bob 148, 150
Giambi, Jason 115, 168, 184
Gibson, Kirk 59
Gideon, Brett 69
Gilkey, Bernard 113
Gillick, Pat 31
Gilson, Hal 8
Gladden, Dan 57
Glavine, Tom 47, 117, 136
Glynn, Gene 206
Gonzalez, Luis 139
Gossage, Goose 25

Grace, Mark 136
Graham, Bruce 62
Graham, Moonlight 174
Grahe, Joe 71–3
Green, Dallas 29–30, 113
Greenberg, Adam 171–6
Grich, Bobby 14–16, 35, 36
Griffey, Ken, Jr. 184–6
Griffin, Mike 91
Grimes, Bob 136
Grimsley, Ross 76
Groat, Dick 8
Gross, Kip 69–71
Grudzielanek, Mark 122
Gubanich, Creighton 133–5
Guerrero, Vladimir 121, 153
Gullickson, Bill 79
Gwynn, Tony 93, 97, 99

Haddix, Harvey 40
Hale, Chip 77
Hall, Bill 194–5
Halladay, Roy 167
Hamilton, Darryl 145
Hamilton, Josh 185
Hammaker, Atlee 42–3, 45
Hammond, Chris 96
Hansen, Craig 179–80
Hardtke, Jason 112–13
Harper, Tommy 22
Harrah, Toby 83
Harrelson, Ken 20
Hart, Mike 155
Hatteberg, Scott 133, 134
Hausman, Tom 39
Hawkins, LaTroy 183, 187
Hearn, Ed 53–4
Heathcott, Mike 132
Helms, Tommy 20
Helton, Todd 164, 182
Henderson, Dave 73, 81–2
Henderson, Rickey 72, 73, 82, 103
Heredia, Felix 136
Hermansen, Chad 141–2
Hernandez, Chuck 71
Hernandez, Keith 54
Hernandez, Ramon 150
Herrmann, Ed 25
Hershiser, Orel 130, 169
Herzog, Whitey 34, 55–6
Heston, Chris 207–8
Higginson, Bobby 124, 165
Hill, Glenallen 136
Hines, Larry 88
Hitchcock, Sterling 141

Hodges, Gil 7–8
Holbert, Ray 96–7
Hollins, Dave 98
Holm, Steve 188–90
Holman, Brad 184
Horner, Bob 44
Hosley, Tim 31
House, Tom 45
Houston Astros 143
Howe, Art 115, 150
Howry, Bob 131–2
Hrbek, Kent 89
Hriniak, Walt 61
Hughes, Travis 169
Huizenga, Wayne 117
Hundley, Todd 113
Hurdle, Clint 42, 183
Hurricane Katrina 176

Iannetta, Chris 188
International League 82
Iowa Cubs 91, 95, 176
Iowa Oaks 27
Izturis, Maicer 201

Jack Murphy Stadium 90, 92
Jackson, Danny 97
Jackson, Reggie 145
Jaha, John 129
Jenkins, Geoff 129–31
Jeter, Derek 167–8
Jewett, Trent 141
Jimenez, Jason 158–9
Joe Robbie Stadium 111, 118
Johnson, Deron 35
Johnson, Lance 113
Johnson, Nick 150–1
Johnson, Ron 190
Jones, Andruw 136
Jones, Bobby 139
Jones, Chipper 136, 137
Jones, Doug 125
Jones, Gary 114, 134–5, 196
Jordan, Brian 153
Junis, Jakob 215

Kahmann, Jim 77
Kaiser, Ken 75
Kansas City Royals 102, 142;
    Hammaker, Atlee 42–3; McGilberry,
    Randy 32–4
Kauffman Stadium 102
Kelly, Pat 121, 209
Kelly, Tom 78, 87, 103
Kendall, Jason 110–12, 194–5

Index

Kern, Jim 25–6
Kile, Darryl 139
Killebrew, Harmon 22
Kingham, Nick 210–13
King, Ray 135–7
Kittle, Ron 48–9
Kniffin, Chuck 182
Knowles, Darold 66
Knudsen, Kurt 78–80
Koch, Billy 165
Koosman, Jerry 7
Kremblas, Frank 192
Kreuter, Chad 82
Kucek, Jack 24–5

Laird, Gerald 169
Lake, Steve 88
Lansford, Carney 139–41
Larkin, Barry 70, 71
LaRussa, Tony 74, 82, 102, 128
Las Vegas Stars 57, 92
Lasorda, Tommy 50
Lau, Charley 49
Law, Vance 38–41
Lawrence, Jim 6
Leach, Jalal 154–7
Lee, David 137–9
Lefebvre, Jim 88, 95
Lembo, Rick 155
Lemke, Mark 113
Lerch, Randy 28–31
Lester, Jon 202–3
Letendre, Mark 64
Leyland, Jim 105, 110, 129, 138, 139, 202
Lieppman, Keith 81
Lillis, Bob 64
Liston, Matt 174
Littell, Mark 34, 122
Little, Grady 135, 181
Litton, Greg 62–5
Lockman, Whitey 17, 18
Lo Duca, Paul 173
Loe, Kameron 170–1
Loiselle, Rich 129
Lombardo, John 169
Lomon, Kevin 118
Loney, James 181
Lopez, Jose 169
Los Angeles Angels of Anaheim/Anaheim Angels/California Angels 14–16, 27–8, 42, 60, 142; Aldridge, Cory 151–4, Alvarez, Juan 139–41; Grahe, Joe 71–3; Machemer, Dave 34–7; Sandoval, Freddy 198–201

Los Angeles Dodgers: Loney, James 181
Loviglio, Jay 138
Lowe, Derek 135
Lowe, Sean 127–8
Luebber, Steve 21–2
Lund, Gordy 48

Machemer, Dave 34–7
Mack, Gary 107
Mack, Shane 103
Mackanin, Pete 70
Macko, Joe 83
MacPhail, Andy 78
Maddon, Joe 141
Maddux, Greg 63, 113, 117
Madlock, Bill 59
Mahler, Rick 44
Malave, Omar 167
Manuel, Jerry 164
Manwaring, Kirt 108, 109
Mariano, Bob 122
Mariano, Bobby 207
Marichal, Juan 24
Marte, Damaso 165
Martin, J.C. 18
Martinez, Edgar 169–71
Martinez, Pedro 121
Martinez, Tino 151
Mateo, Julio 185
Mathews, Greg 54–6
Mathews, Rick 187
Matsui, Hideki 168, 184
May, Lee 20
Mays, Willie 8, 41
Mazzone, Leo 136
McCarty, Dave 89
McCarver, Tim 13
McClellan, Zach 181–3
McCovey, Willie 8, 41
McDowell, Sam 5–7
McGee, Willie 55, 69, 118, 119
McGilberry, Randy 32–4
McGriff, Fred 161
McGuire, Deck 208–10
McGwire, Mark 115–16
McKechnie Field 105
McKeon, Jack 49
McLain, Denny 11
McLaughlin, Bo 121
McMahon, Don 24
McNamara, John 36
McRae, Hal 42
McReynolds, Kevin 57
Mecir, Jim 105–6

Memorial Stadium 15
Mercker, Kent 89
Mesa, Jose 87
Miami Marlins/Florida Marlins; 95, 111; Booty, Josh 116–18; Greenberg, Adam 171–6; Millar, Kevin 128–9
Midwest League 17
Millar, Kevin 128–9, 180, 192
Miller, Damien 149
Milwaukee Brewers 68, 113; Cirillo, Jeff 99–100; Dillard, Tim 192–5; Jenkins, Geoff 129–31; Misuraca, Mike 122–4; Rushford, Jim 160–3; Woodard, Steve 124–7
Mingori, Steve 34
Minnesota Twins 6; Achter, A.J. 205–7; Cordova, Marty 103–4; Luebber, Steve 21–2; McCarty, Dave 89; Reboulet, Jeff 77–8; Trombley, Mike 86–7
Minton, Greg 44
Misuraca, Mike 122–4, 123
Mitchell, Bobby 199
Mitchell, Kevin 64, 90
Molina, Bengie 188
Molitor, Paul 52, 53
Montreal Expos 13, 143; DeHart, Rick 119–22; Forster, Scott 146–7; Sampen, Bill 68–9
Moorad, Jeff 117
Morales, Kendrys 154
Morgan, Joe 44
Morris, Hal 90
Morris, Jack 59
Mulder, Mark 150
Municipal Stadium 87
Munoz, Mike 80
Munson, Thurman 61, 62
Murphy, Dale 44, 71
Murphy, Mike 156, 189
Murton, Matt 171

Nashville Sounds 192
Neel, Troy 81
Nelson, Jeff 75–7
Nen, Robb 166
Nettles, Graig 21
Newman, Josh 182, 186–8
New Orleans Zephyrs 176
New York Mets 12, 18, 68; Denehy, Bill 7–8; Hardtke, Jason 112–13; Hearn, Ed 53–4
New York Yankees 42, 43, 58, 99, 112, 195; Johnson, Nick 150–1; Tewksbury, Bob 51–3
Niekro, Lance 165–6
Niekro, Phil 44–5, 47
Nixon, Otis 126
Nixon, Russ 90, 96
Norfolk Tide 112
Nyman, Nyls 27–8

Oakland Athletics 159; Acre, Mark 100–3; Briscoe, John 74–5; Fox, Eric 80–2; Ortiz, Jose 147–9; Spiezio, Scott 114–16; Tenace, Gene 9–11; Wilson, Tom 149–50
O'Brien, Charlie 147
O'Dowd, Dan 186
Ogea, Chad 115
Oliva, Tony 22
Olivares, Max 72
Oliver, Joe 71, 91
Olivo, Miguel 165
Ordonez, Magglio 150, 201
Ortiz, David 205
Ortiz, Jose 147–9
Ortiz, Junior 87
Otis, Amos 42
Ottawa Lynx 146
Ozark, Danny 31
Ozuna, Marcell 213

Pacific Coast League 17, 34, 48, 58–60, 82, 114, 148, 176, 186
Palmeiro, Rafael 151
Parker, Dave 75
Parrett, Jeff 67
Parrish, Larry 201–2
Parsons, Casey 101
Patek, Freddie 33
Peale, Norman Vincent 51
Pedroia, Dustin 203, 205
Pena, Tony 78
Pendleton, Terry 69
Perez, Tony 20
Perlozzo, Sam 54
Perry, Gaylord 44
Perry, Jim 21–2
Peterson, Fritz 26
Philadelphia Phillies 13, 121; Carter, Andy 97–9; Combs, Pat 65–7; Lerch, Randy 28–31
Phillips, Steve 112
Phoenix Giants 22–3
Piazza, Mike 145
Piniella, Lou 51–2, 69, 71, 86, 106
Pinto, Josmil 207
Pipp, Wally 36
Pitts, Gaylen 118
Pittsburgh Pirates 49, 66; Hermansen,

Index

Chad 141–2; Kendall, Jason 110–12; Kingham, Nick 210–13; Law, Vance 38–41; Wilson, Gary 104–5
Plummer, Bill 8–9, 58
Plunk, Eric 62
Powell, Larry 3–4
Puckett, Kirby 87, 89
Pujols, Albert 207
Pulli, Frank 112

Quade, Mike 98
Quaid, Dennis 44
Quick, Jim 99
Quinn, Bob 25
Quiroz, Guillermo 208

Ramirez, Hanley 179–80
Ramirez, Manny 115, 117
Rapp, Vern 20
Reading Phillies 29
Ready, Randy 98, 196
Reagins, Tony 154
Reboulet, Jeff 77–8
Rettenmund, Merv 35
Reuschel, Rick 64
Reuss, Jerry 11–14, 19
Reyes, Alberto 179
Reynolds, Harold 85
Rhodes, Arthur 85
Richert, Pete 16
Rigney, Bill 22
Ripken, Billy 60
Ripken, Cal 60
Ripken, Cal, Sr. 14
Ritter, Lawrence 3
Ritz Carlton 101
Roberts, Bip 49–50
Robinson, Frank 16, 178
Rodriguez, Alex 151
Rodriguez, Henry 147
Rodriguez, Rich 145
Rodriguez, Sean 199
Roenicke, Ron 200
Romero, Mandy 133
Rose, Pete 7
Row, Macho 98
Rowland-Smith, Ryan 184–6
Royster, Jerry 44, 50, 181
Runge, Paul 152
Runnells, Tom 182
Rushford, Jim 160–3
Ryan, Nolan 36, 45, 56, 83
Ryan, Rosy 22–3
Ryan, Terry 206

Sabean, Brian 189
Sadler, Donnie 134
St. Claire, Randy 146
St. Louis Cardinals 18–19; Franklin, Micah 118–19; Lowe, Sean 127–8; Mathews, Greg 54–6; Reuss, Jerry 11–14; Wisdom, Patrick 213–15
Salt Lake Bees 199
Sampen, Bill 68–9
Samson, David 174–5
Sandberg, Ryne 88
Sanders, Dave 164, 165
Sanders, Deion 108
Sanders, Reggie 141–2
Sanders, Scott 92–4
San Diego Padres 19–21; Holbert, Ray 96–7; Roberts, Bip 49–50; Sanders, Scott 92–4; Shibilo, Andy 157–8; Vosberg, Ed 56–7; Wells, Jared 196–7; Worrell, Tim 89–90
Sandoval, Freddy 198–201
San Francisco Giants 130; Bourjos, Chris 41–2; D'Acquisto, John 22–4; Estes, Shawn 106–10; Heston, Chris 207–8; Holm, Steve 188–90; Leach, Jalal 154–7; Litton, Greg 62–5; Niekro, Lance 165–6
Sanguillen, Manny 40–1
Santiago, Benito 57, 136–7
Santo, Ron 28
Sax, Steve 76
Schaefer, Jeff 60–2
Schilling, Curt 98, 122, 157, 180
Schoendienst, Red 13
Schooler, Mike 76
Schuerholz, John 42
Scioscia, Mike 200
Scott, Donnie 70
Scully, Vin 54
Scurry, Rod 53
Seattle Mariners 34, 170; Boone, Bret 84–6; Campbell, Mike 58–60; Mecir, Jim 105–6; Nelson, Jeff 75–7; Rowland-Smith, Ryan 184–6; Thomas, Justin 197–8
Seaver, Tom 7, 100
Seminara, Frank 90
Sexton, Chris 134
Shea Stadium 54
Shibilo, Andy 157–8
Shildt, Mike 214
Shopay, Tommy 14
Showalter, Buck 149
Simmons, Ted 13
Skeels, Andy 207

Skidmore, Roe 16–19
Skurla, John 62
Smith, Lee 121
Smith, Ozzie 55, 69
Smith, Randy 92
Smith, Steve 105
Smith, Willie 18
Smoltz, John 46–7, 117, 136, 181
Snitker, Brian 47
Snow, J.T. 166
Sosa, Sammy 88, 136, 145
Southern League 163, 208
Sparks, Joe 24, 27, 79
Speier, Chris 65, 149
Spiezio, Scott 114–16
Spradlin, Jerry 90–2
Stanley, Fred 166
Stanley, Mike 133
Stanton, Mike 178
Stargell, Willie 18, 40, 41, 49
Steinbach, Terry 115
Steinbrenner, George 53
Stewart, Jimmy 20
Stewart, Josh 163–5
Stottlemyre, Todd 127
Strop, Pedro 204
Sullivan, John 7, 33
Sutherland, Gary 13
Suzuki, Ichiro 170
Sweeney, Mark 183
Syracuse Blue Jays 79

Tacoma Rainiers 92
Tacoma Tigers 101
Tam, Jeff 149
Tampa Bay Devil Rays/Tampa Bay Rays 184; Jimenez, Jason 158–9
Tanner, Chuck 25, 28, 37, 39
Target Field 204
Tenace, Gene 9–11, 134
Terwilliger, Wayne 78
Tewksbury, Bob 51–3
Texas League 108
Texas Rangers 198; Frye, Jeff 82–4; Hughes, Travis 169; Loe, Kameron 170–1; Witt, Bobby 50–1
Thomas, Frank 76, 132
Thomas, Justin 197–8
Thomas, Lee 66
Thome, Jim 140
Thompson, Rich 199
Thompson, Rob 151
Thompson, Robby 108
Thompson, Tommy 83
Thon, Dickie 66

Three Rivers Stadium 39, 105, 109, 141
Threets, Erick 190
Tidrow, Dick 189
Tiger Stadium 125
Tokyo Dome 145
Toledo Mud Hens 79
Tomko, Brett 158
Torborg, Greg 87
Torborg, Jeff 61
Toronto Blue Jays 82, 125, 159; Chulk, Vinnie 167–8; Woods, Al 31–2
Torre, Joe 12, 19
Torres, Salomon 190
Tosca, Carlos 167
Tovar, Cesar 22
Towers, Kevin 92
Townsend, Heath 182
Trachsel, Steve 94–6, 136
Trammell, Alan 79
Trombley, Mike 86–7
Tropicana Field 159
Tudor, John 56
Turner, Shane 155
Turner Field 136

Uecker, Bob 126
Ullger, Scott 77, 86–7, 89
Uribe, Jose 57, 64

Valbuena, Luis 198
Valentin, Jose 100
Valentine, Bobby 50–1, 83, 113
Valenzuela, Fernando 49, 50
Van Every, Jonathan 190–2
Van Landingham, William 109
Van Slyke, Andy 111
Van Slyke, Scott 208
Varitek, Jason 133, 134, 135
Vaughn, Greg 100
Veterans Stadium 119, 129
Vosberg, Ed 56–7

Wagner, Paul 111
Walbeck, Matt 87–8, 95, 123–4
Walk, Bob 44
Walker, Larry 139, 164
Wallach, Tim 47
Warner, Harry 21
Warthen, Dan 76
Washington, Claudell 44
Washington Nationals 143; Bergmann, Jason 176–9
Washington Senators 14–15
Washington, U L 33
Weaver, Earl 15

Weinbaum, Willie 174
Weinberg, Barry 115–16
Welch, Bob 75
Wells, Casper 201–3
Wells, Jared 196–7
Whitaker, Lou 59
White, Frank 42
White, Jerry 124
Whitehurst, Wally 90
Whitt, Ernie 71
Wickman, Bob 125
Wiggins, Alan 50
Wilkins, Rick 88
Williams, Jimmy 133
Williams, Matt 108, 117, 139
Willis, Dontrelle 172
Wilson, Gary 104–5
Wilson, Roger 111
Wilson, Tom 149–50
Wilson, Willie 42
Wisconsin Timber Rattlers 107
Wisdom, Patrick 213–15

Wise, Rick 140
Witt, Bobby 50–1, 102
Witt, Bobby, Jr. 50–1
Wood, Kerry 144
Woodard, Steve 124–7
Woods, Al 31–2
Woodward, Woody 20
Worrell, Tim 89–90
Worthington, Al 22
Wotus, Ron 189
Wright, Danny 163
Wrigley Field 17, 18, 30, 146–7, 161
Wynegar, Butch 35

Yankee Stadium 52, 53, 106, 167
Yastrzemski, Carl 21
Young, Dmitri 118
Young, Eric 94
Yount, Robin 52, 113

Zahn, Geoff 35

www.ingramcontent.com/pod-product-compliance
Ingram Content Group UK Ltd.
Pitfield, Milton Keynes, MK11 3LW, UK
UKHW041949140426
5217IPUK00014B/722